Back to the Best Books

To Maria,
With love!
Marley

Back to the Best Books

How the Classics Can Change Your Life

Marilyn Green Faulkner

A Unique Guide to 36 Great Books that
Enlighten, Inform and Inspire

Library of Congress Control Number:		2010908871
ISBN:	Hardcover	978-1-4535-0811-4
	Softcover	978-1-4535-0810-7
	Ebook	978-1-4535-0812-1

To order additional copies of this book, contact:
Xlibris Corporation
1-888-795-4274
www.Xlibris.com
Orders@Xlibris.com
79286

*Dedicated with love and gratitude
to my Mother and lifelong reading partner*

Lou Jean Berrett Green

Thanks and Acknowledgments

For the last ten years I have written a column online called "Back to the Best Books," where I invited readers to read the classics together and send comments via email. I have enjoyed reading hundreds of thoughtful responses to great books, some of which are included in this volume. My thanks go out to all the members of the Best Books Club, and to Meridian Magazine editors Scot and Maurine Proctor.

I am indebted to several dear friends who read portions of the manuscript and offered suggestions for improvement. Karen Lusby helped with the author biographies, and Roger Merrill and Sean Graham helped with the design. I'm lucky to have smart children: Kirk, Evan and Megan, Alison and Eric, Andrea and Brian, and Blake read chapters, made notes and pushed me to keep writing. I'm also fortunate to have a wonderful husband, Craig, whose encouragement, inspiration and publishing skills were essential to the success of this project. Finally, I gratefully acknowledge the many great teachers, especially Dr. Arthur Henry King, who have enlightened, informed and inspired me through the years.

CONTENTS

Getting Back to the Best Books: A Novel Idea

"'Oh! it is only a novel!' or, in short, only some work in which the most thorough knowledge of human nature, the happiest delineation of its varieties, the liveliest effusion of wit and humour are to be conveyed to the world in the best chosen language."

Jane Austen—*Northanger Abbey*

Everybody reads novels. Over the course of a lifetime you may read hundreds of them, perhaps without giving much thought to the process. But the novel, that extended work of prose fiction that has become the staple of our reading diet, is a remarkable invention, and in its highest form offers a unique lens through which to view our lives. In his landmark work, *Aspects of the Novel*, E.M Forster makes this intriguing remark:

"We cannot understand each other, except in a rough and ready way; we cannot reveal ourselves, even when we want to; what we call intimacy is only a makeshift; perfect knowledge is an illusion. But in the novel we can know people perfectly, and apart from the general pleasure of reading, we can find here a compensation for their dimness in life. In this direction fiction is truer than history, because it goes beyond the evidence, and each of us knows from his own experience that there is something beyond the evidence, and even if the novelist has not got it correctly, well—he has tried." (E.M. Forster, *Aspects of the Novel*, p. 16)

Each great novel creates a little microcosm of the world. Have you ever had your life taken over by a book? It is a beautiful surrender. Though we may hesitate to admit it, some of us have fictional characters that are dearer to us than many living, breathing people. Just think how many women are in love with Mr. Darcy, though we know he is nothing more than printed words on a page! Did you know that there are actually clubs that revere Sherlock Holmes as a real person and refuse to speak the name of his creator, A. Conan Doyle? Throughout history people have embraced the characters in books as real people; from the hundreds of worried souls on the dock in New York, waiting for the news of Little Nell's death, to the thousands of kids in costume waiting at midnight for the release of the latest Harry Potter novel, characters have the power to move us. Something magical happens when a fictional character makes its way into our minds through the skill of a great author, and the greatest novels continue to exert that power on generation after generation of readers.

Scientists tell us that what we put into our minds on a daily basis has a direct influence on how we perceive our lives. And, face it; most of what we put into our minds is pretty silly stuff. Television, romance novels or the latest bestselling thrillers may be entertaining, but do very little to prepare us for the complicated challenges we face each day. What if we were just a little smarter about what we load into our brains? And what if, as a result, we brought a little more wisdom and insight to our work and our relationships? Deep and thoughtful reading can help us reach a new level of understanding in our daily lives. Since each of us is the sum of what we put in to our minds through the years, it makes sense to improve the quality of our mental nutrition. Systematically replacing ordinary books with great ones over the years may significantly affect our lives. So, how do we choose what to read?

What Makes it Great?

Do you ever wonder what makes a great book great? This was a question I often asked in school, but rarely received a satisfactory answer. There were certain books that everyone agreed were classics, but it wasn't readily obvious to me why this was so. Mark Twain famously defined a classic as, "a book which people praise and don't read." Behind the humor lurks the idea that the classics are a chore: long, boring, difficult books that educated people have struggled through, or at least pretend to have struggled through! Why go to the effort to read the classics?

After a few decades of studying the question, I have learned some things about what makes a great book great. To begin with, great books offer a higher level of language, characterization, and insight than average books, along with a quality of timelessness that makes them relevant to readers in any age. Character usually takes precedence over plot in a classic; what happens in it is less important than who is in it and how they feel and think. The greatest books display an artistry of language that often blurs the line between poetry and prose. A great book is interactive; we bring our best to it and it offers its best to us. We cannot be passive readers; we become inextricably *involved*. Finally, a great book deals with great ideas and makes you think: if a book does not inspire discussion, thought, and even disagreement, it isn't great. It is just entertainment.

When an author combines brilliant artistry with the desire to uplift and edify, the attentive reader achieves a deepened sense of what it is to be human. A great book is designed to change your mind, touch your heart, and lift your spirit. You should emerge from the experience of reading with some new wisdom about the human condition and a deeper perspective about the experiences of your own life. The careful and compassionate observation of the human soul is the gift that a great novel brings us. We cannot live everywhere; we cannot be everyone. But we can read, and by so doing send out a "cord of communion" (to quote Jane Eyre) to another kind of person, and then another, and then another, until we are reinvented by our interconnectedness. Those few authors that have created truly great novels deserve our serious attention; they add to our ability to live creative and thoughtful lives.

A Difficult Pleasure

It is interesting to note that many people will expend terrific effort, time and pain on physical pursuits, and yet resist the mental effort that great literature demands. Serious reading is not a passive activity; it is more like hiking or running, and it is rewarding in the same way. Harold Bloom calls it a "difficult pleasure." As with a long run or a challenging hike, one has to invest a lot of effort in a great book. The vocabulary may be unfamiliar, the imagery confusing, and the length of the book may call for a large commitment of time. Such a book asks a lot of you, but offers in return the same thrill you feel when you reach the top of the mountain or finish that marathon. The "high" one experiences after a great read is comparable to the "high" one experiences after a great run. It's worth the effort!

Every great book changes your life in some way, and a lifetime of reading great books can alter the course of your life. When I was a little girl my mother taught a class for her women's organization titled "*Out of the Best Books,*" using an anthology with readings from the classics. I loved to sit in her room and look through the books, and those readings led us both to the complete volumes from which they were taken. My mother never went to college, but she educated herself through reading the best books, and her children reaped the rewards of her efforts. I grew up understanding that smart people get that way from reading smart books.

A Flabby Brain is Not a Pretty Thing

The brain is a muscle and, like any muscle, it needs to be used in order to grow. We know that television and movies ask very little of our brains, and thus offer us little in the way of mental enrichment. Good books are good for our brains. Since it invariably deals with ideas as well as events, a great book engages both hemispheres of the brain. (You can watch a movie on mental autopilot, but get two or three pages into Dickens or Tolstoy and your synapses will definitely be firing!) Most classics offer challenging vocabulary and symbolism, along with complex plot lines and poetic imagery. In addition, a great book asks us to think about complex problems, make value judgments and question our preconceived notions. Wrestling with such issues in a fictional setting can help us develop a "moral imagination" that may enable us to more creatively approach the knotty problems we face in real life.

That is why it is so important that literature paint an accurate, rather than an idealized representation of the human heart. Franz Kafka said, "A book must be an ice-axe to break the seas frozen inside our soul," and Chaim Potok described the process of writing as "mapping the human heart." The best books show us our true selves, warts and all, yet somehow inspire us to rise above those weaknesses to something finer. To have this kind of life-changing experience, we must reach beyond the level of simple entertainment. Some great books have happy endings, some do not, but each one teaches us something true about ourselves that may lead to more satisfying resolutions of our real-life dramas.

Great books teach us about the shared experience of living, the complexity of the human psyche and the simplicity of the human heart. It is difficult to read great literature and be narrow and prejudiced, and somehow it is easier to step back and understand our own experiences when they can be examined and illuminated through fictional lives. Great books, says David Denby, "speak most powerfully of what a human being can be." This book offers an opportunity to take a fresh look at some great books that can offer insights into our own lives.

How to Use This Book

This volume was prepared to help you approach the classics in a new way. Each of the twelve chapters contains three selections, grouped by life topics (such as coming of age, or romantic love) that you may want to focus on as you read. Choose one book from each chapter, read it, and then discuss it with your book group, a friend, or just write about it in your book journal. Rather than a steady diet of classics, you may want to alternate these selections with more contemporary literature, and in that way this book may last you for several years of reading.

Since the chapters feature a topic of general interest, even those who haven't read the selection can join in the discussion. For this purpose, a plot synopsis is included for each selection. This is followed by a section called "What Makes it Great," touching on just a few elements in the work that elevate it to a higher status. A short biographical sketch of the author is included for your reference, along with sections titled "Did You Know," and "Talk About It," to help you engage in meaningful discussion about the text and its relevance to your own life. I offer some reader reactions, along with some personal reflections in a section called "Take it Personally." Finally, in response to Kafka's challenge, we'll take a plunge into the frozen waters of our souls with an occasional "ice-axe" question, to explore what uncomfortable truths about each of us that these books reveal.

These days it seems that book groups are everywhere, but it's sometimes hard to know just how to discuss a book in a group setting. Using this

book as a guide makes it simple. Have each member present a section and
your discussion will be focused and insightful, with participation from
all. Or have one member prepare and lead the entire discussion using the
sections as desired. If you are reading alone, you might enjoy "writing
back to the book" in a journal. The insights that come as you read great
literature can be life-changing, and are worth saving.

Finally, a note on how these works were selected: In a word, randomly.
Though all of these books have garnered praise and awards, these are not
the thirty-six best books ever written. In fact, some of them may never
make the official canon of classics. My purpose in this volume was to
select a variety of works that share three qualities: they are well written,
they are beloved by readers, and they are fun to read. Most of these books
have also found a distinctive place in our culture that gives them special
relevance. And a couple of them, though they have not yet passed the
"time test" for a classic, are jut so good I couldn't resist sharing them with
you! I've got dozens more I would love to have talked about, but I have
tried to offer a sampling here that will get you searching for classics of
your own. At the end of the volume there are some book lists that may
help you in that quest.

I hope that as you read and discuss these great works of literature,
you will begin to perceive your own reality differently. Your life view will
widen and deepen, and as your "moral imagination" grows, you will find
new reservoirs of wisdom with which to respond to life's challenges. You'll
feel that flabby brain grow sharper and may be inspired to think more
creatively about the complex problems you face. Above all, you'll have the
thrill of reading some of the greatest stories ever told. Could reading better
books actually lead to a better life? What a novel idea. Let's curl up, grab a
book, and see what happens!

Chapter One
Family First

The family. We were a strange little band of characters trudging through life sharing diseases and toothpaste, coveting one another's desserts, hiding shampoo, borrowing money, locking each other out of our rooms, inflicting pain and kissing to heal it in the same instant, loving, laughing, defending, and trying to figure out the common thread that bound us all together.

~*Erma Bombeck*

Beginning with Adam, Eve, and their troublesome offspring, the family has been the central focus of oral and written literature. Each of us belongs to one or more families, and we could all use a little more wisdom about how to manage those tenuous connections. Submitted for your consideration: three unforgettable families, ranging in class and origin from Russian aristocrats to London merchants to Welsh coalminers. The Karenin's, the Forsyte's, and the Morgan's offer portraits of families in crisis, and if there is one thing that we can be sure of in family life it is this: the crises will come. How we face them is up to us. Each of these three novels offers a picture of family life that may enlighten you about your own "little band of characters," and encourage you to strengthen the ties that bind you together.

Conscience and Compassion:
Anna Karenina, by Leo Tolstoy

"Happy families are all alike, every unhappy family is unhappy it its own way." With this famous line Leo Tolstoy begins a tale that encompasses all of the triumphs, struggles and crises that occur in families: fidelity and infidelity, faith and disbelief, toil and leisure, sibling rivalry and devotion, birth and death. For Tolstoy the story of *Anna Karenina*, a wealthy member of the Russian gentry who falls into an affair that ends tragically with her suicide, provided a way to examine the family dynamic from every angle. Into its pages he poured all of his philosophical searching about the meaning of life, religion, social justice and familial love. After finishing it he renounced all of his earlier works and remarked, "I wrote everything into *Anna Karenina*, and nothing was left over." At its publication most critics praised Tolstoy for his careful handling of a difficult subject, though some questioned his motives, and wondered whether it was possible to write a moral book about the subject of immorality. It was, and from the day of its publication to this, *Anna Karenina* has captivated readers all over the world.

Synopsis

Anna Karenina is actually the story of two marriages, one in decline and one in ascendance. Anna and her husband, Karenin, lead the average life of an aristocratic couple, caring for their son and attending to social duties, until Anna meets the dashing soldier Vronsky, with whom she falls passionately in love. Vronsky has been courting a young woman named Kitty who is also pursued by a man named Levin. When Vronsky becomes enamored of Anna he abandons Kitty and she falls ill. Eventually, she renews her relationship with Levin and they marry. The tragic decline of the Karenins' marriage is juxtaposed upon the steady progress of the relationship between Kitty and Levin. Anna seeks a divorce from her husband (which never actually occurs) and abandons her son to go with Vronsky to Italy, where she becomes pregnant with his child. Eventually

Did You Know?

Unlike English names, Russian names are gender specific. Karenin is the family name of Anna's husband, but a suffix is added for the wife's name to make it feminine; thus, Anna Karenina. One of the great challenges in reading Russian literature is dealing with all of the names. Besides a shifty surname, everybody seems to have two or three given names and a couple of nicknames as well! Many novels kindly list the cast of characters at the front of the book: most helpful. Still, fortitude is required to keep it all straight. Don't say I didn't warn you.

they return to Russia where she is ostracized from society because of her affair. She becomes increasingly paranoid and depressed and eventually throws herself under a train. Meanwhile, Levin and Kitty have a son and grow to truly love and value each other.

What Makes it Great?

There is nothing remarkable about the plot of *Anna Karenina*; countless novels have been written about infidelity in marriage. So what makes this book a classic? To begin with, Tolstoy has an incredible gift for description, writes beautiful prose (even in translation) and creates finely detailed, multi-dimensional characters. But there is something more. The genius of a great novel is its ability to literally immerse you in the lives of its characters, and each novelist employs various tactics to this end. One way that Tolstoy accomplishes this is through his sheer volume of detail. After several hundred pages of confusing Russian names, long digressions into philosophy, and more details about Russian daily life than we may have wanted, we find that we have become more than observers of Anna's world, we're members of the family! We've been required to expend some effort to stay with the story, and through the creative and active involvement of our brains, our imaginations, and our emotions, we have come to feel like participants in this drama. This transformation has occurred because the novel is simultaneously stimulating the mind, emotions, imagination, memory and understanding. To paraphrase Walter Cronkite, *we are there.*

From the opening lines, Tolstoy pulls us inextricably into the everyday existence of this extended family. Notice how he opens the narrative with a disarming description of the infidelity of a minor character—foreshadowing the tragedy to come—yet treating it in a light manner, drawing us in with his casual tone. Nothing about the opening warns us that this is a story of a tragic love that ends in suicide. We sense no danger; certainly the situation is serious, but not dire; some resolution may yet be possible:

"Everything was upset in the Oblonskys' house. The wife had discovered an intrigue between her husband and their former French governess and declared that she would not continue to live under the same roof with him. This state of things had now lasted for three days, and not only the husband and wife but the rest of the family and the whole household suffered from it. They all felt there was no sense in their living together, and that any group of people who had met together by chance at an inn would have had more in common than they." (1)

Oblonsky's marital troubles and the resulting emotions felt by his wife and children are so succinctly expressed here that one is startled. We're not even to the second paragraph and we have heard so much, so soon! Because of the light, easy tone, we feel interested in this situation, we want to see what will happen, and thus Tolstoy has captured us. When Anna enters the picture we already feel a part of her extended family. The author has let us in a side door (perhaps through the servant's entrance) and we are part of the action as it unfolds. Time and again when the tension grows overwhelming Tolstoy will lighten up and treat us to a day scything wheat with the servants, or sledding on a snowy hillside. He has a way of making everything interesting; we love to share in this world. Then suddenly, he jolts us, making us look beyond the action to the deeper meaning of events. Here, for example, Vronsky (Anna's lover) finds that he is irritable and easily offended, and suddenly realizes that his grumpiness is symptomatic; it is a result of his guilt. This easy move from events to their deeper meaning is a mark of greatness:

"He was angry with everybody for their interference, just because he felt in his soul that they were right . . . The recollection of incidents often repeated rose vividly in his mind, where lies and deceptions revolting to his nature had been necessary. He remembered most vividly having more than once noticed her feeling of shame at the necessity for this deception and lying. And he experienced a strange feeling which since his union with Anna sometimes overcame him. It was a feeling of revulsion against something, against Karenin, or against himself, or against the whole world—he hardly knew which. But he always drove away this strange feeling." (168)

Good People, Bad Choices

This is not a book about bad people. It is a book about good people who make bad choices and suffer the consequences, and we suffer with them. In the closing scenes, Anna Karenina moves toward the train station and her doom. On one level, we can easily trace the events in the plot that have led up to this moment: her affair with Vronsky, her separation from her child, the slow mental collapse brought about by her tormented conscience. Yet at the same time we are asked to do more: through the use of foreshadowing Tolstoy causes us to remember an earlier moment in the novel, hundreds of pages back, when another person fell beneath the wheels of a train, and this device causes us to reflect on the cyclical nature of the story, and, by extension, of life. We experience, through Anna's tormented mind, the despairing twists of logic that drive a fine, bright person to suicide, and finally are forced onto the tracks ourselves. "What will she do?" is replaced by "What would I do?" Even as she throws herself onto the tracks she questions her decision, and we are drawn right into her dying thoughts:

"A feeling seized her like that she had experienced when preparing to enter the water in bathing, and she crossed herself. The familiar gesture of making the sign of the cross called up a whole series of girlish and childish memories, and suddenly the darkness, that obscured everything for her, broke and life showed itself to her for an instant with all its bright past joys . . . . And at that same moment she was horror struck at what she was doing. 'Where am I? What am I doing? Why?' She wished to rise, to throw herself back, but something huge and relentless struck her on the head and dragged her down. 'God forgive me everything!' she said, feeling the impossibility of struggling . . ." (695)

Crossing the Fragile Line

Tolstoy draws us further into the dilemma as he has Levin, the hero of the tale and father of a happy family, entertain thoughts of suicide as well. We realize that it is not just the tragedies of life that make us desperate, but also the fleeting, fragile nature of its joys. Tolstoy juxtaposes Anna's downward spiral of misery upon the upward spiral of happiness growing in Levin and Kitty's life, and we are reminded of the countless small decisions that have led to the tragic conclusion of one narrative and the happy resolution of the other. With a few subtle changes, all could have ended differently. Tolstoy said, "Art is a human activity having for its purpose the transmission to others of the highest and best feelings to which men have risen." In order to accomplish this, the best fiction may also show us, in heartbreaking detail, how human beings fail.

There are a few books that, when completed, will never be forgotten. For me, *Anna Karenina* was such a book, as it has been for millions of thoughtful readers. And that cumulative vote makes it a classic.

Quotations taken from *Anna Karenina*, by Leo Tolstoy. A Norton Critical Edition. W.W. Norton and Company, New York, 1995.

Talk About It

Why do women, more than men, feel that they must sacrifice their happiness for their families, and are we still critical of women who put themselves first? Would our reaction to Anna Karenina be different if she was a man?

About the Author: Leo Tolstoy

Leo Tolstoy was a man of passionate extremes, vacillating between self-indulgence and self-denial throughout his life. Born in 1828 to an aristocratic family in central Russia, Tolstoy spent his early years living an idyllic life on the family estate, coddled by aunts and grandparents after the death of his mother. Then, just after the family moved to Moscow so that the boys could attend school, his father died suddenly, and Leo seemed to lose his emotional balance. At age sixteen, Tolstoy entered the university to study Arabic languages, yet fell into a pattern of dissipation, gambling, and debt. He struggled over the next several years, repeatedly writing to his aunts about his resolution to reform, and then falling again into his bad habits. Eventually he entered the army with his brother and served in several campaigns.

At the age of 34, Tolstoy fell in love with Sonya Behrs, the 19-year-old sister of a friend, and changed his life for the better. Together they had twelve children, and Sonya became his personal assistant, typing manuscripts and helping him finish his landmark novels, *War and Peace* and *Anna Karenina*.

Tolstoy suffered bouts of depression, questioning his own motives and his desire for security and prosperity. Eventually he gave up all of his possessions, including the family estate, to live as a peasant, surrounded by acolytes who believed in his teachings. Estranged from Sonya and rejected by all but his youngest daughter, Tolstoy eventually died in a train station in 1910. Thousands paid their respects at his simple funeral.

Though friends told him that his rambling, introspective style would make his books irrelevant in the literary tradition, *Anna Karenina* and *War and Peace* were recently cited in Time Magazine's "Ten Greatest Books of All Time," in places one and three respectively.

Sources:

The Literature Network

Orwin, Donna T. *The Cambridge Companion to Tolstoy.* Cambridge University Press, 2002.

People as Possessions:
The Forsyte Saga, by John Galsworthy

The Forsyte Saga is a trilogy of novels written over a period of fifteen years (1906-1921) in which John Galsworthy created an unparalleled picture of London society around the time of the First World War. The struggle between the possessor and the possessed, between those who live only to acquire and those who love beauty, replays itself in the lives of three generations of Forsytes.

One of those books that defined an era, the *Forsyte Saga* captures a period of time that is gone forever. The motorcar was all the rage, technological advances were causing a general decline in religious faith, and new forms of communication meant that men and women were forced out of the isolation that had served to cushion their prejudices and antiquated ideas.

Synopsis

Soames Forsyte, acknowledged leader of the Forsyte clan, is an avaricious, merciless man that epitomizes the materialistic, grasping side of society. He sees everything and everyone as a possible possession or investment. His beautiful wife Irene is his prized trophy; though she despises him, he sees only her value as an asset. The drama revolves around their excruciatingly uncomfortable marriage and its consequences in the lives of all of the extended family through three generations. The fashionable, moneyed Forsytes represent a dying breed of aristocracy, clinging to their possessions and customs even as the world is in upheaval around them. Soames Forsyte refuses to acknowledge that his miserable wife deserves anything but proper clothes and the other accoutrements of her station. His bewilderment and rage at her rebellion forms the crux of the action, while the growing attachment between Irene and his cousin Jolyon Forsyte creates the rivalry that will change their lives.

Did You Know?

The *Forsyte Saga* was made into an outstanding miniseries (with Damian Lewis especially chilling as Soames Forsyte.) There are two parts with hours of episodes, so stock up on popcorn and treats and settle in for a marvelous marathon. However, the televised version offers only a glimpse of Galsworthy's genius. You must read the original to get all those wonderful words.

What Makes it Great?

The brilliance of the *Forsyte Saga* lies in Galsworthy's searing portraits of family life, often funny and always insightful. Here, for example, is his description of the engagement party that opens the novel, a perfect example of Galsworthy's wry, nuanced tone. No one in the family approves of the intended groom (and in fact the marriage will never take place) but the loyal Forsytes are there in "full plumage."

"When a Forsyte was engaged, married, or born, the Forsytes were present; when a Forsyte died—but no Forsyte had as yet died; they did not die; death being contrary to their principles, they took precautions against it, the instinctive precautions of highly vitalized persons who resent encroachments on their property." (4)

One unique quality of this work is the way its bemused, satirical style melts into a voice of great compassion in moments of crisis: the deaths, crucial moments of decision, and the declarations of love and hate on which the narrative turns. Galsworthy has an uncanny knack for capturing the voices of children, women and the elderly. Here he invites us into the thoughts of little Jolyon Forsyte (the fourth generation of that name) as he contemplates his beautiful mother. At the age of nine he is really seeing her for the first time, as children do at about that age, and words like "goldy" and "beautifulness" create an authentically childlike voice without a trace of sentimentality. Galsworthy's gift of restraint is evident here; there is often as much in what he doesn't say as in what he says:

"While he was eating his jam beneath the oak tree, he noticed things about his mother that he had never seemed to see before, her cheeks for instance were creamy, there were silver threads in her dark goldy hair, her throat had no knob in it like Bella's and she went in and out softly. He noticed, too, some little lines running away from the corners of her eyes, and a nice darkness under them. She was ever so beautiful . . . this new beautifulness of his mother had a kind of particular importance, and he ate less than he had expected to." (619)

Another great quality of this work lies in its searing social statements. John Galsworthy was satirizing his own social class and, considering the time in which he wrote, he took he took a courageous stance on the rights of women. Much of the story concerns the tumultuous triangle involving Soames Forsyte, his wife Irene, and his rival for her affections, his cousin Jolyon. It is noteworthy that Galsworthy's concern is not so much the inferior political or social status of women, but the fact that their emotional needs were completely overlooked. Irene is not ill treated or abused: on the contrary, she lives in comfort and style. Yet she is desperately unhappy, and this *matters*. Her unhappiness is a complete mystery to Soames; in his self-satisfied, myopic existence a woman who needs something more than status and security is beyond his ken. In a revealing scene, they sit together in stony silence at the dinner table, and Soames begins to realize, perhaps for the first time, that there are things that money cannot buy:

"Could a man own anything prettier than this dining table, with its deep tints, the starry, soft-petaled roses, the ruby colored glass, and quaint silver furnishing; could a man own anything prettier than the woman who sat at it? Gratitude was no virtue among the Forsytes, who, competitive, had no occasion for it; and Soames only experienced a sense of exasperation amounting to pain, that he did not own her as it was his right to own her, that he could not, as by stretching out his hand to that rose, pluck her and sniff the very secrets of her heart." (70)

Though Soames is a man of impeccable breeding, scrupulous manners and perfect hygiene, Galsworthy describes him in bestial terms, brilliantly revealing his brooding undercurrent of violence. Using such eerie verbs as "plucking" and "sniffing," Galsworthy exposes the soul of a man who must possess what he admires, even if it destroys, and foreshadows the terrible moment when Soames, in the height of his frustration, forces himself sexually upon his wife and earns her undying hatred. Galsworthy was well aware that such scenes were not uncommon among married people of his day, and his revelation of such an ugly truth reveals as much about Galsworthy's courage as it does about the society he chronicles.

There is a curious turn in the last two installments of the narrative that only adds to the work's greatness, in my opinion, as the villainous Soames becomes a more sympathetic character. In the fifteen-year gap between the writing of the first novella and the last, Galsworthy grew older, wiser and, like many of us, less critical of his own social group. Though he continues to indict the Forstyes for their skewed priorities, he presents them in a more human and vulnerable light as time marches forward and their sins are visited upon their children and grandchildren.

The rights of women, the double standard of justice as applied to the rich and the poor, the evils of the First World War and the class confrontation between master and laborer all found a place in Galsworthy's fiction. His shrewd observation of extended families and their impact on each other is relevant in any age.

Quotations taken from *The Forsyte Saga*, by John Galsworthy. Oxford University Press, London. 1999.

Talk About It

It is said that money can't buy happiness, but it can certainly purchase whatever comes second! The Forsyte's are rich. Is money an essential part of their problems?

About the Author: John Galsworthy

Born in 1867 to upper-class British parents, John Galsworthy was raised in luxury, attended the finest schools, studied law, and was in due course called to the bar. Yet after an unlucky love affair, he became restless and decided to travel instead. A chance meeting with Joseph Conrad on a voyage to the South Sea inspired him to write. After several unsuccessful attempts, he found his voice with *The Man of Property*, a novel based on his own life experiences. This epic story of the large, prosperous Forsyte family grew to fill three novels, written from 1906 to 1921. In 1932, Forsyte was awarded the Nobel Prize in literature, "for his distinguished art of narration which takes its highest form in *The Forsyte Saga*."

The trilogy was a glaring criticism of Galsworthy's own social class; the author based the character of Soames Forsyte on his cousin, whose wife left him and later married Galsworthy. The novel's pivotal scene, where Soames forces himself on his wife and earns her undying hatred, was actually based on an event in his wife's first marriage. Over fifteen years and the First World War elapsed between the first and second novels, and Galsworthy's own maturation process is evident in his more sympathetic approach to the character of Soames as the novels progress.

Later authors such as Virginia Woolf and D.H. Lawrence attacked Galsworthy for embracing the very values he criticized in his books. Like Dickens, Austen, and Eliot, Galsworthy satirized his own society without rejecting it. Yet, he lent his prodigious talent to many causes, bringing problems of social injustice to light. In fact, his play, *Justice*, led Winston Churchill to advance prison reform in England.

Galsworthy died from a brain tumor in 1933, six weeks after being awarded the Nobel Prize.

Sources:

Cooper, Robert M. *The Literary Guide & Companion to Southern England*. Ohio University Press, 1998. pp. 323-324.

Wikipedia

Family, Faith and Innocence:
How Green Was My Valley, by Richard Llewellyn

"I am going to pack my two shirts with my other socks and my best suit in the little blue cloth my mother used to tie round her hair when she did the house, and I am going from the Valley." (1)

Granted, I am one of those people who blubber easily, but I cannot read these opening words of Richard Llewellyn's beautiful novel without tearing up, for bound up in this sentence (as in a cloth) are all the components that make this book a sweet and memorable read. There are the homely details of family life; a housewife's head scarf, a best suit, a pair of extra socks. There is the hint of all of the work that goes into the raising of a large family (in this case, one with nine children) and the hair of the gentle Mrs. Morgan going slowly white under that blue cloth. Then, there is the valley, the symbol of a world of innocence and faith that Huw Morgan loves and lives to see destroyed by the physical and spiritual pollutions all around him. This story of a Welsh coal mining family is unapologetically sentimental, yet is balanced by an unflinching realism that rings true to life.

Synopsis

How Green Was My Valley is set sometime around the turn of the century, and tells the story of the Morgans, a poor but respectable mining family of the South Wales valleys. The story is told through the eyes of the youngest son, Huw Morgan. Huw's academic ability sets him apart from his elder brothers and enables him to consider a future away from the mines. All five brothers and his father are miners, and after the eldest brother, Ivor, is killed in an industrial accident, Huw moves in with his sister-in-law, Bronwen, with whom he has always been secretly in love. Later, Huw's father is also killed in the mine. One of Huw's three sisters, Angharad, makes an unhappy marriage to a wealthy mine owner and never overcomes her clandestine relationship with the local minister. After everyone Huw has known either dies or moves away, he decides to leave as well, and tells us the story of his life just before he leaves his childhood home, which is about to be swallowed up by the slag heap of the mine, symbol for the refuse of a troubled society.

What Makes it Great?

The *Dictionary of Literary Biography* comments on Llewellyn's simple, heartfelt style, and on the unusual status that he has in the modern literary community:

"Richard Llewellyn is one of the more prolific authors of the twentieth century, with a total of twenty-three novels written in a little less than forty years, together with two stage plays and contributions to diverse film scripts, all produced in a crowded and varied life. Yet he stands apart from other novelists of his period, belonging to no movement or literary tradition and, indeed, professing never to read modern novels. As a consequence of this independence, his work has received little or no academic attention as yet, while newspaper and magazine reviewers find difficulty in assessing it. Llewellyn appears to have influenced few writers of any significance in the English language. However, he continues to command a large, worldwide popular audience, and sales of his novels remain high.

"Part of Llewellyn's significance is due to his unique stance. His work is a personal statement made in a singular style, refreshingly uninhibited by the pursuit or expansion of modern philosophies, modes of thinking, and fashionable ideas." *(Dictionary of Literary Biography)*

An example of this strange and wonderful style is Huw's description of his father's death in the mines. Long before it became fashionable to "think green" Llewellyn invites us to view the earth as a living creature, reaching up and taking the lives of men that threaten her existence. As his father gasps under the crushing weight of the rocks and earth after a cave-in, Huw struggles to find a way to help him breathe easier. Llewellyn uses a brilliant personification of the earth as a wounded, angry mother and all the creatures that live on her surface as a blanket, the weight of which is smothering his father:

"But the earth bore down in mightiness, and above the Earth, I thought of houses sitting in quiet under the sun, and men roaming the streets to lose voice, breath and blood, and children dancing in play, and women cleaning house, and good smells in our kitchen, all of them adding more

Did You Know?

The scene in which Huw is beat by the schoolmaster for speaking Welsh refers to policies that tried to force everyone in the United Kingdom to speak English. In the later 19th century virtually all teaching in the schools of Wales was in English, even in areas where the pupils barely understood it. Government policy fostered a program called "Welsh Not." A board with the letters WN cut into it was hung around the neck of any child heard to speak Welsh, and the last child wearing the sign each day was punished. Through the efforts of Welsh reformers this policy was changed in the early 20th century.

to my father's counter-pane. There is patience in the Earth to allow us to go into her, and dig, and hurt with tunnels and shafts and if we put back the flesh we have weakened she is content to let us bleed her. But when we take and leave her weak where we have taken, she has a soreness and an anger that we should be so cruel to her and so thoughtless of her comfort. So she waits for us, and finding us, bears down and bearing down, makes us a part of her, flesh of her flesh, with our clay in place of the clay we thoughtlessly have shoveled away." (443)

This simple, organic approach to the Earth feels more akin to Eastern or First-nation philosophy than the musings of a Welsh Protestant. Llewellyn's ability to see into the universal heart of man makes his characters somehow modern and transcends the time frame of the narrative. The timeless perspective, and the unique manner of his expression, makes it great.

A Song of the Heart

The Welsh are a deep and ancient people, with an incomprehensible language and a natural flair for poetry and song. If you have been to Wales you have heard the Welsh sing, and you never forget it. Every little town has its choirs and bands. Music plays an important role in the daily life of the Morgan family. Though they spend their days in the belly of the mine, they soar, through song and language, in their leisure hours, and Llewellyn captures this joy.

Huw is a bright boy whose only struggle in school is against the bullying by other boys who are threatened by his intelligence, and the prejudice of his schoolmasters toward the Welsh. In Victorian times there was a concerted effort to stamp out the Welsh language, and children were punished for speaking their native language in school. Huw's blind rage at the schoolmaster's cruel persecution causes his final expulsion from the school and his rejection of the intellectual life it promised. The terrible sadism rampant in the school system of that day is expressed most eloquently in the description of the schoolmaster's face after he has beaten Huw with such violence that he has broken the stick:

"I looked at him as I slipped from Mervyn Phillip's' back, and found him pale, wet about the forehead, with a blueness about the mouth, and a shifting of muscles pulling one side of his face, and a pinkness in his eyes, and trembling in the hands that he tried to have quiet by linking his fingers. His eyes stared hard at me, moving over my face, but I kept my eyes on his. His tongue put wet about his mouth and his breath pulled him up short as though reins had been jerked, and then I turned away from him and got my legs to bring me to my seat." (207)

As Huw Morgan waits for the slagheap to swallow his childhood home, he remembers a world untouched by the complexities of modern life. No one locked a door; there were no policemen or jails in the community. Neighbors monitored each other, sometimes severely, and the church was the center of social and spiritual life. Women kept the house and did the dishes, and men worked in the mines. Children spoke when they were spoken to and were beaten for disobedience. For the most part, they were happy, yet the slow influence of civilization, both good and bad, crept inexorably in just as the slag from the mines crept down the hill toward their homes. Unions, immorality, theaters, education and technology combined to destroy their innocent way of life forever.

How Green Was My Valley is an unabashedly sentimental story, and for that it has been discounted by academics as inferior. These cynical, sterner critics are missing something I think. The older I get the more I believe that a little sentimentality—a good cry for that which has been lost in life—can be very healing for the soul, and this cathartic experience is at the heart of *How Green Was My Valley*. I'm usually put off by a book that

I suspect is trying to make me cry, but this novel does not strike me that way. It's sentiment is honest and true.

Huw is a strange character, hot-tempered and passionate, yet unable to marry or settle on one woman; fiercely intelligent, yet stubborn and unwilling to use his mind to achieve something above the level of the mine. His long illness as a child gives him the perspective of the outsider, and he sees the lives of his family with a level of objectivity unavailable to the rest of the group. As the novel draws to a close he reflects that, though much has been lost, nothing that we hold in our hearts is ever really gone. "There is no fence or hedge around time that is gone," he says. "You can go back and have what you like if you remember it well enough." His beautiful retelling of a special childhood may take you back to an innocent time of your own, gone, but never lost.

(Quotations taken from *How Green Was My Valley*, by Richard Llewellyn. Dell Publishing Co. New York, 1988.)

Talk About It

How can family members find unity, or should they even try when they are so different? This large family is made up of such diverse characters, which eventually grow apart. How have you maintained unity in your family while appreciating the diversity therein?

About the Author: Richard Llewellyn

Richard Dafydd Vivian Llewellyn Lloyd was born in 1906 in Hendon, North London. His English birthplace contradicts Llewellyn's own lifelong claim he was born in St. David's, Wales, though he was of Welsh blood and Welsh themes pervade his writings. At age sixteen, he entered the workforce as a dishwasher in a London hotel. During this time he also worked in the motion picture industry. In 1924, Llewellyn joined the British army and served six years in India and Hong Kong.

After leaving the service he worked a succession of jobs, including a defining period of time as a coal miner in South Wales. Llewellyn's experience in the mining communities proved to be inspiration for his first novel. He worked on this project for twelve years before taking leave from a screenwriting job in Hollywood to complete the manuscript for *How Green Was My Valley*. Published to international acclaim in 1939, the novel was honored in the United States with the National Book Award. In 1941, the book was made into an Oscar-winning film starring Walter Pidgeon and Maureen O'Hara.

Though he penned many more novels, including three sequels to this first work, nothing Llewellyn wrote approached the success of his earliest book. He stood apart from other novelists of his time, taking part in no movement or literary tradition, and professing never to read modern novels. During his life, he worked as a journalist, covering the Nuremburg Trials, and continued as a screenwriter for Twentieth Century-Fox and MGM. (He wrote the screenplay for my favorite John Wayne movie, *The Quiet Man*.) A Welsh national, Llewellyn lived in several countries and married twice. He died in Dublin in 1983.

"Richard Llewellyn." *Encyclopedia Britannica*. 2009. Encyclopedia Britannica Online. 28 Sep. 2009

Family First: Take it Personally

At the age of nineteen I read *Anna Karenina* for the first time and felt (as Tolstoy intended me to feel) that I had lived Anna's life with her, every step of the way. I could no longer think of myself as a person who would never step onto those tracks, for I had been there with her. I could see and feel what she *should* have done, and yet empathize with her inability to do it. Tolstoy was teaching me conscience and compassion at the same time. For a moment, at nineteen, I was lifted beyond my years and my limited understanding into a greater level of wisdom. That new depth of insight was then available to me as my own life unfolded. Now, thirty-five years later, I have recently reread *Anna Karenina*, and find that I can combine its insights and beauties with experiences and thoughts from over three decades of living since my last encounter with the novel, adding new levels of enrichment to the experience.

Not everyone has had the same experience! One member of the Best Books Club recalled reading Anna Karenina: "I was fed up with Anna at the end and was ready to push her under the train if she didn't jump! But, I was eighteen, and male." Certainly different characters will reach out to different individuals. Will Anna reach out and draw you in as she did me? It remains to be seen. To me the purpose of a great book is not to show us what terrible things happen to people as a result of their mistakes, though many do that. It is, instead, to help us enter the mind and heart of another person and truly see how it feels experience those consequences without actually having to live through them. Rather than a list of life lessons and moral platitudes, the act of knowing another person—sharing that perfect knowledge that is impossible in real life—sheds a new light on our own life-narratives, and is the hallmark of greatness in a work of fiction. All three of the books in this chapter deal with the deep divisions that can occur in families. So, here goes the ice-axe question: Do you have an enemy in your family circle? How did this happen? Can the situation be remedied, or is the relationship broken beyond repair? Is it your fault?

"A book must be an ice-axe to break the seas frozen inside our soul." Kafka

Chapter Two
Growing Pains

"Doing all the little tricky things it takes to grow up, step by step, into an anxious and unsettling world."

Sylvia Plath

"When you grow up your mother says, 'Wear rubbers or you'll catch cold.' When you become an adult you discover that you have the right not to wear rubbers and to see if you catch cold or not."

Diane Arbus

There's never been a better time to be a girl: the future is full of career and educational opportunities, and political equality is finally a reality for many, and on the horizon for others. At the same time, the sheer abundance of choices makes the life of a young woman more complicated than it has ever been. To paraphrase Dickens, it is the "best and the worst of times" to grow up female.

Women have always struggled to balance the pull of hearth and home with the work of the world. They have fought to protect their children, keep the love of a husband and take their place in society at large. These three women come of age in three completely different worlds, Communist China, Medieval Norway and Depression-era New York, yet they face similar challenges with courage and grace. In their life sagas women may find both a kindred soul and a new perspective. And men may find some much-needed insight into the women in their lives.

Coming of Age in an Age Gone By:
A Tree Grows in Brooklyn, by Betty Smith

Some authors, it seems, were born to write one great book, and such was the case with Betty Smith. In 1943, at the age of forty-seven, she penned a semi-autobiographical account of her Brooklyn upbringing. The book, *A Tree Grows in Brooklyn*, sold 300,000 copies in its first six weeks. That year everyone in America, from cabbies to college professors, was reading and talking about the remarkable story of Francie Nolan, a poor girl struggling to survive with her family in turn-of-the-century New York. Betty Smith became an instant celebrity, and eventually won the Pulitzer Prize.

Though she wrote three other novels and several plays, Smith never achieved the level of success and critical acclaim that attended her first major literary effort. Fifty years after its debut, *A Tree Grows in Brooklyn* remains a perennial favorite for schools and book clubs, with over a million copies sold. In 1995 The New York Public Library chose it as one of the "Books of the Century."

Synopsis

We meet Francie Nolan, age eleven, reading on the fire escape of her Brooklyn tenement flat, her only companion a curious tree that grows out of the cement and curls around her lonely perch. Francie is a masterpiece of characterization; an unforgettable combination of artistic sensitivity and pure immigrant pluck. Some days Francie and her little brother Neeley wander the streets in search of junk to sell for pennies. Other days they are sent on various (often terrifying) errands for their hard-working janitress mother, Katie. Francie's father, Johnny Nolan, is a loveable Irish drunkard whom Francie cannot respect, though she idolizes him for his charm and talent. Her mother holds the family together with her hard work and determination, while her father lends it romance through his music and idealistic dreams.

Though the bare bones of the story line suggest a romanticized portrait of city life, Smith's narrative is full of the grim realities that accompany poverty and ignorance. Infant mortality, alcoholism, depression, disease and depravity dog the steps of the Nolan family, and nothing about their lives is sugar-coated or drenched in dreamy nostalgia. The novel follows Francie through her teenage years, and comes to a close as she prepares to leave home and make her way in the world. A true "coming-of-age" story, its primary focus is the growth of one child in a relentlessly difficult environment. Through Francie's eyes, we see a world both familiar in its scenes of family life and foreign in its wrenching struggle to survive.

What Makes it Great?

Two factors that may account for the lasting appeal of this novel are its delight in detail and its ruthless honesty. Smith has a marvelous eye for the little things that make Francie's situation unique and interesting to the rest of us. She notices everything, and my favorite moments in this story are those that chronicle the details of a daily life I would never otherwise understand. For example, I liked the description of one week's worth of dinners made from six loaves of stale bread. Here is Saturday's feast:

"Saturday supper was a red letter meal. The Nolans had fried meat! A loaf of stale bread was made into pulp with hot water and mixed with a dime's worth of chopped meat into which an onion had been cleavered. Salt and a penny's worth of minced parsley were added for flavor. This was made up into little balls, fried and served with hot ketchup. These meat balls had a name, *fricadellen*, which was a great joke with Francie and Neeley." (44)

Smith is not a poetic writer, but she is a powerful one, and her descriptions have the searing accuracy that marks the finest prose. Here, for example, is the moment when Francie finally summons the courage to confront her young father after his death from the effects of alcoholism. Notice Smith's careful attention to the kinds of things that a young girl would notice, such as his face, his mustache, and his tie. This, combined with the avoidance of any form of sentimental whitewashing, creates a moment that feels completely real: as with Anna Karenina on the tracks, we are there, with Francie, palms sweating, heart pounding, approaching the coffin:

"Francie stood there with her eyes on the ground, afraid to look. Finally she lifted her eyes. She couldn't believe that papa wasn't living!

> # Did You Know?
>
> After the publication of her novel, Betty Smith received thousands of letters from people who felt that she had captured something essential about growing up poor in America. She wrote, "Now, any time of the day, Box 405 is filled with letters from people who have read my book. Most letters begin: "This is my first fan letter. I've just read your book and I must tell you . . ." Or: "I've never lived in Brooklyn but someone must have told you the story of my life because that's what you wrote." Smith answered every letter, and said she felt a personal connection to each person who was touched by her book.

He wore his tuxedo suit, which had been cleaned and pressed. He had on a fresh dicky and collar and a carefully tied bow tie. There was a carnation in his lapel and, above it, his Union button. His hair was shining and golden and as curling as ever. One of the locks was out of place and had fallen down on the side of his forehead a little. His eyes were closed as though he were sleeping lightly. He looked young and handsome and well-cared for. She noticed for the first time how finely arched his eyebrows were. His small mustache was trimmed and looked as debonair as ever. All the pain and grief and worry had left his face. It was smooth and boyish looking . . . It was queer to see papa's hands so quiet when she remembered them as always trembling . . . She stared steadily at his hands and thought she saw them move. Panic churned up in her and she wanted to run away . . ." (288)

Poverty isn't Pretty

Many novels tend to portray poverty in one extreme or another: either poverty destroys lives, and engenders hopelessness and crime, or poverty is painted as an ennobling ideal from which sturdy young souls emerge. Betty Smith manages something altogether different. Her startling combination of realism and idealism shocked some critics, yet it accounts

for the lasting popularity of the novel. When asked why she wrote
so frankly about issues many considered too daring to discuss, Smith
responded, "I had no axe to grind. I just wanted to write, but it seems
I didn't know my own strength." Reaching beyond the domestic trials
of the poor, Smith explores the social context of poverty as well: class
struggle, the power of the unions, and the fraud and deception practiced
on the illiterate immigrant population are all chronicled through the
experiences of the Nolan family.

In the face of this grim reality, Smith ably captures the resilience and
the indefatigable resolve of these people to rise and improve their status
through education and thrift. Though she has only finished grade school,
Francie's mother has her children read one page of Shakespeare and a page
from the Bible every night, and by so doing pushes them onto a higher
plane of learning. Brooklyn's poor are the backbone of a rising nation, and
Francie embodies the best of their kind.

In the end, this is not primarily a book about social issues, or
Brooklyn, or even about poverty. It is a story of a girl growing out
of her childish dreams and into the life of a woman, and because it
touches upon this universal theme it has found a universal audience.
Francie takes enough of her idealism with her into adulthood to earn
our love and respect, yet of necessity must say goodbye to the child
that sat on the steps by the tree. In a sweet final scene she sees a new
occupant on her old step. As she dresses in her high heels, stockings
and linen dress she has that moment that defines the "coming of age"
novel as, whispering good-bye to her former self, she closes the window
on that chapter of her life.

Novelist Anna Quindlen comments on why this novel is gritty, yet
great: "In Francie's beloved Brooklyn, a rapist stalks the hallways, young
women give birth out of wedlock and are reviled and even attacked, the
nice old man in the junk store is not someone a child should risk being
alone with . . . So why is this not a grim book, with Francie's beloved
father crying through delirium tremens and her teacher giving her "C"s
in English when she dares to write about that real-life horror . . . ? Part of
it is certainly because we know Francie has triumphed." (*A Tree Grows in
Brooklyn*, Introduction, *x*)

The generation that lived through the Great Depression is nearly gone now, but the benefit of their experiences is needed more than ever. *A Tree Grows in Brooklyn* should be required reading for all of us baby boomers and our carefully coddled offspring.

Quotations taken from *A Tree Grows in Brooklyn*. Harper Modern Classics, New York. 2001.

Talk About It

Betty Smith was criticized for including many of the grim details of poverty in her novel. These days, she would be criticized for not including enough of the bad stuff! What do you think? Did she get it right?

About the Author: Betty Smith

Betty Smith was born Elisabeth Lillian Wehner in 1896, in Brooklyn to German immigrants. She married twice and was the mother of two girls. While her first husband attended law school at the University of Michigan, she enrolled in college courses, though she had not graduated from high school. There she honed her skills in journalism, literature, writing, and drama, winning a prestigious Hopwood Award. Throughout her life, Smith worked as a dramatist, receiving many awards and fellowships including the Rockefeller Fellowship and the Dramatists Guild Fellowship for her work in drama.

In 1943, at the age of forty-seven, she wrote a semi-autobiographical account of her Brooklyn upbringing, *A Tree Grows in Brooklyn*. It sold 300,000 copies in its first six weeks. Betty Smith became an instant celebrity, and eventually won the Pulitzer Prize.

Smith often said that she wrote the novel, "not as it was, but as it should have been." She worked with George Abbott on the musical adaptation of the book, and continued to work as a dramatist throughout her life. She died in Connecticut at the age of 75.

Sources: Yow, Valerie Raleigh. *Betty Smith: Life of the Author of* A Tree Grows in Brooklyn. Wolf's Pond Press, 2008.

A Life Worth Celebrating:
Kristin Lavransdatter, by Sigrid Undset

It happens this way: you're young, in love, and you cannot listen to your better judgment telling you that you are making a mistake. Against the advice of everyone who knows better, you marry that charming man with a weak character. Each passing year shows you the folly of your choice, yet you make the best of it and build a life together.

Or perhaps it happens this way: you are a parent, and you have a child who is the special treasure of your heart, yet she chooses to marry a man whom you cannot respect. Later, when you are older and your grandchildren come for a visit they are unruly, as ill mannered as their father, and hard to enjoy, yet you watch their faces as they sleep and revel in their perfect beauty.

Then again, perhaps it happens this way: you have a spouse you love dearly, yet between you there are long-standing resentments that are hard to get past. On some days however, the two of you feel so much joy and fulfillment in the children you have raised and the life you have built together that you wonder why those tense times must plague your relationship.

As you grow older your faith in God grows, but your faith in mankind suffers. Or vice versa. Finally you lay dying, and all of the trials, resentments, fears and challenges seem as nothing to you. There is only your faith, the love between you and your spouse, and your quiet joy in the lives of your children and their children.

I could be talking about moments in your life or the lives of those close to you. In reality, I am recounting scenes from a remarkable trilogy of novels titled *Kristin Lavransdatter*, by Sigrid Undset. In an epic narrative tracing the life of one fourteenth century Norwegian woman, Undset holds a mirror up to life that reflects the timeless nature of the trials, joys and fears we all face. Sigrid Undset was the first woman to win the Nobel Prize for Literature, awarded to her in 1928 for this remarkable trilogy. Some critics hailed her heroine, Kristin Lavransdatter, as the first "real woman" in literature, and she emerges from these pages as a fully realized human being, with a noble heart and many flaws.

Synopsis

We first meet Kristin as the young, slightly spoiled daughter of a Norwegian nobleman who refuses her father's choice of a husband and instead marries a weak, moody man. We follow her progress through her long, difficult marriage, the joys and sorrows of raising seven sons, the onset of old age, and to the close of her life. Along the way we are introduced to an unforgettable cast of supporting characters.

As does any good historical novel, *Kristin Lavransdatter* immerses us in the details of life in another age. We know what's for dinner, how it is eaten and what the room looks like where it is served. We come to understand the church, and the strange combination of pagan superstition and Christian faith that guided the people of that day. Kristin's weaknesses, joys and sorrows are so deftly shown through dialogue and inner monologue that we begin to feel that we know her intimately, and cannot help but love her as others do. The narrative shifts effortlessly from political intrigues to the most mundane details of rural life, from deep spiritual insights to moments of selfishness and stress. In other words, we are given a whole life, not the varnished version of a life presented with a hidden agenda.

What Makes it Great?

One of the characteristics of this great book is the way it combines historical accuracy with emotional veracity. Many works of "historical fiction" give us a picture of life in another age; yet offer us only cardboard cut-outs for characters. Undset, a diligent student of history, definitely has her facts right, but her writing soars as well. As Kristin's life unfolds we are drawn both into her family and into her time, as the world of medieval Norway becomes as familiar to us as our own. Few historical novels accomplish this with such grace; we are scarcely aware of the transformation, but we begin thinking and reacting like Norwegians in that distant age. The character of Kristin is multi-faceted. We are never sure what she is going to do or say but we never tire of finding out. Her insatiable love of life sees her through one trial after another, and fuels the lifelong passion in her relationship with her husband, Erlend. Much

Did You Know?

The first major translation of Undset's work, by Charles Archer, has a quaint, old-fashioned tone. Archer used a medieval-sounding jargon for his translation that can be hard to follow at times, yet this is the translation I first read and I found it charming. Since that time another translation by a woman named Tiina Nunnally has taken precedence. Nunnally (using the theory that even medieval Norwegians would not sound medieval to each other) uses a more contemporary colloquial style that will be easier to read. Her translation is said to be more accurate and less precious than Archer's, though Undset's genius shines through both.

like Tolstoy, Undset has a gift for bringing us in the side door of a family and finding us a spot at the dinner table. We are privy to the thoughts and emotions of each family member, yet always our main focus is on Kristin and her stormy path.

Juxtaposed against the ongoing battleground of Kristin's marriage is the steady relationship of her father and mother. Undset beautifully contrasts their insurmountable difficulties with the deep joys of the long, faithful partnership between Lavrans and his wife. When, after thirty-four years of marriage, Lavrans becomes ill and knows he must die, these two stoic souls are finally able communicate without barriers (yet still with a dignified restraint) in one of the most beautiful exchanges I have ever read. (Its spare beauty reminds me of the last sweet exchange between Cordelia and King Lear.) In a quiet moment together, Lavrans places on her finger his own ring, one that he had requested never to be taken from his finger. Ragnfrid gazes down at her betrothal ring, her wedding ring, and now this last, which she realizes is to be worn after his death.

"She felt it—with this last ring he had wedded her again. When in a little while, she sat over his lifeless body, he willed she should know that with this ring he had espoused to her the strong and living force that had dwelt in that dust and ashes ... Through the pitchy darkness that was coming she saw the glimmer of another, milder sun, she smelt the scent of the herbs in the garden at the world's end ..."

Lavrans laid his wife's hand back in her lap, and sat down on the bench, a little way from her, with his back to the board, and one arm upon it. He looked not at her, but gazed into the hearth-fire.

When she spoke again, her voice was calm and quiet:

"I had not thought, my husband, that I had been so dear to you."

"Aye, but you were"; he spoke as evenly as she." (505)

Here is a sample of a more recent translation, showing Tiina Nunnally's skillful use of alliteration and poetic imagery. Here, news spreads of the death of Arne, Kristin's first love:

"It was a biting, cold night, the snow creaked underfoot, and the stars glittered, as dense as frost, in the black sky. After they had gone a short distance, they heard shouts and howls and furious hoof beats south of the meadows. A little farther along the road the whole pack of riders came storming up behind them and then raced on past . . . a few of them understood the news that Halvdan had yelled after them; they dropped away from the group, fell silent, and joined Lavran's party . . . the dark houses looked as if they were streaked with blood . . . One of Arne's little sisters was standing outside, stamping her feet, with her arms crossed under her cloak. Kristin kissed the tear-stained face of the freezing child. Her heart was as heavy as stone, and she felt as if there was lead in her limbs as she climbed the stairs to the loft where they had laid him out." (86)

Finding Ourselves in Kristin's World

Kristin Lavransdatter is a work that invites you into another world, yet leaves you with many insights about your own. I don't know anyone who hasn't loved this book (I speak of it as one book because my old hardbound version has all three novels bound together) and I have recommended it to many. One critic called it "the finest historical novel our 20th century has yet produced," and another claimed, "As a novel it must be ranked with the greatest the world knows today."

As we look to the classics for wisdom about our own lives, Kristin's experiences can be illuminating. Most marriages are more like Kristin's than those portrayed in romance novels. Both partners struggle with personal weaknesses that undermine the success of the union, and those struggles can stretch through generations. There are no really evil characters in this novel; no villain is threatening the happiness of Kristin's home. As Pogo so eloquently said; "We have met the enemy, and he is us." Recognizing that fact can make us more compassionate toward those we love, and who struggle to love us.

Quotations taken from *Kristen Lavransdatter*, Alfred A. Knopf, New York. 1951.

Talk About It

Did Kristin Lavransdatter marry the wrong man? Is there a "Mr. Right" for everyone, or does that person change as we change? What advice would you give to a young person choosing a mate?

About the Author: Sigrid Undset

Sigrid Undset was born in Kalundborg, Denmark in 1882, but her family moved to Norway when she was two years old. Her father was an archeologist and her mother served as his illustrator and secretary, and Sigrid grew up among the artifacts of her native land. Since her father was Norwegian and her mother was Danish, she was comfortable in both societies. When her father died in 1893 the family struggled financially, so Sigrid left school and took a job in an electrical company, where she worked for ten years. In the evening she would write, and completed two novels set in the medieval world she loved. A publisher encouraged her to write something more modern, which she did, producing a book of short stories about office workers that sold reasonably well.

This gave her the opportunity to try her hand at the historical novel again. Her best-known work is *Kristin Lavransdatter*, a trilogy about life in Scandinavia in the Middle Ages. The book was published from 1920 to 1922 in three volumes, and portrays the life of one woman from birth until death. For this and other work, Undset was the first woman to be awarded the Nobel Prize in Literature in 1928.

In the face of the Nazi invasion Undset fled Norway for the United States in 1940 but returned after World War II ended in 1945. She donated all of her Nobel Prize money to charity, and even sold her Nobel medal to raise money for Finnish children in distress after the war. She was married twice, raised three children, one of them severely retarded, and late in life converted from Lutheranism to Catholicism. She died in Norway in 1949, at the age of sixty-seven.

(Kristin Lavransdatter, Introduction, and Wikipedia)

A World Apart:
Wild Swans: Three Daughters of China,
by Jung Chang

Though events on the world stage in the decade since September 2001 have been devastating, they have also been educational. For example, the average American now has a visual impression of the living conditions in Iraq. We know the difference between the political climate in Fallujah and Baghdad. We know who the Kurds are and where Kuwait is, and share strong opinions about elections in Afghanistan. Sadly, this cultural literacy comes rather too late. After the atrocities of 9/11 the intelligence community found themselves hopelessly ignorant—only a few agents spoke Arabic—and no one seemed to know much about this new enemy that knew so much about us. We were left to play catch-up with deadly consequences. One wonders, if only we had understood a bit more about the embattled region that now claims the lives of American soldiers every day, would things be different now?

There are other troubled and troubling regions in the world, regions that are increasingly the focus of the nightly news. One of these is China, that vast land with over a billion people, about which most of us know very little, yet whose financial power in the Western economies is growing at an alarming rate. An ancient empire with a long history of corruption, China fell to Mao Zedong and his forces after World War II and continues today as one of the last bastions of old-style Communism. Though Chairman Mao's Cultural Revolution has metamorphosed into a China that welcomes capitalist investment, the tragedy of Tiananmen Square looms as a reminder that in China, capitalist investment does not necessarily come in tandem with freedom, or even basic human rights.

How shall we understand a people as complex as the Chinese? One of the best ways is through studying the lives of individuals as they move through its history. There have been a handful of outstanding autobiographical works written by Chinese exiles, and among the best is Jung Chang's, *Wild Swans: Three Daughters of China*. Published in 1991 to great acclaim, this dense, fascinating account of three generations of women in China was the best selling non-fiction book ever published in Britain. It has since sold over ten million copies worldwide, has been translated into over thirty languages, and continues to be a favorite with readers.

Synopsis

Chang's history begins with the story of her maternal grandmother, who was sold as a concubine to a warlord at the age of fifteen. Her narrative explores the stark contrast between the grandmother, given as a concubine to a local warlord, and the life of her daughter, a zealous member of the Communist party who marries a fellow Communist and tries to be loyal to Mao at all costs. Unfortunately, the shifting political tides and her husband's fanatical obedience to the party exact a terrible toll in her life. Their daughter (the author) is also a fervent communist in her youth, but becomes disillusioned as she sees the cruelty of party leaders, who torture and harass her father until he is a broken man. She eventually leaves China, and becomes the first Chinese woman to receive a doctoral degree outside China. The saga of these three lives offers a fascinating glimpse into the history of a nation.

What Makes it Great?

Like Francie Nolan and Kristin Lavransdatter, Jung Chang is a character in her own life. This is not a simple biography, it's a novel constructed from real lives. Chang's ability to shift between historical fact and the novelistic description of detail is remarkable. The opening scene, a horrendous description of foot binding, alerts us to the fact that we have entered a strange new world:

"My grandmother's feet had been bound when she was two years old. Her mother, who herself had bound feet, first wound a piece of white cloth about twenty feet long round her feet, bending all the toes except the big toe inward and under the sole. Then she placed a large stone on top to crush the arch. My grandmother screamed in agony and begged her to stop. Her mother had to stick a cloth into her mouth to gag her. My grandmother passed out repeatedly from the pain." (24)

Did You Know?

Chang's latest work, a biography of Mao, was co-authored by her husband Jon Halliday and portrays Mao in an extremely negative light. The couple travelled all over the world to research the book which took twelve years to write. They interviewed hundreds of people who had known Mao including George Bush, Sr., Henry Kissinger, and Tenzin Gyatso, the Dalai Lama.

This horrific torture suffered by daughters at the hands of their otherwise devoted mothers is hard to comprehend, and is more disturbing when we learn that this process lasted several years. (Even grown women could not untie their feet, for they would immediately begin to grow.) Yet what was the choice? Mothers, who, in pity, released their daughters from the torment and allowed their feet to grow to normal size saw them unable to attract suitable husbands, or suffer the contempt of the husband's family. This fundamental lack of choice—the sense that women were confined to a certain role and could not escape—is brilliantly presented through the ritual of foot binding. It became a metaphor for me as I read about these remarkable women and men, who were willing to reshape their minds to conform to a regime that demanded unquestioning loyalty, even at the expense of reason and common sense. Here, for example, is a description of her grandmother's response when she is informed that she will be given as a concubine to a wealthy warlord:

"The first my grandmother knew of her impending liaison was when her mother broke the news to her a few days before the event. My grandmother bent her head and wept. She hated the idea of being a concubine, but her father had already made the decision, and it was unthinkable to oppose one's parents. To question a parental decision was considered 'unfilial'—and to be unfilial was tantamount to treason. Even if she refused to consent to her father's wishes, she would not be taken seriously; her action would be interpreted as indicating that she wanted to stay with her parents. The only way to say no and be taken seriously was to commit suicide." (30)

Reading about the strength of parental authority in this society helped me understand the unflinching obedience that the next generation offered to the Communist regime. Mao was the new father, and children willingly betrayed their own blood relations in their blind loyalty to the Chairman.

Is it Really a Novel?

Chang is bringing us the inner thoughts of her characters, so we know that she is, in a sense, recreating rather than just reporting the outward facts of their lives. This blurring of the line between factual people and fictional characters can be unsettling in a story about real people, but this kind of creative reconstruction of reality is something we all do, even about our own lives, and Chang does it beautifully. One of the delights of this unusual memoir is Jung Chang's ability to isolate sweet moments that are unique to Chinese society, yet seem familiar to all of us. As Chang grew to womanhood, she became caught up in the Communist philosophy and its attendant lifestyle. Like other young Communists, she cut off her hair, wore shapeless clothing, and eschewed all things feminine as *bourgeois*. Yet each morning, she watched her beautiful old grandmother (the former concubine) care for her hair in the traditional Chinese fashion:

"My grandmother kept her hair tied up neatly in a bun at the back of her head, but she always had flowers there . . . She never used shampoo from the shops, which she thought would make her hair dull and dry, but would boil the fruit of the Chinese honey locust and use the liquid from that. She would rub the fruit to produce a perfumed lather, and slowly let her mass of black hair drop into the shiny, white, slithery liquid. She soaked her wooden combs in the juice of pomelo seeds, so that the comb ran smoothly through her hair, and gave it a faint aroma . . . . I remember watching her combing her hair. It was the only thing over which she took her time." (265)

Precious moments like this make Jung Chang and her family real for us. They are no longer nameless faces among a billion Chinese, they are a family: women, men and children who love each other and hope for all the same things we do. When the Cultural Revolution shatters this family, we feel shattered as well. Chang's father, a devoted Communist, comes under condemnation for no particular reason, and the Red Guards (young people given free reign by Mao to terrorize the populace) storm his home. As part of the program of public humiliation, they cause him to kneel and watch as they destroy his prized collection of ancient Chinese manuscripts:

"Mrs. Shau slapped my father hard. The crowd barked at him indignantly, although a few tried to hide their giggles. Then they pulled out his books and threw them into huge jute sacks they had brought with them. When all the bags were full, they carried them downstairs, telling my father they were going to burn them . . . My father had spent every spare penny on his books. They were his life. After the bonfire, I could tell that something had happened to his mind." (330)

Wild Swans is compulsively readable. (I determined to skim much of it and found myself reading every word.) Chang has a remarkable eye for detail and a strong sense of where her narrative must lead us. Whether these stories have been embellished is impossible to tell, but her account offers us a way to track China's journey from Monarchy to Communism and see that world through new eyes. There may be no way to understand a billion Chinese people, but we can understand one woman, then one family, and in so doing may take the first step across the cultural gulf that divides us.

Quotations taken from *Wild Swans: Three Daughters of China*. Touchstone, New York. 1991.

Talk About It

Jung Chang offers us a picture of China under the emperors and warlords, and a picture of China under Communism. Which do you think was worse?

About the Author: Jung Chang

Jung Chang was born in 1952 in the Sichuan Province of China. Her parents were both Communist Party officials, and, as her father was greatly interested in literature, she developed a love of reading and writing, even composing poetry as a child. As Party officials, the Chang family enjoyed a good life with many privileges in the early days of the Cultural Revolution. However, Chang's parents became disillusioned with Chairman Mao and, as a result, were singled out and publicly humiliated by the party. This led Chang, who had become a Red Guard at age 14, to lose her idealistic commitment to the party as well. Her depiction of the Chinese people as having been "programmed" by Maoism would ring forth in her subsequent writings.

After various jobs ranging from country doctor to electrician, Chang left China in 1978 to study in Britain on a government scholarship. She became the first person from the People's Republic of China to be awarded a doctoral degree from a British university; her degree was in linguistics. The publication of Jung Chang's first book, *Wild Swans,* made her a celebrity. Chang's unique style, using a personal description of the life of three generations of Chinese women to highlight the many changes that the country underwent, proved to be highly successful. The book has sold over 10 million copies worldwide and is banned in mainland China.

Source: Wikipedia

Growing Pains: Take it Personally

These three novels speak to women in a unique manner. The overwhelming reader response to Betty Smith's book has already been mentioned, but I received many impassioned responses from Best Book Club members about all three of these books. One Book Club member summed up her experience with "her Kristin" this way:

"I read the Kristin Lavransdatter trilogy the first time because I liked the cover—I admit it. At first I thought, what does a woman from the Middle Ages in Norway have to do with me—a woman in the 1970's in Orange County, California, and then I discovered my Kristin. She still feels like an old friend. I have re-discovered her many times, as a new wife, a new mother, and now as I am entering my 40's. I see something different in her and discover something different in me—with each read."

In response to *Wild Swans*, another reader commented, "Times may change, but through the ages women face the same trials, heartbreaks, and responsibilities that are unique in our roles as daughters, mothers and wives. Reading this book, I received insight into my own life and future."

Among the many insights we might take away from these narratives would be the following ice-axe question: In what ways have our own parents bound our feet? What painful experience from your youth continues to cause you pain and does damage to your present and future? Can you see any way to address the issue and lessen its negative impact in your life?

Chapter Three
Boys to Men

"What is genius?—It is the power to be a boy again at will."

James M. Barrie

"The boy is father to the man."

Proverb

How does it feel to be a boy growing up? Today, more than ever, it is vital to understand the boys in our sphere of influence and help them come of age with dignity and integrity. The decline of the traditional family has removed the male role model from many homes, requiring greater support at this crucial developmental stage from extended family, friends and mentors. Psychologist Michael Gurian warns that our boys are a threatened demographic:

"It seems impossible for us to fully comprehend the state of male adolescence in our culture, yet it is essential we do so. There is hardly any social or personal health indicator in which adolescent boys do not show the lion's share of risk today. Decades ago, our females suffered more in more high-risk areas, and now our adolescent males are suffering privation we have not fully understood." (*A Fine Young Man*, Introduction)

The *bildungsroman*, or coming of age novel, follows the progress of the boy to the man. Three great authors from widely different cultural perspectives open a window into the lives of boys as they come to grips with a world of racial hatred, religious intolerance and moral degeneracy. They emerge changed forever, into fine young men.

Boys Gone Wild :
The Adventures of Tom Sawyer, by Mark Twain

Mark Twain remains as colorful a figure in our collective consciousness as any of the characters he created. In fact, the man we remember as Mark Twain was himself a character, carefully created and promoted by the brilliant Samuel Clemens. His first novel, *The Adventures of Tom Sawyer,* is remarkable in many respects, for here we see the world through the eyes of a boy, rather than the traditional rugged hero of the American novel. And what a boy he is! Tom Sawyer leaps off the page as a complete and complex personality, with all the infuriating cockiness and endearing insecurity of the pre-pubescent male.

Synopsis

Tom Sawyer, an orphan, lives with his Aunt Polly in a small town on the Missouri River in the mid-1800's. He is full of mischief: he plays hooky from school, cheats to win prizes in Sunday School and generally misbehaves in any way he can devise. His best friend is Huck Finn, the ragged, homeless son of the town drunk, (with even worse morals) and together they get into one scrape after another. Eventually the two miscreants land in big trouble by accidentally straying onto the scene of a homicide and becoming the targets of Injun Joe, the grave-robbing murderer of Doctor Robinson.

Tom and Huck run away to a local island, then make a dramatic appearance at their own funeral after they are declared dead. They suffer illness, start a band of pirates and Tom has quarrels with his first love, Becky Thatcher. When the wrong man goes on trial for the murder of Dr. Robinson, Tom and Huck (though sworn to secrecy about it) are consumed with guilt. Eventually, on a church picnic, Tom and Becky become lost in a cave, while Huck discovers a plot by Injun Joe to hurt a local widow. Huck foils the plot, Tom saves Becky, Injun Joe gets his just desserts and the boys find the treasure that Injun Joe had concealed in the cave. They all live happily ever after, except poor Huck, who is adopted by the grateful widow and has to wear real clothes and go to school!

What Makes it Great?

One of the secrets to Mark Twain's enduring popularity is his remarkable voice. The first line of this book is the shortest first line in all of literature, and a pure stroke of genius. Here it is: "Tom!" With this one word Twain lets us know that our hero is no saint; he's a boy who gets yelled at—a lot. Tom is always in trouble, always has a new angle, and is the kind of kid you don't want your child to play with. You have to love him. Twain instantly establishes a warm relationship with the reader as he invites us to remember our own childhoods by stepping into Tom's world. These days Tom would be evaluated by counselors and placed on medication for Attention Deficit Disorder, but in Twain's day he was simply a mischievous, all-American boy, and Twain obviously revels in his naughtiness:

"He was not the Model Boy of the village. He knew the model boy very well though—and loathed him. Within two minutes, or even less, he had forgotten all his troubles. Not because his troubles were one whit less heavy and bitter to him than a man's are to a man, but because a new and powerful interest bore them down and drove them out of his mind for the time—just as men's misfortunes are forgotten in the excitement of new enterprises. This new interest was a valued novelty in whistling, which he had just acquired from a Negro, and he was suffering to practice it undisturbed. It consisted in a peculiar bird-like turn, a sort of liquid warble, produced by touching the tongue to the roof of the mouth at short intervals in the midst of the music—the reader probably remembers how to do it, if he has ever been a boy. Diligence and attention soon gave him the knack of it, and he strode down the street with his mouth full of harmony and his soul full of gratitude. He felt much as an astronomer feels who has discovered a new planet—no doubt, as far as strong, deep, unalloyed pleasure is concerned, the advantage was with the boy, not the astronomer." (4)

In an era when novels featured sugar-sweet children and all-wise adults, Tom Sawyer emerges as a complex, charming, infuriating, fascinating character in the process of transformation. Notice how in just a few lines (during the time when the "lost boys" are hiding out on the island) Twain shows us all the warring factions in the heart of a growing boy: the love of indolence, competitive games, and a primitive superstition, combined

Did You Know?

Mark Twain wrote this book in response to a type of literature that he despised: the book with a "moral message." These stories include "The Story of a Bad Little Boy Who Lived a Charmed Life" (1865) and "The Story of a Good Little Boy Who Did Not Prosper" (1870) in which "bad boys" get into mischief and suffer the consequences. By creating Tom, the all-American bad boy with a good heart, Twain turned these moralistic stories on their heads.

with a still-latent obsession with a girl, which he considers a shameful weakness:

"Next they got their marbles and played "knucks" and "ring-taw" and "keeps" till that amusement grew stale. Then Joe and Huck had another swim, but Tom would not venture, because he found that in kicking off his trousers he had kicked his string of rattlesnake rattles off his ankle, and he wondered how he had escaped cramp so long without the protection of this mysterious charm. He did not venture again until he had found it, and by that time the other boys were tired and ready to rest. They gradually wandered apart, dropped into the "dumps," and fell to gazing longingly across the wide river to where the village lay drowsing in the sun. Tom found himself writing "BECKY" in the sand with his big toe; he scratched it out, and was angry with himself for his weakness. But he wrote it again, nevertheless; he could not help it. He erased it once more and then took himself out of temptation by driving the other boys together and joining them." (255)

Stepping into Manhood

Like most great children's books this is a novel full of adult subject matter, replete with the themes of death, religious dogma in opposition to simple goodness, and the natural honor that exists in man before civilization corrupts him. Twain is so familiar and quotable that it is easy to laugh at the humor and miss the bitter subtext of the novel, which offers a harsh criticism of the way "society" fails its young. Tom is carefully taught to adopt the religious hypocrisy and racial hatred rampant in his culture, and his resistance to these teachings causes most of his trouble. He vacillates between half-hearted attempts to accept societal norms and an instinctive rejection of all authority. When Tom and Becky become hopelessly lost in the cave however, Tom begins to grow up. His mischievousness has brought his beloved into real danger; and now there are no adults around against whom to rebel. For the first time, our hero begins to show real courage rather than mere bravado:

"At last Becky's frail limbs refused to carry her farther. She sat down. Tom rested with her, and they talked of home, and the friends there, and the comfortable beds and, above all, the light! Becky cried, and Tom tried to think of some way of comforting her, but all his encouragements were grown threadbare with use, and sounded like sarcasms. Fatigue bore so heavily upon Becky that she drowsed off to sleep. Tom was grateful. He sat looking into her drawn face and saw it grow smooth and natural under the influence of pleasant dreams; and by-and-by a smile dawned and rested there. The peaceful face reflected somewhat of peace and healing into his own spirit, and his thoughts wandered away to bygone times and dreamy memories. While he was deep in his musings, Becky woke up with a breezy little laugh—but it was stricken dead upon her lips, and a groan followed it.

"Oh, how COULD I sleep! I wish I never, never had waked! No! No, I don't, Tom! Don't look so! I won't say it again."

"I'm glad you've slept, Becky; you'll feel rested, now, and we'll find the way out."

"We can try, Tom; but I've seen such a beautiful country in my dream. I reckon we are going there."

"Maybe not, maybe not. Cheer up, Becky, and let's go on trying." (367)

This willingness to "go on trying," in the face of overwhelming odds, sums up Tom's greatness, and epitomizes the pioneering spirit that conquered the frontier. It is another mark of Twain's brilliance; in the face of prejudice, hatred and heartless cruelty, he persists in a childlike faith in the essential goodness of the human spirit. This relentless optimism is one more reason why Mark Twain holds an enduring place in the hearts of readers everywhere.

Quotations taken from *The Adventures of Tom Sawyer*. Penguin Classics Edition, New York. 1986

Talk About It

Tom Sawyer and Huck Finn would be labeled juvenile delinquents in our day. Have we lost something in the attempt to eradicate bad behavior in boys, or are we better off today with the advances in child psychology?

About the Author: Mark Twain

Samuel Clemens was born in 1835, the son of a genteel but unsuccessful father who died of pneumonia when he was eleven. Clemens was the sixth of seven children, only three of which survived childhood. He was raised on the banks of the Missouri River in a tiny town called Hannibal, later to be immortalized as the fictional town of St. Petersburg in his writing. At the time, Missouri was a slave state, a theme to be explored so well in his work.

He was always writing, and had his first story published while still a teenager. His early years were spent as a printer, a journalist, and as a steamboat pilot. His first great success as a writer came when his humorous tall tale, "The Celebrated Jumping Frog of Calaveras County", was published. He adopted the name Mark Twain and followed the example of Artemus Ward, a famous humorist of the time, giving lectures on his experiences in the West.

During his family's seventeen years in Hartford, Connecticut, Twain wrote some of his best-known works: *The Adventures of Tom Sawyer* (1876), *The Prince and the Pauper* (1881), *Life on the Mississippi* (1883), *Adventures of Huckleberry Finn* (1884), and *A Connecticut Yankee in King Arthur's Court* (1889). *The Adventures of Huckleberry Finn* is known as The Great American Novel. William Faulkner called Twain "the father of American literature."

During his lifetime, Twain became a friend to presidents, artists, industrialists, and European royalty. He died in 1910 and was buried in his wife's family plot in New York. A 12-foot (i.e., two fathoms, or "mark twain") monument marks his grave.

Sources:

James M. Cox. *Mark Twain: The Fate of Humor*. Princeton University Press, 1966.

Everett Emerson. *Mark Twain: A Literary Life*. Philadelphia: University of Pennsylvania Press, 2000.

Mapping the Human Heart:
The Chosen, by Chaim Potok

"Long ago, in *The Chosen,*" Chaim Potok writes, "I set out to draw a map of the New York world through which I once journeyed. It was to be a map not only of broken streets, menacing alleys, concrete-surfaced backyards, neighborhood schools and stores . . . a map not only of the physical elements of my early life, but of the spiritual ones as well." (Chaim Potok, *"The Invisible Map of Meaning: A Writer's Confrontation," Triquarterly, Spring 1992)* With his glimpse into the lives of the Hasidic Jews of New York, Chaim Potok transports us to a world completely strange, yet strangely familiar.

Synopsis

The Chosen is the story of two young men growing up in Brooklyn just before the onset of World War II. Through a chance encounter between their baseball teams they form a friendship that changes both their lives. Reuven Malter, an orthodox Jew, and the son of a passionate Zionist and dedicated scholar, acts as narrator. Danny Saunders, a Hasidic Jew, is a brilliant boy with a photographic memory who is the son and heir of a Tzaddik, the leader of a Hasidic sect. He is being raised by his father under a code of silence, meaning, that with the exception of Talmudic discussions, Reb Saunders never speaks to his son directly. This seemingly cruel treatment is designed to "teach him the suffering of the world" and prepare Danny to assume his father's place as the head of the congregation. Though the two boys see each other as complete cultural strangers, to the outside world they are simply both Jews.

As these boys become acquainted we come to understand, with Reuven, something about Hasidism, the ultra-conservative sect that originated in Poland in response to the persecutions suffered by Jews hundreds of years ago. A Tzaddik, a mystical leader who is rabbi, prophet and even a Messianic figure to his followers, leads each group of Hasidic Jews. They dwell in a world closed even to other Jews, and as Reuven enters this world through his friendship with Danny, we have the rare opportunity to experience a fascinating culture within a culture. Danny resists the future that is mapped out for him: he is unwilling to follow in his father's footsteps and longs to study psychology. We follow the boys through their high school and college years, as they come to terms with their fathers, their faith and their futures.

What Makes it Great?

Potok's great strength is not in description or plot; it is in character. The greatness of this novel, and its enduring appeal, lies in the quirky characters of the two boys and two fathers at its center. Both Danny and Reuven are irresistible in their sincerity, idealism and intelligence. It's not easy being Jewish in any age, and Potok gives us an inside look at the myriad challenges that they face. These boys and their fathers entrance us; we cannot look away. Here, for example, is the moment when Reb Saunders explains to Reuven (and by extension to Danny) why he imposed the code of silence that has caused Danny so much pain and sorrow:

"My father himself never talked to me, except when we studied together. He taught me with silence. He taught me to look into myself, to find my own strength, to walk around inside myself in company with my soul . . . . One learns of the pain of others by suffering one's own pain, he would say, by turning inside oneself, by finding one's own soul. And it is important to know of pain, he said. It destroys our self-pride, our arrogance, and our indifference toward others. It makes us aware of how frail and tiny we are and of how much we must depend upon the Master of the Universe . . . .

"Reuven, I did not want my Daniel to become like my brother, may he rest in peace. Better I should have had no son at all than to have a brilliant son who had no soul . . . . And I had to make certain his soul would be the soul of a tzaddik no matter what he did with his life." (278, 279)

Did You Know?

When Potok was 14, he read Evelyn Waugh's novel *Brideshead Revisited,* and the experience altered him forever. He explained in a *Newsday* interview, "I found myself inside a world the merest existence of which I had known nothing about, I lived more deeply inside the world in that book than I lived inside my own world, for the time it took me to read it." This sensation of being transported to a parallel reality captivated Potok, and he struck out to learn how to achieve the same effect with his own words.

A Man of the World

Chaim Potok says that he wrote *The Chosen* in order to come to terms with his own Jewish upbringing, particularly the fundamentalist viewpoint that taught him to see the Jewish race at the center of world history. Raised in an unquestioning orthodox home, Chaim graduated from his local Yeshiva and was ordained a rabbi. It was at this point that his life changed completely, when he was sent to Korea for two years as a chaplain. Of this experience he says, "When I went to Korea I was a very coherent human being in the sense that I had a model of what I was—I had a map. I knew who I was as a Jew. When I went to Asia, it all came unglued. It all became relativized. Everything turned upside down." (Chaim Potok, personal interview) He came to believe that religious dogma is meaningless unless it leads us to deal more compassionately with others. He said: "A theology that is not linked directly to a pattern of behavior is a blowing of wind and macabre game with words. And a pattern of behavior that is not linked to a system of thought is an instance of religious robbery." (ibid.)

Chaim Potok's father had taught him that Jews suffered because they were God's chosen, yet over a million Koreans had been senselessly slaughtered during the war. He wondered, were they also chosen in some way, or was all the suffering of the Jews meaningless? Potok had been taught to believe that paganism was evil, yet in the faces of devout Buddhists in prayer he recognized the same intensity that he knew in the faces of the faithful Jews in his synagogue. How could God hate these sincere, devout people?

Through his experience in Korea Potok came to believe that by helping readers see into another culture, he could help them get a new perspective on their own. One of his early inspirations was James Joyce, who wrote only about his hometown of Dublin. Joyce said, "If I can get to the heart of Dublin I can get to the heart of all the cities in the world. In the particular is contained the universal." As we get into the heart of a lonely Hasidic boy we learn some universal truths about the human struggle, and find curious parallels between his world and our own.

Reuven's father tells him, "Human beings do not live forever, Rueven, we live less than the time it takes to blink an eye, if we measure our lives against eternity. So we may be asked what value is there to a human life. There is so much pain in the world. What does it mean to have to suffer so much if our lives are nothing more than the blink of an eye? I learned a long time ago, that the blink of an eye in itself is nothing. But the eye that blinks, that is something. The span of life is nothing. But the man who lives that span, he is something. He can fill that tiny span with meaning, so that its quality is immeasurable, though its quantity may be insignificant. A man must fill his life with meaning; meaning is not automatically given to life. It is hard work to fill one's life with meaning. A life filled with meaning is worthy of rest. I want to be worthy of rest, when I am no longer here . . ." (147)

Potok's greatness lies in his simple faith in mankind and in his ability to evoke the tender, halting steps from boyhood into manhood. At the same time, he believes in allegiance to a cause larger than ourselves, so that we will be "worthy of rest" when the time comes. Few goals are worthy of greater dedication.

Quotations taken from *The Chosen. Random House*, New York. 1967.

Talk About It

Reuven and Danny are both Jews, yet their cultures are so different that they feel like strangers. The effort to include all of the diverse cultures that make up our schools and communities can be confusing. To what extent should we attempt to accommodate the different cultures that surround us? Is it even possible to do so?

About the Author: Chaim Potok

Chaim Potok, born Herman Harold Potok, was reared in an Orthodox Jewish home by Polish immigrant parents. His parents also gave him his Hebrew name Chaim, meaning "life" or "alive." Born in 1929 in New York City, he attended religious schools. However, as a young man he became fascinated by less restrictive Jewish doctrines, particularly the Conservative side of Judaism. He attended Yeshiva University and earned degrees in English and Hebrew literature. Potok was eventually ordained a Conservative rabbi. He joined the U.S. Army as a chaplain and served in South Korea from 1955 to 1957, which he described as a transformative experience.

In 1967, Potok began his career as an author and novelist with the publication of *The Chosen*, written while he lived with his family in Jerusalem. It stands as the first book from a major publisher to portray Orthodox Judaism in the United States. After spending six months on the bestseller list, the book has remained extremely popular. Chaim Potok "wrote of what he knew best, Jewish-Americans in the 20th century struggling with two contradictory yet valid points of view." (Shirley Saad, UPI). The conflict can best be summed up in Potok's own words, "Is it possible to live in a religious culture and a secular culture at the same time?"

The Chosen was made into a film, released in 1981, which won the top award at the World Film Festival, Montreal. The novel was also adapted into a stage play by the author. He went on to publish a sequel to the book, *The Promise*, and many other fiction and non-fiction works.

In 1958, Potok married Adena Sara Mosevitzsky, a psychiatric social worker, whom he met in 1952 at Camp Ramah in the Poconos. They had three children: Rena, Naama, and Akiva. He died of brain cancer in 2002.

Source:*Wanderings: Chaim Potok's History of the Jews*, Chaim Potok, Knopf, New York, 1978.

Art Imitates Life Imitates Art:
The Power of One, by Bryce Courtenay

What makes us cling so tenaciously to life? What is the importance of
each individual? These are the questions at the heart of a stirring novel
by Bryce Courtenay, *The Power of One*. This autobiographical story of
an English boy raised in South Africa is a daunting account of one small
life pitted against a world of hatred and strife. In an environment where
survival seems impossible, this lonely little boy finds a way to triumph over
his enemies and remain true to his friends.

Synopsis

Peekay is in a difficult position. As an English boy sent to a South
African boarding school at the age of five, he finds himself the whipping
boy for the Afrikaaner students, Nazi sympathizers who hate the British
for the atrocities of the Boer war. Peekay is too young to understand the
motivations for the hatred and persecution that he meets at every turn, and
his bewilderment is heart rending. The torments he suffers at the hands of
his cruel schoolmates are recreated for us in grim detail.

As a defense against constant persecution, Peekay becomes a boxer, and
learns to hold his own physically against those who threaten him. Through
the influence of some gentle teachers over many years, he also becomes
a horticulturist, a musician, and an academic scholar. What he does not
become is a bitter, twisted man, because of the influence of these two
or three guiding personalities in his life. Since his father is dead and his
mother is emotionally childish, Peekay must find mentors to guide him.
His Zulu nanny gives him love, and the conductor he meets on the train
to school gives him a quest: to become the welterweight champion of the
world. Peekay finds himself in the middle of a political and racial storm, as
the Afrikaaners are forced to round up Germans (with whom they actually
sympathize) as prisoners of war, while offering the English token support
along with private hostility. A German doctor/horticulturist/musician
befriends the lonely boy and teaches him to be proud of his good mind
rather than try to hide it. Much of the book deals with Peekay's attempts to

Did You Know?

One of the most impressive things about this novel is the age of the author when he wrote it. Bryce Courtenay didn't begin writing fiction until he was fifty-five years old, and his novel has had an impact on millions of people throughout the world. His story is clearly written with a purpose: to help us believe in the value of each individual and in the power of each individual to triumph over adversity and make a positive contribution to the world.

soften the harsh effects of war on this old man. In the meantime he learns to fight, and pursues his boxing career with the same zeal as his studies, becoming a legend along the way through some remarkable successes.

The violence of apartheid is a central issue in this novel. Peekay observes the workings of a violent culture in the prison, where the white wardens abuse black inmates, most of whom have had little education or opportunity. When Peekay and Morrie try to fight the hatred towards black culture by establishing a night school, they learn just how tenacious the cycle of violence is when imbedded into a culture. Though Peekay faces almost insurmountable obstacles, his courage and tenacity shine through at every turn.

What Makes it Great?

The greatness of this novel lies in its message, which has inspired millions. Its central theme is first revealed to us as Peekay rides toward his future on the train. Along with a goal to become a fighter, the conductor offers Peekay a mantra that seems to speak directly from the tracks and guides his life thereafter:

"I stood there watching the early morning folding back. It can be very cold in the lowveld before the sun rises, and without a blanket I soon began to shiver. I tried to ignore the cold, concentrating on the lickity-clack of the carriage wheels. I became aware that the lickity-clack was talking to me: *Mix-the-head with-the-heart you're-ahead from-the-start. Mix-the-head with-the-heart you're-ahead from-the-start,* the wheels chanted until my head began to pound with the rhythm. It was becoming the plan I would follow for the remainder of my life; it was to become the secret ingredient in what I thought of as the power of one." (104)

When it comes to actual technique, Courtenay is a good writer but not a great one. He has some fine descriptive passages, but is somewhat weak when it comes to really fleshing out a believable character. His good characters are a little too good to be true, and the bad ones are over-the-top evil. (The Zulu nanny, for example, exudes love and wisdom, while his white, Evangelical Christian mother is simply weak and hypocritical. Neither has the balancing traits that real people would have.) His strength lies in his ability to evoke a landscape and a culture that is completely unfamiliar to most of us, and use it as a backdrop for the more familiar emotional landscape that we all share. Here is a description of some lonely moments on a hillside, mourning the loss of his nanny, that reveals both his strengths and weaknesses as an author:

"As I sat on the rock high on my hill, and as the sun began to set over the bushveld, I grew up. Just like that. The loneliness birds stopped laying stone eggs, they rose from their stone nests and flapped away on their ugly wings and the eggs they left behind crumbled into dust. A fierce, howling wind came along and blew the dust away until I was empty inside.

I knew they would be back but that, for the moment, I was alone. That I had permission from myself to love whomsoever I wished. The cords that bound me to the past had been severed. The emptiness was a new kind of loneliness, a free kind of loneliness. Not the kind that laid stone eggs deep inside of you until you filled up with heaviness and despair. I knew that when the bone-beaked birds returned I would be in control, master of loneliness and no longer its servant. You may ask how a six-year-old could think like this. I can only answer that one did." (142)

It is natural for the narrator to be somewhat defensive, because it really is a bit of a stretch to believe that a six-year-old could elucidate such thoughts as these. With that nit-picking aside, I recommend this novel because of its untiring optimism in the face of overwhelming evil. Peekay finds beauty, grace and humor in the most trying circumstances. In an evil world he happens upon good people who become trusted friends. His ability to assimilate information and his persistence give him an advantage that overshadows his liabilities of size and status, and his stubborn belief in the power of one person to effect change has inspired millions of readers.

Note: Though it concerns a very small child, this is not a children's book. It contains a good deal of foul language and some graphic violence. Yet when the book came out in 1989 teachers were so impressed with its inspiring message that they petitioned the author to create a version more suitable for children. Thus, an expurgated version of this novel is available, and I would recommend it for parents who want to share it with children, and for those who will find the swearing offensive.

Quotations taken from *The Power of One*. Ballantine Books, New York. 2008.

Talk About It

Bryce Courtenay (Peekay) was certainly the victim of bullying—an issue very much in today's headlines—and he found his own way of combating it. Have you or your children experienced this kind of persecution and, if so, how would you recommend dealing with it?

About the Author: Bryce Courtenay

The Power of One is a fictionalized story of Bryce Courtenay's childhood in South Africa. Courtenay was born illegitimately in Johannesburg in 1933 and spent his early years on an isolated farm in a small village. Like his fictional hero, Peekay, five-year-old Courtenay learned to box as a means of self-defense in private school. After the boy's move to Barberton, a drunken German music teacher, Doc, gave young Courtenay his true childhood education, filling his mind with the wonders of nature as they roamed the high mountains. Courtenay acknowledges it was the best education he was ever to receive. He won a scholarship to a fine South African boarding school and later went on to study journalism in London.

Forbidden to return to South Africa after he started a weekend educational program for native Africans in the hall of his prestigious boy's school, Courtenay moved to Sydney, Australia. He married a woman named Benita and had three sons, Brett, Adam, and Damon. Damon, a hemophiliac, contracted HIV from a blood transfusion during the early days of the disease. After Damon died tragically of AIDS, Courtenay wrote *April Fool's Day*, the compelling novel that commemorated his son and brought attention to the AIDS epidemic.

Bryce Courtenay began writing fiction at age 55 and published *The Power of One* in 1989. It became one of Australia's best-selling books by any living author. Courtenay is also in demand as a motivational speaker. Before his literary career, he worked in advertising as a copywriter and creative director.

Sources:

Suite 101.com/ world literatures

www.brycecourtenay.com

Boys to Men: Take It Personally

One member of the Best Books Club that invariably has something interesting to say is Phillip Harris, an Englishman now residing in Texas. Chaim Potok is a particular favorite of this thoughtful and erudite reader. Of these three coming-on-age sagas he offers the following perspective:

"All three writers are not really writing about boys becoming men, but rather boys having the spirit to rebel against the perceptions of their time and their struggle to become individuals of meaning. Mark Twain is the American Charles Dickens—a social reformer dressed as a superb raconteur—and this is what him so engaging and his books timeless. We of the twenty first century, with all our fancy toys, long for the old days. Bryce Courtney has the same gift. He places a timid but staunch personality in the midst of one of the most despicable episodes in modern history with the foreknowledge that the reader will know and be comforted by the eventual historical outcome.

"Chaim Potok's approach is different. His book is a declaration from the heart. The characters are almost incidental to the story. It is what they believe and practice that makes the book so riveting. Rueven's father's declaration about the meaning of life is the central theme of the book (and also "the promise.") It is difficult to read this passage without the tears marking the page."

What do we learn about boys from these three novels? Perhaps it is simply an appreciation of the conflicting emotions that rage within each young man's heart. Not only the longing for acceptance and love, but the yearning to be part of a cause greater than oneself is a driving force in the life of a young man, that can lead him to great achievements, or to acts of destruction, depending on the influences at hand. These novels encourage us to take a closer, more compassionate look at the young men in our lives.

Chapter Four
Road Trips

"The World is a book, and those who do not travel read only a page."

~St. Augustine

"Travel is fatal to prejudice, bigotry, and narrow-mindedness, and many of our people need it sorely on these accounts. Broad, wholesome, charitable views of men and things cannot be acquired by vegetating in one little corner of the earth all one's lifetime."

~Mark Twain

The picaresque novel (from the Spanish *"pícaro"*, for "rogue" or "rascal") is a type of prose fiction that depicts the adventures of a roguish hero getting by on his or her wits in a dangerous and foreign society. Though this type of novel originated in Spain, there are examples of it in every language, and these are three marvelous examples. Rudyard Kipling takes us down the dusty Grand Trunk road in India and William Faulkner takes us joyriding down the equally dusty back roads of Mississippi. Then Mark Twain takes us down the Mississippi River on a raft with Jim and Huck, on a journey toward human understanding. Our three intrepid travelers, though taken by surprise at the dangers they face, prove equal to the challenge as they find a way to survive without sacrificing those ideals that will inform their adult lives. So, take to the road with Kim, Lucius, and Huck, and come home changed for the better.

A Good Boy On a Bumpy Road:
The Reivers, by William Faulkner

William Faulkner is the most famous American author that no one reads. My basis for saying this is an unofficial poll I have been conducting ever since I married into the Faulkner family (no relation to the author.) I simply ask everyone who comments on the name (usually to ask if I receive royalties) if they have actually read Faulkner, and they invariably answer in the negative! It's not exactly scientific, but I think my poll reflects a pretty realistic view of this famously difficult writer.

Nearly everyone, it seems, has dabbled in Dickens and struggled through some Shakespeare, but the works of Faulkner, winner of the Nobel Prize for Literature and two Pulitzer Prizes, appear to be largely uncharted territory. One Faulkner scholar explains: "For many readers Faulkner remains an Everest too steep and craggy to climb. His dense, at times overwrought prose, his exceedingly complex plots; the intertwined genealogies that connect his books to each other, and the sheer immensity of his *ouvre*—these and other challenges scare people away." (Jonathan Yardley, "William Faulkner's Southern Draw: *The Reivers*," *The Washington Post*, January 6, 2004, p. C01)

We know Faulkner is great, but we don't know *him*. It's time to change that, and an easy place to start is with the last book he wrote. *The Reivers* was published a month after Faulkner's death in 1962 and won for him (posthumously) his second Pulitzer Prize. It is the most accessible and the most hopeful of all his works, both a serious moral tale and a very funny story.

Synopsis

Like most of Faulkner's novels, *The Reivers* is set in rural Mississippi, in a fictional county called "Yoknapatawpha." (Try saying that five times quickly!) Though he began by writing of more exotic locales, Faulkner was advised by a friend to write about the place he knew best. He said, "Beginning with *Sartoris* (his third novel) I discovered that my own little postage stamp of native soil was worth writing about and that I would never live long enough to exhaust it." (*Lion in the Garden*, 255.)

"Reiver" (pronounced 'reever') is an old Scottish word meaning "robber," and this rollicking novel is actually the story of a series of thefts. The bit of larceny that starts everything in motion happens when "Boss" Priest, the venerable family patriarch, leaves town with his wife, son and daughter-in-law for a funeral. He entrusts his eleven-year-old grandson Lucius to the care of his black servants, and his beautiful new Winton Flyer automobile (one of only eleven in Mississippi) to the care of his white hired man, Boon Hogganbeck. To say Boon loves this automobile is a gross understatement, and Boon, left alone with the car, the key, and four empty days, cannot resist the temptation to take it to Memphis, an eighty-mile journey over dirt roads. Young Lucius comes along as his willing hostage, along with the black servant Ned, who stows away in the rumble seat. If you've read Dickens's, *The Pickwick Papers*, or the adventures of Mr. Toad in *The Wind in the Willows*, you are familiar with kinds of crazy misadventures that distinguish a picaresque novel. Just about everything that can go wrong does. Lucius ends up staying in a house of prostitution, and the stolen car gets traded (don't ask me how or why) for a stolen racehorse named Lightning. The racehorse must be ridden in a race to win back the car, and Lucius must ride it. Meanwhile the days pass, and Grandfather will be coming home soon. Inevitably Lucius and Boon will come to the bar of justice, but not before Lucius has taken his first steps toward manhood, and learned a great deal about life that he didn't want to know.

What Makes it Great?

Chief among Faulkner's many strengths are his use of dialogue and his unique voice. In his larger novels Faulkner employs a style of dialogue that can be hard to follow; characters' thoughts are mixed up with the action in a way that has one going back over the previous page more often than not, trying to figure out what really happened and what was just imagined. In *The Reivers*, we are treated to the greatness of Faulkner's genius without all that mental work. The action comes in a straightforward fashion, through the down-home folksy voice of Lucius, now grown to be an old man himself. The delightful narration has that kind of wandering digressive quality that makes your grandfather's stories both fascinating

Did You Know?

William Faulkner's famed acceptance speech for the Nobel Peace Prize is a profound commentary on the meaning of literature: "The human heart in conflict with itself . . . alone can make good writing because only that is worth writing about, worth the agony and the sweat . . . leaving no room in his workshop for anything but the old verities and the truths of the heart, the universal truths lacking which any story is ephemeral and doomed—love and honor and pity and pride and compassion and sacrifice . . . [Man] is immortal, not because he alone among creatures has an inexhaustible voice, but because he has a soul, a spirit capable of compassion and sacrifice and endurance. The poet's, the writer's duty is to write about these things. It is his privilege to help man endure by lifting his heart . . ."

and infuriating, coupled with a wonderfully dry sarcasm about everything modern. Faulkner critic Malcolm Cowley described this as "a sort of homely and sober-sided frontier humor that is seldom achieved in contemporary writing." Here is the firmly tongue-in-cheek description of the beloved Winton Flyer:

"So he bought the automobile, and Boon found his soul's lily maid, the virgin's love of his rough and innocent heart. It was a Winton Flyer . . . You cranked it by hand while standing in front of it, with no more risk (provided you had remembered to take it out of gear) than a bone or two in your forearm; it had kerosene lamps for night driving and when rain threatened five or six people could readily put up the top and curtains in ten or fifteen minutes, and Grandfather himself equipped it with kerosene lantern, a new axe and a small coil of barbed wire attached to a light block and tackle for driving beyond the town limits." (28)

Along with the hilarious adventures of its heroes, *The Reivers* deals with some very serious themes—morality, Christian virtue and racism—and does so with the same gift of understatement that characterizes its humor. Lucius, the cherished eldest son of a prosperous family, has been strictly raised to behave as a "gentleman." (He must work every Saturday morning while his fellows play ball.) He worships his old grandfather, Boss Priest, a man that embodies for him all the virtues that the title "Boss" implies. Shielded from evil by a loving family, Lucius has simply assumed that he is a "good boy." Yet, from the moment that he consents to accompany Boon in the stolen car, he wages a losing battle with his conscience.

What Lucius doesn't realize is that the stolen car is just the beginning, and he will be thrown into a situation far more perilous that he could have imagined. For Boon is on his way to Memphis to visit a prostitute in a "bawdy" house, and through him Lucius is exposed to the seamy underside of city life. He meets the alcoholic proprietor of the house, the crooked lawmen who frequent it, and the despicable, voyeuristic nephew who acts as the worst possible guide to this strange new world. Then there is the prostitute herself, Corrie, whose obvious goodness immediately wins his heart. Corrie is the kind of person of whom Jesus was speaking when he told the Pharisees, "The publicans and the harlots go into the kingdom of God before you." (Matthew 21:31) She's an angel in disguise.

Too Much, Too Soon

Through Otis (the despicable nephew) Lucius learns the tragic history of Corrie's life, and becomes her champion. Eventually he is overwhelmed by the revelation of so much, so soon. He says, "I knew too much, had seen too much. I was a child no longer now; innocence and childhood were forever lost, forever gone from me." Meanwhile, Corrie is watching this young boy, kept afloat in a veritable cauldron of evil only by his moral values. For, though he may have made a mistake in coming along for the ride, Lucius is indeed a "good boy," and proves himself so with every new challenge. My favorite moment in the book (and one I have shared with my own sons) occurs when the owner of the house offers Lucius a beer.

"Is yours a beer-head too?"

"No sir," I said. "I don't drink beer."

"Why?" Mr. Binford said. "You don't like it or you can't get it?"

"No sir," I said. "I'm not old enough yet."

"Whiskey, than?" Mr. Binford said.

"No sir," I said. "I don't drink anything. I promised my Mother I wouldn't unless Father or Boss invited me."

"But your mother's not here now," he said. "You're on a tear with Boon now. Eighty—is it?—miles away."

"No sir," I said. "I promised her." (107-108)

The quiet moral courage of the young boy causes Corrie to rethink her own life. Orphaned and forced into prostitution at a young age, she now realizes that she can choose to change, and does.

Corrie's transformation, and Lucius's fearless defense of her against grown men, (even against the man who loves her) form one of the very serious and inspiring themes of this novel. Another is its portrayal of blacks and whites in the deep South. Ned McCaslin is a wonderful character; as the "natural" descendant of a white plantation owner and a black slave, he has a unique perspective on the delicate racial balance of the South. He has no rights, yet he has the respect of his white overseers, and cannily forms a tenuous friendship with Sam, the white railroad worker, based on their mutual financial interests. Foremost among the black characters, however, is old Uncle Parsham, a mirror image of Lucius's revered Boss Priest. Lucius chooses to stay with Uncle Parsham rather than with a white family, and Faulkner's account of the family meal is a perfect example of his subtle yet eloquent message of equality.

"Bow your head," and we did so and he said grace, briefly, courteously but with dignity, without abasement or cringing: one man of decency and intelligence to another: notifying Heaven that we were about to eat and thanking It for the privilege, but at the same time reminding It that It had had some help too; that if someone . . . hadn't sweated some, the acknowledgment would have graced mainly empty dishes, and said Amen and unfolded his napkin and stuck the corner in his collar *exactly as Grandfather did*, and we ate." (164, Italics added.)

Faulkner's life spanned the Jim Crow years of segregation in the South, and the novel, set in 1905, reflects the rampant prejudice of the time. Against this backdrop Faulkner treats his characters with perfect equality. Both black and white characters are equally complex, neither all good nor all bad, and this respect for the humanity of the black man was revolutionary in its time. Though this is a novel about a child, it is not for children. Like most coming-of-age novels, *The Reivers* attempts to teach us lessons we may have missed in our upbringing, lessons about honesty, fairness and the value of each living soul. The final scene, where Lucius confesses all to his grandfather, stops just this side of sentimentality, and invariably moves me to tears. *The Reivers* is a great favorite of mine, and provides a door into the works of a great author.

Quotations taken from *The Reivers*. 1st Vintage International Edition, New York. 1962.

Talk About It

Have you had a life-changing road trip? How has travel changed your life perspective? Where in the world do you still want to go, and why?

About the Author: William Faulkner

Born in 1897 to an old Southern family, William Faulkner grew up in Oxford, Mississippi, where he attended public school only fitfully after the fifth grade; he never graduated from high school. In 1918, after the U.S. Army rejected him for being underweight and too short (5 feet, 5 inches), Faulkner enlisted in the Canadian Air Force and later the British Royal Air Force during the First World War. He studied for a time at the University of Mississippi, and temporarily worked for a New York bookstore and a New Orleans newspaper. Apart from trips to Europe and Asia and a few brief periods in Hollywood as a scriptwriter, he remained on a farm in Oxford.

Faulkner created a fictional Southern county similar to his own, the imaginary Yoknapatawpha County and its inhabitants. The created human drama in Faulkner's work is built after the model of actual, historical drama extending over almost a century and a half. Each story and each novel contributes a part to the whole.

William Faulkner married Estelle Oldham in 1929, and they lived in Oxford until his death on July 6, 1962. He was a quiet, dapper, courteous man, mustachioed and sharp-eyed. He steadfastly refused the role of celebrity: he permitted no prying into his private life and rarely granted interviews.

Faulkner was awarded two Pulitzer Prizes: one for his 1954 novel, *The Fable*, the other for his 1962 novel, *The Reivers*. In addition to developing an impressive body of fiction, Faulkner enjoyed notable success with his screenplays, including his adaptations of Ernest Hemingway's novel, *To Have and Have Not*, and Raymond Chandler's novel, *The Big Sleep*.

Source: Blotner, Joseph. *Faulkner: A Biography*. New York: Random House, 1974. 2 vols.

Certain Is the Way:
Kim, by Rudyard Kipling

It is interesting to trace the route one takes to finding a new favorite book. For example, I would never willingly have read anything by Rudyard Kipling, whom I viewed as, at worst, a political poet of British Imperialism and, at best, merely an author of children's books. It took a portrait of *Kim* in another novel to spark my interest enough to overcome my initial prejudice. Laurie R. King's brilliant mystery series featuring Sherlock Holmes and his young partner, Mary Russell, crosses the lines between fictional and historical characters without hesitation. In *The Game*, Holmes and Russell are sent to India to find Kimball O'hara, the protagonist of Kipling's greatest novel. This sparked my interest in *Kim*, and I was well rewarded with a wonderful reading experience. (By the way, if you love a mystery and are a Sherlock Holmes fan, I recommend the Russell/Holmes series as well!)

Synopsis

Kim is the story of a young boy caught in a clash of cultures. The illegitimate son of an Irish soldier and an Indian woman, orphaned at a young age and somehow abandoned in the Indian backcountry, he is taken up by a Tibetan lama, then eventually becomes a spy for the British. Rudyard Kipling, raised in England and India by parents who helped him see across cultural divides, creates in the character of Kim an irresistible combination of Indian pragmatism and British idealism.

The road trip begins when Kim attaches himself to a Tibetan lama, on a pilgrimage to find a sacred river that will lead him to enlightenment. Fascinated by this new character, as detached as he is from the social constraints of caste and country, Kim becomes the old man's servant, and the relationship that they forge is one of the sweetest in literature. (The unselfish concern of Kim for the old man and vice versa is a refreshing contrast from the parasitic way Little Nell's grandfather literally sucks the life out of her.)

Did You Know?

Kipling was a true imperialist, and his blatant racism caused him to fall out of favor with his countrymen. For Kipling, the term "white man" indicated citizens of the more highly developed nations. He felt it was their duty to spread law, literacy, and morality throughout the world. Kipling referred to less highly developed peoples as "lesser breeds" and considered order, discipline, sacrifice, and humility to be the essential qualities of colonial rulers.

As a true child of both cultures, Kim's usefulness to the government becomes apparent, and he is educated at the British schools while the lama continues his search. These are the less exciting sections of the book, and we sigh with relief when Kim sheds his schoolboy garments and escapes to the back roads for every holiday. Eventually Kim and the lama help unveil a dastardly plot by subversives and Kim is started on a career as an intelligence officer. The lama, meanwhile, finds the river, and enlightenment, in an unexpectedly spiritual finish.

What Makes it Great?

Kipling's gift for description is stunning, and the relationship between the two protagonists is endlessly satisfying. When these come together the novel simply shines. Much of the narrative involves the efforts of Kim to provide and care for the old man, always with this deep undercurrent of sincere regard and deep affection. And it is here, walking with these two unlikely companions in the streets of some small village on the Grand Trunk Road, that we can see, and smell, and hear, and taste Kipling's India:

"And now we have walked a weary way," said Kim. "Surely we shall soon come to a parao (a resting-place). Shall we stay there? Look, the sun is sloping."

"Who will receive us this evening?"

"That is all one. This country is full of good folk. Besides,"—he sunk his voice beneath a whisper,—"we have money."

The crowd thickened as they neared the resting-place which marked the end of their day's journey. A line of stalls selling very simple food and tobacco, a stack of firewood, a police station, a well, a horse-trough, a few trees, and under them, some trampled ground dotted with the black ashes of old fires, are all that mark a parao on the Grand Trunk; if you except the beggars and the crows—both hungry." (63)

Another facet of this novel is the insight it lends us about Eastern philosophy. The lama's beautiful faith, so different from our Western striving for perfection, consists in the effort to abandon all desire or selfish intent. We may "acquire merit" by doing good to others, but there can be no ego involved. When an English priest discovers Kim's Irish parentage, the lama is told that he must give up the boy to the white "sahibs." Both Kim and the lama are devastated, and their different natures become apparent as Kim considers an escape while the lama seeks to understand how he has failed:

"Said Kim in English, distressed for the lama's agony: "I think if you will let me go now we will walk away quietly and not steal. We will look for that River like before I was caught . . ."

"Good heavens, I don't know how to console him," said Father Victor, watching the lama intently . . . They listened to each other's breathing—three—five full minutes. Then the lama raised his head, and looked forth across them into space and emptiness.

"And I am a follower of the Way," he said bitterly. "The sin is mine and the punishment is mine. I made believe to myself—for now I see it was but make-belief—that thou wast sent to me to aid in the Search. So my heart went out to thee for thy charity and thy courtesy and the wisdom of thy little years. But those who follow the way must permit not the fire of any desire or attachment, for that is all illusion." (91-92)

Poetic Prose

Kipling's poetry appears in bits and snatches at the beginning of each chapter, and offers perspective and commentary on the action as it unfolds. Whether in verse or prose, poetic insights abound in *Kim*, and take the novel to a higher plane than one would expect. Here, for example, is an intriguing stanza taken from a poem titled "The Prodigal Son:

> Here come I to my own again—
> Fed, forgiven and known again—
> Claimed by bone of my bone again,
> And sib to flesh of my flesh!
> The fatted calf is dressed for me,
> But the husks have greater zest for me;
> I think my pigs will be best for me,
> So I'm off to the styes afresh. (77)

What an insightful glimpse into the mind of the addict, or the wanderer of any kind who, when welcomed home and supported on all sides, slides quickly into relapse. When he's not concentrating so hard on meter and rhyme, Kipling's prose is also poetic and a delight to read. Simple descriptions have a lyrical quality that sings, as in the passage where the lama returns to the Himalayas, his beloved "hills:"

"Glancing back at the huge ridges behind him and the faint, thin line of the road whereby they had come, he would lay out, with a hillman's generous breadth of vision, fresh marches for the morrow; or, halting in the neck of some uplifted pass . . . would stretch out his hands yearningly towards the high snows of the horizon. In the dawns they flared windy-red above stark blue . . . All day long they lay like molten silver under the sun, and at evening put on their jewels again." (230)

Morten Cohen comments, "In a sense, Kim's quest is everyone's: the quest for identity, the quest for selfhood. It is a universal theme . . . And, in the end, the quest is more important than the discovery. The quest involves reaching out, searching, and by reaching out and searching, the boy is shaped into the man. There is more meaning in trial than there is in triumph. The knowable, the definable, is dross; the real worth of life is entangled in the unknowable, the magical, the mystical." (*Kim,* Bantam Classic Edition, Introduction, xv)

Quotations taken from *Kim.* Bantam Classics Edition, New York. 1983.

Talk About It

In our day Eastern philosophy has made its way into our culture through yoga, meditation and the popularity of such figures as the Dalai Lama. But can we truly be both eastern and western in our life-view, both accepting fate as it comes and also striving to change our circumstances through sheer will power? Are we kidding ourselves when we attempt to assimilate both philosophies?

About the Author: Rudyard Kipling

Joseph Rudyard Kipling was born in Bombay (now Mumbai), India in 1865. Indian servants cared for him and taught him the Hindi language. At age five, his parents boarded him in England with paid foster parents. This custom among English parents living in India sought to remove their children from the heat and deadly diseases of the colony. But, it was an unhappy five years as he felt abandoned and was physically abused and neglected in turn. He found solace in literature and poetry, voraciously reading the magazines and books his parents sent him. After enrolling in school at age 12, he was made editor of the school journal. The family's limited finances prevented Kipling from attending a university. He returned, instead, to India and worked as a journalist in Lahore.

Kipling's first book of fiction, consisting of forty stories, was published in 1888. The following year, he returned to England. His popularity grew as his stories proliferated. He lived in the United States briefly, returning again to England. He wrote *The Jungle Book* (1894), children's stories that gained a wide international audience. For his finest novel, *Kim* (1900), Kipling revisited the subject of India, and an Irish orphan who adapts "early and completely to Indian ways."

Considered one of the most popular writers in English in the late nineteenth and early twentieth centuries, Kipling was known for both his verse and his prose. George Orwell recognized him as "a prophet of British Imperialism," a subject immediately followed with controversy. However, as the age of the European empires withdraws, Kipling proves an incomparable interpreter of how empire was experienced. He was the first English writer to receive the Nobel Prize for literature and remains the youngest laureate (at age 42) in that prize area. He died in 1936.

Sources:

Pinney, Thomas. H. C. G. Matthew and Brian Harrison. ed. 'Kipling, (Joseph) Rudyard (1865-1936)'. *Oxford Dictionary of National Biography*. Oxford University Press, September 2004.

A Ride Down the River of Life:
Adventures of Huckleberry Finn

The same issues that were introduced in *The Adventures of Tom Sawyer* are raised in the sequel, *Adventures of Huckleberry Finn*, with the added theme of racial harmony, a courageous move on Twain's part and one that caused the book to be banned in many places. This story of Tom's best friend, Huck Finn, has the young white boy risking life and limb to help a black slave escape. The irony of political correctness is such that *Huckleberry Finn* has become controversial again in our time, and now for the opposite reason, namely, that Twain's use of the offensive word, "nigger," makes the book unacceptably racist. True, it is a jarring word, but, as Toni Morrison so brilliantly asserts, the word is inextricable from the novel, since Huck would not have referred to a black man in any other term. Morrison makes the point that Huck's love for the runaway slave Jim represents racial harmony, but not racial equality. Neither Huck, nor Twain, could truly conceive of the black man as an equal. That Twain portrays Jim as human, fallible and with the same emotional complexity as his white characters, represented a great leap forward in literature, and one which we can celebrate while eschewing the epithet.

Synopsis

At the close of "*The Adventures of Tom Sawyer*," Huck and Tom end up wealthy young men, but Huck's $6,000 share of Injun Joe's treasure is too much temptation for Huck's despicable father. He kidnaps Huck and holds him prisoner, trying to pry the money out of him. When Huck finally escapes he teams up with Jim, a runaway slave in search of his family, and they take a raft down the Mississippi river. Along the way they find a house lost in a flood and ransack it for valuables. They encounter feuding families and become embroiled in the dispute. Later they meet up with two con men named the King and the Duke and get into trouble with them. The King sells Jim and he ends up back at Aunt Polly's house. Huck and Tom rescue him and all ends well.

Did You Know?

Mark Twain has the final word on any effort to find a deeper meaning in his works. He begins this book with the following "author's notice:"

Persons attempting to find a motive in this narrative will be prosecuted; persons attempting to find a moral in it will be banished; persons attempting to find a plot in it will be shot.
Author's Notice.

Huck's journey down the river is a journey of inner discovery as well. His conversations with Jim reveal Huck's deep-seated prejudice and Jim's great moral sense. Though he has little of the snobbery of his white neighbors, Huck simply cannot see Jim as a man like himself until it is almost too late. When Huck finally risks everything to rescue his friend Twain shows us an ideal of racial equality that was unheard of his day.

What Makes it Great?

Huck Finn is a remarkable creation, all boy, yet everyman as well. Through Huck's eyes Twain teaches us to see the world in a new way. He manages the impossible task of preserving Huck's dialect, mannerisms and vocal style while tackling themes that range from domestic abuse to moral integrity, and from democracy to religious faith. A pivotal moment in the narrative occurs when Huck, who delights in pranks, convinces Jim that he dreamed their frightening passage down part of the river. Jim, trusting as always, tries to interpret the dream, and suddenly realizes that the young man he considers his true friend has made a fool of him. Watch how Twain, while capturing the Negro vernacular perfectly, shows us the black man rising in dignity and the white boy seeing him, for the first time, as a man, with the same feelings, yet with even greater integrity than himself:

"Jim looked at the trash, and then looked at me, and back at the trash again. He had got the dream fixed so strong in his head that he couldn't seem to shake it loose and get the facts back into its place again right away. But when he did get the thing straightened around he looked at me steady without ever smiling, and says: "What do dey stan' for? I'se gwyne to tell you. When I got all wore out wid work, en wid de callin' for you, en went to sleep, my heart wuz mos' broke bekase you wuz los', en I didn' k'yer no' mo' what become er me en de raf'. En when I wake up en fine you back agin, all safe en soun', de tears come, en I could a got down on my knees en kiss yo' foot, I's so thankful. En all you wuz thinkin' 'bout wuz how you could make a fool uv ole Jim wid a lie. Dat truck dah is TRASH; en trash is what people is dat puts dirt on de head er dey fren's en makes 'em ashamed." Then he got up slow and walked to the wigwam, and went in there without saying anything but that. But that was enough. It made me feel so mean I could almost kissed HIS foot to get him to take it back. It was fifteen minutes before I could work myself up to go and humble myself to a nigger; but I done it, and I warn't ever sorry for it afterwards, neither. I didn't do him no more mean tricks, and I wouldn't done that one if I'd a knowed it would make him feel that way." (98)

There are many moments of pure hilarity as well. Here for example, is Huck's take on the various Christian virtues as they are taught to him:

> On Bible learning with the Widow Douglas: "After supper she got out her book and learned me about Moses and the Bulrushers and I was in a sweat to find out all about him; but by and by she let it out that Moses had been dead a considerable long time; so then I didn't care no more about him, because I don't take no stock in dead people." (10)

> On right choices: "What's the use you learning to do right, when it's troublesome to do right and ain't no trouble to do wrong, and the wages is just the same?" (104)

On church attendance: "There warn't anybody at the church, except maybe a hog or two, for there warn't any lock on the door, and hogs likes a puncheon floor in summer-time because it's cool. If you notice, most folks don't go to church only when they've got to; but a hog is different." (121)

There are also moments of majestic descriptive power, such as Huck's picture of a sudden storm in Chapter Nine:

"It would get so dark that it looked all blue-black outside, and lovely; and the rain would thrash along by so thick that the trees off a little ways looked dim and spider-webby; and here would come a blast of wind that would bend the trees down and turn up the pale underside of the leaves; and then a perfect ripper of a gust would follow along and set the branches to tossing their arms as if they was just wild; and next, when it was just about the bluest and blackest—fst! It was as bright as glory and you'd have a little glimpse of tree tops a plunging about, away off yonder in the storm, hundreds of yards further than you could see before; dark as sin again in a second, and now you'd hear the thunder let go with an awful crash and then go rumbling, grumbling, tumbling down the sky towards the under side of the world, like rolling empty barrels downstairs, where it's long stairs and they bounce a good deal, you know." (113)

Mark Twain, the man William Dean Howells referred to as "the Lincoln of our literature," uses the backwoods vernacular of an unlearned boy to teach a higher set of ideals about human behavior. And he put a nation on notice when he had the white boy say of the black slave, "I do believe he cared just as much for his people as white folks does for their'n."(23) Finally, when threatened with eternal damnation for breaking the law and aiding the runaway slave, he takes a stand between the false teachings of society and his inner voice.

"I was a-trembling, because I'd got to decide, forever, betwixt two things, and I knowed it. I studied a minute, sort of holding my breath, and then says to myself:

"All right, then, I'll GO to hell." (30)

This young boy, on a journey to discovery with a runaway slave, took a nation along for the ride, and changed the course of history.

Quotations taken from *Adventures of Huckleberry Finn*. Penguin Classics Edition, New York. 1986

Talk About It

Political correctness could be called the new Puritanism of our day. What is the limit? Is Huck Finn an objectionable book because of its use of an objectionable word? What are the justifications for keeping it in the canon?

Road Trips: Take it Personally

Huck Finn has had an impact on my thinking. When quite young I remember hearing a quote from the novel in a sermon about prayer:

"I about made up my mind to pray, and see if I couldn't try to quit being the kind of a boy I was and be better. So I kneeled down. But the words wouldn't come. Why wouldn't they? It warn't no use to try and hide it from Him. Nor from ME, neither. I knowed very well why they wouldn't come. It was because my heart warn't right; it was because I warn't square; it was because I was playing double. I was letting ON to give up sin, but away inside of me I was holding on to the biggest one of all. I was trying to make my mouth SAY I would do the right thing and the clean thing, and go and write to that nigger's owner and tell where he was; but deep down in me I knowed it was a lie, and He knowed it. You can't pray a lie—I found that out." (221)

This great quote speaks eloquently on two levels. On its face, it's an excellent lesson about the dangers of lying to oneself, and, by extension, to God. But it's more than just a Sunday School lesson. Huck has been taught, in church, that it is right to turn in a runaway slave, and so he is trying to feel right about that, even though in his heart he can feel that it is wrong. Twain is saying something deeply profound through this simple boy's prayer, indicting an entire society for teaching its young people that wrong is right, and causing their moral confusion. Are we teaching our children right or wrong traditions?

This leads to another **ice-axe question**: where does racial prejudice come from, and can we see it in ourselves? Do you have racial prejudices that no amount of education or training can obliterate? Where do they surface? For example, if your child wanted to marry someone of a different race or culture, would you object? Why?

Chapter Five
True Romance

And think not you can direct the course of love, For
love, if it finds you worthy, directs your course.

Kahlil Gibran

Romance is the fiction that owes no allegiance to the God
of things as they are. In the novel the writer's thought
is tethered to the realm of probability, but in romance it
ranges at will over the entire region of the imagination.

Ambrose Bierce

The search for love is at the center of human existence. So it's no
surprise that romance fiction is the best-selling genre of popular literature,
accounting for $1.4 billion in annual sales and outselling both religious/
inspirational books and science fiction/ fantasy, according to the Business
of Consumer Book Publishing. But are we looking for love in all the
wrong places? These three novels take a look at what we really ought to
be seeking when it comes to romance, taking us to a deeper level than the
romance novel ever dared. Jane Eyre teaches us that the route to a perfect
union may be a long and treacherous one of self-denial. And according to
E.M. Forster and A. S. Byatt, you may have to truly change your mind,
that is, your whole way of thinking, before you can recognize that soul
mate. So open your eyes and your heart and read on. Love may be just
around the corner.

Beyond the Counterfeits of Love:
Jane Eyre, by Charlotte Bronte

When Ja*ne Eyre* was first published in 1847, it was an immediate success, and at the same time, very controversial. Readers loved the tiny, feisty heroine and critics admired the mastery with which Bronte tackled a variety of thorny issues, such as the educational system, organized religion, and class prejudice. However, there seemed to be a rebelliousness about Jane, and about the novel, that frightened some, and the book was immediately attacked for its insistence on the idea that personal fulfillment is an acceptable goal for a woman, just as it is for a man. Though this seems hardly revolutionary stuff to us today, the defiant tone of the heroine shocked polite society.

Synopsis

Jane Eyre, an orphan taken in by her wealthy uncle, suffers an unhappy childhood. Bullied by her cousins and treated coldly by her aunt, she eventually rebels and is sent away to one of the infamous schools in Northern England. There she suffers cold, privation and humiliation at the hands of corrupt schoolmasters, yet also finds her gifts through the kindness of a few teachers and friends. She is eventually hired as a governess by Edward Rochester of Thornfield manor, a gruff yet charismatic man who is raising the French daughter of a former lover. Almost immediately she falls under his spell, and as their friendship deepens it blossoms into romance.

But Mr. Rochester has a secret: someone is hidden in the attic of the manor. It is only on the morning of their wedding that Jane learns that the hidden lunatic in the attic is the first Mrs. Rochester. Though Edward begs her to live with him as a mistress, Jane refuses and runs away. She suffers near starvation on the road and is eventually taken in by a minister and his sisters, to whom she is actually related. The minister proposes to Jane and wants to take her to India as a missionary/wife, but at the last moment Jane senses Mr. Rochester calling to her and travels home to Thornfield, only to find it burned to the ground. Mr. Rochester, blind and maimed from his attempt to save his first wife's life, lives in a cottage nearby. They are reunited and marry, and eventually have a child.

What Makes it Great?

A great book has many layers, and the closer one examines the work the more one finds. Perhaps it might be useful to take an in-depth look at just one scene of this magnificent novel to appreciate the beauty of the language and the layers of symbolism it offers the reader. The climactic scene of the narrative takes place in the garden at Thornfield manor, Mr. Rochester's ancestral home. The name itself ("Thorn field") already has us thinking about Adam's curse and his expulsion from Eden. Before Jane's arrival, Thornfield had been a cursed place for Mr. Rochester. Now, in this great scene, Bronte brings her two lovers into their own garden of Eden through language, symbolism and Biblical and mythological allusions.

The scene opens on Midsummer Eve, a deeply symbolic night for the English, (still just a few hundred years away from their Druidic roots), and it truly is a Midsummer Night's dream, with all the magic Shakespeare ever imagined about to commence. Jane describes her desire to enjoy the beautiful grounds, but, aware that Rochester is watching from the house, she steals into the orchard to be alone. "No nook in the grounds more sheltered and more Eden-like; it was full of trees, it bloomed with flowers . . ." Well, now we are with Jane (our Eve) in Eden, and all of our senses are called into play. Flowers and their fragrances are described, our sight is drawn to the lovely rising moon, and each sound of bird and breeze is carefully described. As Bronte, the master craftsman, slips quietly into the present tense we are drawn right into the garden with Jane; with her, we smell a familiar fragrance, Mr. Rochester's cigar. (Until the recent past, this was one fragrance that was distinctly and exclusively masculine.) Adam has arrived.

And of course, he is eating fruit! He wanders among the trees and vines, sampling this cherry and that plum, and stoops to examine a great moth. (Watch out Jane, moths are drawn to flame. There is fire imagery everywhere.) As Jane attempts to escape she is accosted not by his person, but only by his voice. He speaks without turning and she is as much his captive as the moth. Jane wonders how he knows she is there: "could

Did You Know?

Though Jane's strong sense of self-worth seems only natural to us, it shocked polite society of the time. The book was immediately attacked by critics for its insistence on the idea that personal fulfillment is an acceptable goal for a woman just as it is for a man. Mrs. Rigby, a popular columnist of the day, wrote of the orphan Jane Eyre:

"She has inherited in fullest measure the worst sin of our fallen nature—the sin of pride ... and she is ungrateful too. It pleased God to make her an orphan, friendless, and penniless—yet she thanks nobody, and least of all Him ... on the contrary, she looks upon all that has been done for her not only as her undoubted right, but as falling far short of it." (Quarterly Review 84, December 1848)

his shadow feel?" she asks herself. It is the first reference to the spiritual communication she senses between them. Since we are in Eden we are not surprised that they seat themselves at the base of a great tree.

Smell, sight, hearing, taste and touch. Bronte has called into play all of the physical senses, and were the scene to end here with our lovers entwined in an embrace, it would take its place as a great romantic scene. But it is here, seated in their own quiet Eden, that Bronte takes us onto a higher plane, as intellectual and even spiritual senses come into play. First, she employs that remarkable facility that separates us from the beast: human conversation. Jane and Rochester begin to talk. At first he tries to draw her out by pretending that he must marry Blanche Ingram and send Jane away, which causes her to drop her ever-present reserve. Her true feelings begin to pour out, and what was begun as an attempt to manipulate Jane's emotions evolves into an intimate communication. As Rochester talks, Bronte captures one of the deepest expressions of human intimacy, what she calls "a cord of communion." As they discuss their imminent parting, Rochester asks, "Are you anything akin to me, do you think, Jane?" She is too emotionally overcome to respond, so he goes on:

"Because,' he said, 'I sometimes have a queer feeling with regard to you—especially when you are near me, as now: it is as if I had a string somewhere under my left ribs, tightly and inextricably knotted to a similar string situated in the corresponding quarter of your little frame. And if that boisterous channel, and two hundred miles or so of land come broad between us, I am afraid that cord of communion will be snapt; and then I've a nervous notion I should take to bleeding inwardly." (299)

This is a beautiful description of the feeling of kinship that exists between a man and a woman who are truly "in love." They feel, in short, like a family even before they are one. We've gone way beyond the giddy, deceptive affections that have selfish gratification at their center. Jane and Rochester would instinctively understand that all the talk about people who love but can't commit is silliness: there is no love without commitment.

In Bronte's view, there can also be no love without equality; a very courageous view for her day. She has her heroine respond to what she considers insincerity on Rochester's part with a stinging reminder of her own self-worth:

> "Do you think, because I am poor, obscure, plain and little,
> I am soulless and heartless?—You think wrong!—I have
> as much soul as you,—and full as much heart! And if God
> had gifted me with some beauty, and much wealth, I should
> have made it as hard for you to leave me, as it is now for
> me to leave you. I am not talking to you now through the
> medium of custom, conventionalities, or even of mortal
> flesh:—it is my spirit that addresses your spirit; just as if
> both had passed through the grave, and we stood at God's
> feet, equal—as we are!" (300)

A Rebel with a Cause

With no one to teach her the wrong ideas, Jane understands instinctively that lasting relationships are based on equality, and that there is no place in a true marriage for intimidation or fear. Though she calls Rochester her Master and rejoices in his masculine strength, he, in turn, avers that he is mastered by her and rejoices in her equal, yet deliciously different, feminine strength. This balance does not come immediately, but as a result of the (literally) fiery trials through which they pass together. Like most of us, these lovers only glimpse the possibility of true union in the moonlit orchard. There is much pain and sorrow between that beginning and their final happiness.

Though she mistrusts orthodox religion, Jane Eyre is a deeply spiritual person who longs for a life of usefulness and service. She is, however, unwilling to accept the harsh cruelty of her masters as treatment that is naturally due her as an orphan. She persists in believing that she should be treated on an equal level with others, and is willing to treat them in the same way. Above all, she longs for a spirit-to-spirit relationship with a partner who knows her as she knows him, with whom she can share a productive life. She does not wish to be owned, coddled or catered to, nor does she wish to sacrifice her life in serving a brutish tyrant. She seeks a partnership of mutual respect between equals. This was not what Victorian society prescribed, but it must have been what an overwhelming number of women really longed for, because *Jane Eyre* was embraced by the public immediately and has been an enduring favorite ever since.

Quotations taken from *Jane Eyre*. Penguin Classics Edition, London. 1996.

Talk About It

Jane Eyre struggles to be on an equal footing with the men in her life. She eventually becomes a caretaker for the man she loves, since he has been blinded and maimed. Is this really a happy ending? Have women today achieved equality with men?

About the Author: Charlotte Bronte

Charlotte Bronte was born and raised on a remote parsonage on the lonely moors of Yorkshire, England. Within this cold, austere home lived Patrick Bronte and his four surviving children: Branwell, Charlotte, Emily and Anne. Their mother died soon after the birth of the last child, and two older sisters died from tuberculosis contracted at the boarding school they attended, a school that would become the model for the dreaded Lowood Academy in *Jane Eyre*.

The Bronte children were very bright, artistic and deeply curious about the world. By contrast, Mr. Bronte was remote, severe, and largely ignored his children, so they turned to each other for companionship and intellectual stimulation. Over the years Charlotte and her sisters invented elaborate fictional worlds, writing stories and poems to entertain each other. Charlotte's first novel, *The Professor*, was rejected for publication, but while caring for her father after a surgery, Charlotte wrote *Jane Eyre*, under the pseudonym Currer Bell. The novel was an instant success and Currer Bell was an overnight sensation. Who was he, or was he a she? No one knew for sure.

Over the next few years the Bronte sisters published their novels under pseudonyms and stayed hidden in their Yorkshire sanctuary. They did not realize that their home was a breeding ground for the disease that had taken their elder sisters, and both Emily and Anne died within a year of each other. Charlotte was devastated, and soon she married Arthur Bell Nichols, a curate and long-time friend. She became pregnant, and then succumbed to a long illness in 1855. Small of stature, pale and plain, Bronte resembled her heroine Jane in both spirit and body, though her life did not have the triumphant ending she could create in fiction. In the one hundred and fifty-four years since the publication of *Jane Eyre*, millions of readers have been grateful that, with all her tribulation, Bronte found the courage to exercise her tremendous creative talent.

Source: *The Life of Charlotte Bronte*, by Elizabeth Gaskell. Penguin Classics Edition, London. 1997.

Through a Glass Darkly:
A Room with a View, by E.M. Forster

The business of seeing is a strange process. We know that something mechanical occurs when light hits the retina of the eye, and images are communicated to the brain. That, however, is just the beginning of sight. From quite a young age, we also understand that sight is an inward process as well, and look beyond the surface of faces and objects for their spiritual significance. Perched precariously between the innocence of prewar England and the disasters to come, a young man named Edward Forster penned a novel about a young girl learning to see for herself, and poured into it all of his "insights" (a lovely word) about the clash between civility and nature, between keeping up appearances and living with a vision. He called it *A Room with a View.*

Synopsis

Set in the turn-of-the-century English countryside, the novel recreates an idyllic world that is gone forever. Games of lawn tennis, tea in the garden, calls paid to neighbors and returned within ten days; all the conventions of genteel suburban life are chronicled here in delightful detail. There are the Emerson's with their "anti-religious" views, and the snobby Vyse's in London who give dinner parties attended by "the grandchildren of famous people." We meet the ancient Miss Alan's, who traverse the globe armed with Baedeker guides and plenty of digestive bread, the bitter, suspicious spinster cousin Charlotte, and a host of others, Italians and English, all drawn with careful, loving care by a master of characterization.

The central figure of the tale is Lucy Honeychurch, an average girl with a pretty face and an unusual talent for music. Mr. Beebe, the celibate clergyman who acts as intermediary between the disparate cast of characters at home and abroad, muses about what might happen if Lucy ever learns to "live as she plays." Such a development would not be possible in England, but on a tour of Italy with her cousin, Lucy comes face-to-face, first with death, then with physical attraction, then with love, and finally with herself. She meets an eccentric man named Emerson, and is shocked when his son George arouses in her a feeling of immediate physical and spiritual attraction, a passion so foreign to her that she attributes it to her Italian surroundings.

Lucy's first impulse is to flee Italy and her new emotional state, and soon, safely back in England, she replaces one chaperone for another; she becomes engaged to Cecil Vyse, snobby, controlling, yet socially desirable. But the winds of fate blow even as far as Windy Corner, and George turns up in her English neighborhood, as full of passion and primal energy as in Italy. Lucy must choose. Whether she will have the courage to bring her new viewpoint home with her, and whether she will be able to reconcile her youthful passion with social propriety becomes the focus of the story, told in a tone of comic irony remarkable in an author so young.

What Makes it Great?

E.M. Forster was raised in a setting very like Windy Corner, coddled by his mother and maiden aunts after his father's death. He has a pitch-perfect ear for dialogue, which makes it a pleasure to listen in on the Honeychurch's at home, or the Vyse's in their stuffy, London flat. Forster uses dialogue to help us see into the hearts of these people, but we must attend to the subtle shifts in conversation. No one will shout the message to us here, except old Mr. Emerson, who eschews all forms of "civilized" communication and wishes only to speak from the heart. (It is he who possesses the wardrobe upon which is inscribed this curious motto: "Mistrust all enterprises that require new clothes.") His loud ranting offends everyone but Lucy, who sees in his indelicacy "something beautiful."

The novel is organized rather like a play, with humorous chapter headings that describe the scene to follow. My favorite is Chapter Six, titled: "The Reverend Arthur Beebe, the Reverend Cuthbert Eager, Mr. Emerson, Mr. George Emerson, Miss Eleanor Lavish, Miss Charlotte Bartlett, and Miss Lucy Honeychurch Drive Out in Carriages to See a View; Italians Drive Them." The two exceptions are titled simply, Fourth Chapter and Twelfth Chapter. These two chapters

Did You Know?

E.M. Forster was only twenty-eight years old when he published *A Room with a View*, and its tone reflects the hope and optimism of a young idealist. Forster has been called the expert on spinsters, clergymen and "nervous old ladies," and peoples his novel with the kind of people who raised him, in a nostalgic representation of an era disappearing even as he began to write. D.H. Lawrence called Forster "the last Englishman."

record events of deeper significance: the death of the Italian that brings Lucy and George together, and the swim in the "Sacred Lake," where Freddy, George and the clergyman Beebe go "skinny-dipping" and encounter Cecil, Lucy and Mrs. Honeychurch in a hilarious clash between nature and civilization. Though Forster makes us laugh in these scenes, his message is serious: The trappings of civilization—our manners, civilities, customs and prejudices—keep us from truly connecting with each other and with the best that lies within us. Lucy, upon hearing that the Emerson's will be moving to her neighborhood, rehearses over and over how she will behave when she again meets George. When, instead of meeting at church or a garden party, she stumbles across him, naked as Adam and whooping like an Indian at play in the bathing pool, all her rehearsal is in vain. She simply bows to him, Forster says, "across the rubbish that cumbers the world." What a gorgeous sentence that is.

There is a bit of Lucy Honeychurch in all of us, isn't there. It can be difficult as a young person, trying to establish a personal ideology, to get in touch with the essential requirements of our innermost souls. Lucy must travel to Italy to appreciate that her home is where she is most herself. Ironically, Cecil, though impeccably British, is hopelessly out of place in her home while George slips easily into the routine of things. In Windy Corner, Forster creates a haven of safety, flawed yet perfect in its way, as our own homes should be, with a loving family that helps us find our inner vision through acceptance, unconditional love and an occasional dose of the truth about ourselves. Forster uses the house at Windy Corner to personify the strength of a good family:

"Whenever Mr. Beebe crossed the ridge and caught sight of these noble dispositions of the earth, and, poised in the middle of them, Windy Corner,—he laughed. The situation was so glorious, the house so commonplace, not to say impertinent. The late Mr. Honeychurch had affected the cube, because it gave him the most accommodation for his money, and the only addition made by his widow had been a small turret, shaped like a rhinoceros' horn, where she could sit in wet weather and watch the carts going up and down the road. So impertinent—and yet the house "did," for it was the home of people who loved their surroundings honestly. Other houses in the neighborhood had been built by expensive architects, over others their inmates had fidgeted sedulously, yet all these suggested the accidental, the temporary; while Windy Corner seemed as inevitable as an ugliness of Nature's own creation. One might laugh at the house, but one never shuddered." (178)

The Craft of the Novelist

In *A Room with a View*, we are able to see the novelist's development in process, as Forster was a young man at the time and just beginning to put his tools to use. It is a pleasure to turn from this early work to *Howard's End* and then *A Passage to India*, and see this novelist working at the height of his craft. Forster is always concentrating on the most average of people, who, in his words, are "too confused to be wicked and too mild to be great. They are simply people." People like most of us. But for Forster, their emotional lives are deeply important. In a climactic moment in the narrative, (once again seen through Mr. Beebe's eyes) he mirrors Lucy's mood with a description of the Surrey skies, dark and lowering, and paints a breathtaking image of light and dark in collision.

"The sky had grown wilder since he stood there last hour, giving to the land a tragic greatness that is rare in Surrey. Grey clouds were charging across tissues of white, which stretched and shredded and tore slowly, until through their final layers there gleamed a hint of the disappearing blue. Summer was retreating. The wind roared, the trees groaned, yet the noise seemed insufficient for those vast operations in heaven. The weather was breaking up, breaking, broken, and it is a sense of the fit rather than of the supernatural that equips such crises with the salvos of angelic artillery. Mr. Beebe's eyes rested on Windy Corner, where Lucy sat, practicing Mozart. No smile came to his lips, and, changing the subject again, he said: "We shan't have rain, but we shall have darkness, so let us hurry on. The darkness last night was appalling." (166)

Forster's own life was, to use his expression, "a muddle," and he appears never to have achieved the happiness he granted to Lucy and George. In them he created a union of body and soul that symbolized the complete harmony of civilization and nature. It is "a consummation devoutly to be wished" and a beautiful expression of the heights attainable in the midst of everyday realities. Once you gaze at the scenes in this little world, you cannot help but enjoy the view, and may gain some insight into the workings of your own windy corner.

Quotations taken from *A Room With a View*. Bantam Classics Edition, New York. 1988.

Talk About It

There is a lot of talk about nature in these novels. The moon follows people, lightning strikes trees and the wind carries voices. Do you think this strengthens the impact of the story or makes it less believable?

About the Author: E.M. Forster

E.M. Forster was raised in an idyllic English country house, much like those in his novels. He was born Edward Morgan Forster on January 1, 1879. His father, an architect, died soon after his birth, so Forster was raised by his mother, along with various aunts and governesses. A precocious boy, he started writing stories at the age of six and remained committed to the passion of writing throughout his life. He attended Cambridge and, after receiving an inheritance from a great-aunt, traveled the world with his mother.

Forster spent time in India and other regions of the Far East, which he chronicled in his last great novel, A *Passage to India.* He wrote for the London literary journal *The Athenaeum.* His first novel, *Where Angels Fear to Tread* (1905), set in Tuscany, was followed by *The Longest Journey* (1907), and then *A Room With a View* (1908.) While he started writing *Maurice* in 1912, it was not officially published until after his death in 1971. This novel deals with the treatment of homosexuals as criminals, which Forster deplored, and sheds light on his personal predilections.

After the death of his mother he maintained residences at Cambridge and in London. In the 1950's he helped write the libretto to Benjamin Britten's opera *Billy Budd,* based on Melville's 1924 novel of the same name. In 1953 he was awarded the Order of Companions of Honor and in 1969 given Queen Elizabeth's Order of Merit. At the age of ninety, on June 7, 1970, Edward Morgan Forster died at the home in Coventry of friend and long-time companion Robert Buckingham.

Source: Wikipedia, *A Room With a View,* Introduction.

Finding our Present in the Past:
Possession by A.S. Byatt

"The book was thick and black and covered with dust." It is not a coincidence that the first two words of this remarkable novel are, "the book." *Possession* is a book about books, about the study and love of literature and the strange obsession with the lives of literary figures shared by academics, historians, and the randomly curious public. It tells the story of a quiet literary scholar, Roland Michell, who finds a lost letter from the great Victorian poet R.H. Ash to another famous poet of the day, Christabel LaMotte. As he is an Ash scholar, Roland takes the letter to a LaMotte scholar named Maude Bailey, and together they begin a search to uncover the relationship between the two. It is a discovery that will have repercussions in the academic world and in their own lives. If you tend to lose yourself in second-hand bookstores, are ravenously curious about the lives of the authors whose works you read, or simply love a great romantic mystery, you will love this book, which won the Booker prize, England's highest literary award.

Synopsis

Roland Mitchell is a poor grad student pursuing a doctorate on the famous Victorian poet, Randolph Henry Ash. As a research assistant he spends hours in the library researching arcane facts, and one day stumbles across a letter written by Ash to another famous poet of the time, Christabel La Motte. On an impulse, he steals the letter, and goes to the leading La Motte scholar, Maude Bailey, for help. As they research old documents and piece together the relationship between the poets, they fall in love as well. Others, including jealous academic rivals and private collectors, get wind of the momentous find and the story culminates on a dark and stormy night as the body of Ash is exhumed in order to find the truth about the past.

Roland and Maud discover a cache of letters that prove that Ash and La Motte were indeed lovers, and their story is recounted in bits and pieces as the modern researchers uncover the clues. Their poetry is recreated as well, and infuses the narrative with a mythical beauty. Roland and Maude must come to grips with their mutual obsession with the past and decide if it can be the basis for a future together.

What Makes it Great?

The marvel of this novel is that Byatt creates not just two poets, but also two complete bodies of work. Calling on her extensive knowledge of Victorian literature, she intersperses the narrative with poetry, prose, tales, and even literary criticism about the works of these fictional characters. It is, to use an over-taxed phrase, a *tour de force*, and the poems are beautiful in their own right. Here are just a few lines from the fictional Ash:

> In certain moods we eat our lives away
> In fast successive greed; we must have more
> Although that more depletes our little stock
> Of time and peace remaining.

A.S. Byatt is herself a formidable scholar of literature who left a teaching career at London College in 1983 to write full-time. One day while in the British Museum Library, she spotted a well-known Coleridge scholar. It occurred to Byatt that much of what she knew about the Romantic poet had been filtered through the mind of that scholar. She mused about the effect that such a single-minded pursuit must have on a person. "I thought," she said, "it's almost like a case of demonic possession, and I wondered—has she eaten up his life or has he eaten up hers?" (A.S. Byatt, personal interview) Years later while studying Robert Browning, she became interested in the effect that his relationship with his wife (the more famous and more readable poet Elizabeth Barrett Browning) would have had on his work, and vice versa, and considered writing a novel about their lives. Soon the two ideas would combine for one great work.

Fearing the legal implications as well as the artistic restrictions of writing about real people, Byatt decided instead to create a pair of Victorian poets and link them to a pair of modern literary scholars. She remembered D.H. Lawrence's advice: "I thought: I have to have two couples, which he says is the beginning of any novel." She also decided she

Did You Know?

Byatt once said, "I write novels because I am passionately interested in language. Novels are works of art which are made out of language, and are made in solitude by one person and read in solitude by one person . . . ." In *Possession* there is a marvelous passage about the act of reading that describes an emotion dear and familiar to any serious reader:

"Now and then there are readings that make the hairs on the neck, the non-existent pelt, stand on end and tremble, when every word burns and shines hard and clear and infinite and exact, like stones of fire, like points of stars in the dark . . ." (512)

would try to instill her novel "with the kind of warmth of a Shakespearean comedy." Her romantic poet, Randolph Henry Ash (loosely modeled on Robert Browning) writes dramatic monologues with deep mythological and psychological underpinnings. The fair, mysterious Christabel LaMotte resembles Christina Rosetti, with her mystical, lyrical verse and her fascination with ancient folk tales and legends. I confess that my first time through this novel I went to my *Norton Anthology of English Literature* and looked for R.H. Ash, only to find that he did not actually exist! It amazed me that the author could switch from one style to another and write such beautiful verse in different voices. The third time through the book, I was also sensitive to the way the poetry illuminates the narrative.

Liberated Women?

For those who are involved in (and perhaps discouraged by) the academic climate of today, *Possession* offers a clear-eyed look at modern literary scholarship. In particular Byatt is interested in the largely negative effect of the feminist movement on literary studies. Herself the mother of four children and a successful career woman, Byatt is keenly aware of each woman's struggle to balance the different roles in her life, and is certainly an ardent advocate for the rights of all people. She sees, however, a curious parallel between modern women and their Victorian counterparts and suggests that in the fight for their freedom, women may have "thrown the baby out with the bathwater."

Byatt seems to suggest that, while the Victorian woman was trapped by the notion that her proper place was only to mother children and nurture and support men, the modern woman may be equally trapped by the opposite notion, that she must live free of these very natural female roles. Thus Christabel LaMotte is symbolized by the princess in the glass coffin, beautiful but unable to break free of her bonds. Yet her modern counterpart, renowned scholar and feminist Maude Bailey, is presented as a kind of "ice queen," equally unhappy and trapped in a role that feels unnatural to her. She self-consciously hides her long, blonde hair under a scarf; her beauty is a source of shame, and her life (characterized by her surgically sterile apartment) is lonely and unfulfilling. Byatt introduces another feminist scholar, the vulgar American Leonora Stern, in a further attempt to show the kind of backwards Puritanism that exists in academia today, where morality and virtue are the new taboo, and fundamental truths have been deconstructed and dissected until nothing remains but tolerance.

The very "modern" Roland and Maude seem almost childish in their inability to form meaningful relationships, and this emotional paralysis stems from the shifting philosophies of today: "Roland had learned to see himself, theoretically, as a crossing-place for a number of systems, all loosely connected. He had been trained to see his idea of his 'self' as an illusion . . ." As Roland and Maude attempt to uncover "the truth" about the two poets, they learn important truths about themselves as well, and they break free of the modern relativism that has bound them.

Literary Study and the Search for Truth

The characters that swarm like scavengers around the relics of the lives of the two Victorian poets represent the desolation of our modern morality. Like Shakespeare, Byatt is showing us this empty world for a reason, however, to encourage us to recover certain truths that have been trampled in the rush for social progress. Roland Mitchell and Maude Bailey feel strangely uncomfortable in their modern setting and turn to the past for answers.

As they connect to the lives of these poets through their letters, they find strength within themselves to live more meaningful lives. Byatt's genius for metaphor connects the two couples, linking the present to the past. Notice the use of color: greens for the feminine and grays and blacks for the masculine characters. Connection is made through objects: Cropper wears Ash's watch, Maude wears LaMotte's brooch. Symbols of confinement and release are paired: the glass coffin and the library cubicle, the green Beetle and the serpent Melusine, the short-lived Eden of Yorkshire and Roland's forbidden garden.

As the story builds toward its climax, the images pile up, as it were, until everything and everyone meets in one place, in one very cinematic scene, to uncover the truth. Yet, even with all the romantic drama, Byatt never loses contact with books, with the fact that it is through reading and writing that human beings connect with their finer selves.

Those who write biography or study history know that every life has a story, but also that we can never tell the story exactly as it was. There is no final truth in history, but only interpretation and recreation. We read the journals of our ancestors and wonder what was not said that would have been most enlightening, as we try to extract a vision of their reality from the clues left to us. Roland and Maude, after years of studying these poets, are torn between a desire to protect their privacy and an insatiable curiosity to find out what really happened to them. In a highly readable series of events we are pulled deeper and deeper into these interconnected lives, switching from past to present and back to the past. Finally, after all is revealed, Byatt shares one more crucial detail with the reader that is never revealed to the other characters. It is her way of letting us know at the last that the full story of any other life will always be, to some extent, a mystery.

Quotations taken from *Possession*. Vintage Books, New York. 1990.

Talk About It

Through her modern couple, Byatt seems to say that in our search for freedom and equality, we have lost a fundamental sense of identity. Do you think this is true, and if so, why? Was her Victorian couple equally as confused, or less so?

About the Author: A. S. Byatt

Courtesy of A.S. Byatt

Antonia Susan Drabble Byatt was born in Yorkshire in 1936. Her Quaker parents were a judge and an English teacher. A self-described "greedy reader," Byatt spent her often-bedridden asthmatic childhood reading fiction: Dickens, Austen, and Scott. Greedy reading made her want to write. World War II marked the end of her childhood; she was evacuated to the countryside and then to a Quaker boarding school. A solitary and slightly awkward child, she withdrew to the basement boiler room to write. Byatt was educated at Cambridge (as one of the first women admitted), Bryn Mawr College, and Oxford. At Cambridge, she found an atmosphere of "moral seriousness" that placed English literature at the center of university studies.

Byatt lectured in English and literature at the University of London, Central School of Art and Design, and University College, London. She left in 1983 to write full-time. A number of her books deal with nineteenth-century concerns, thinkers, and authors, especially themes of Romantic and Victorian literature. Her short stories merge naturalism and realism with fantasy. She married twice and is the mother of four children, one of whom was killed in a car accident at age 11. *Possession* won the Booker Prize in 1990, and Dame Byatt's latest work, *The Children's Book* (2009), was shortlisted for the same award.

Sources: *www.asbyatt.com*
www.contemporarywriters.com
www.salon.com
Wikipedia

True Romance: Take it Personally

In his famous discussion of Eros in the book *The Four Loves*, C.S. Lewis offers a slightly different take on romantic love: "To be in love is both to intend and to promise lifelong fidelity. Love makes vows unasked; can't be deterred from making them." (*The Four Loves*, p. 158) Every person who is in a committed relationship understands the feeling of kinship, the "cord of communion" that springs to life between two people (who might otherwise be comparative strangers) and compels them to create a family, rather than just pass each other by. This sense of kinship is both spiritual and physical, and it is essential to the deepest kind of human intimacy. It is rarely discussed in fiction, but it is what we're all either seeking, or feel lucky to have found.

In my college days when I had a new boyfriend, I'd take him home to meet the family, and invariably break up with him as a result! It was always in my home, among the minutiae of daily life, that I could see things most clearly. If the exciting new beau was out of place in my home—my real world—the romance lost its luster. Lucy Honeychurch finds the same thing to be true. We tend to think of romantic love as something outside our daily reality, something exciting and different. Yet in all three of these works lovers recognize each other as somehow already familiar—the lover feels like family—and this feeling confuses them. They have trouble realizing that the thing they are seeking is that very familiarity.

This leads to an ice-axe question for the ages: are we expecting the wrong things from romantic love? Are we expecting excitement, thrills and constant variety when in fact, our souls yearn for simplicity, familiarity and reliability? Have romance novels and movies taught us to expect the opposite of what we really want? There is an old saying that our frustrations are determined by our expectations. What do we really expect, and is it what we really want? Since love is at the center of our lives, it might be worth thinking about.

Chapter Six
Action Figures

And thus the native hue of resolution
Is sicklied o'er with the pale cast of thought;
And enterprises of great pith and moment,
With this regard, their currents turn awry,
And lose the name of action.

Hamlet I:iii

My husband Craig is one of those guys that can't sit still. It's useless to take him on vacations that involve sitting around by the pool; he doesn't last ten minutes before he's off on an adventure. Predictably, he has little patience for most of the Victorian literature that I love. In fact he refers to my books as "tea-drinkers," because they expend so much verbiage on elaborate descriptions of the food, clothing and furnishings that by the time something actually happens he has long since ceased to care! He would concur with Hamlet about the dangers of too much *thinking* and not enough *doing*.

This chapter is for Craig and all those like him who love to read but squirm at the mere mention of Austen or Bronte. Each of these books features unforgettable characters, stirring plots, and loads of historically accurate detail. From the impossibly dangerous (and claustrophobic) seafaring battles with Captain Jack Aubrey, to the hidden caves where the Count of Monte Cristo finds his treasure, to the muddy trenches of the First World War, men of courage and action continue to thrill and inspire. Even sedentary types like myself love to be swept along for the ride, as long as we're home in time for tea!

Collateral Damage:
The Count of Monte Cristo, by Alexandre Dumas

History can be viewed as a series of revolutionary moments, where the existing hierarchy was upended by the sheer determination of a few brave heroes. One imagines the fierce determination on the faces of the men surrounding King John as the Magna Carta was signed. We can picture the desperate expressions of the Paris mob that stormed the dreaded Bastille Prison, or the icy resolve of George Washington as he crossed the Delaware to continue a seemingly hopeless battle against overwhelming odds. Yet none of these moments, however daring, can compare for sheer bravado to the day when a poor carpenter's son climbed a hillside, sat on a rock, and calmly uttered a series of statements that turned his culture's code of ethics inside-out and transformed the history of the world forever.

"Ye have heard that it hath been said, An eye for an eye, and a tooth for a tooth: But I say unto you, That ye resist not evil: but whosoever shall smite thee on thy right cheek, turn to him the other also . . . Ye have heard that it hath been said, Thou shalt love thy neighbour, and hate thine enemy, But I say unto you, Love your enemies, bless them that curse you, do good to them that hate you, and pray for them which despitefully use you, and persecute you; That ye may be the children of your Father which is in heaven . . ." (Matthew 5:38-44, *King James Version*)

In the Sermon on the Mount, Jesus presented an ideal of behavior so contrary to the natural inclination of mankind that we continue to ignore it and substitute a more comfortable compromise in its stead. Who among us truly loves his enemies, turns the other cheek, and does not seek revenge against those that persecute us? Our sense of justice recoils at the idea.

As a result of our obsession with fairness, we cling to the notion that our ills are caused by someone or something that must be ferreted out and punished. If our relationships fail, we blame our spouses, or our upbringing. If we commit crimes, the fault is in our economic system. It's the government who forces us to cheat on our taxes and our employer whose unfair practices lead us to fail at our work. In those rare cases when we truly are the innocent victims of evil we may spend a lifetime nursing the pain and increasing the damage by attempts to even the score. With the bitter Shylock, we ask, "If you wrong us, shall we not revenge?"

(*Merchant of Venice*, III, i, 66) Yet, as Shylock learned, revenge has a way of backfiring, damaging us more than those we seek to punish.

The almost irresistible lure and the devastating effects of revenge are the central themes of Alexandre Dumas' classic tale of adventure, *The Count of Monte Cristo*. *The Count of Monte Cristo* appeared in serialized version over the course of about eighteen months in 1844 and 1845. In 117 chapters, (nearly 1500 pages) Dumas introduces a fascinating array of characters in a tumultuous combination of murder, intrigue, betrayal, duels, and death-defying adventure.

Synopsis

Edmund Dantes, a young soldier in the French army, is betrayed by his three best friends and sent to prison for many years, where he is driven to the brink of suicide. At a crucial moment, he meets the prisoner in the next cell, a strange man with great knowledge to teach him and a hidden treasure to leave him. Following his escape from prison, Dantes finds the treasure and returns to France, where he dwells like a Sultan, with slaves and servants to do his bidding. His arrival in Paris as the Count of Monte Cristo causes a sensation, and it is there that he begins to work his revenge on his three mortal enemies, one of whom is now married to his former fiancé.

As a result of his tutelage in the prison, the "Count" now possesses knowledge, wealth, strength and resourcefulness. He also believes that he is the agent of Providence, sent to mete out justice to those who have sinned, and he engages in an elaborate scheme to humiliate and ruin each of the men involved in the betrayal. In the end, however, he finds that revenge is a poison that infects all it touches. Not only his enemies, but their innocent children are victims of his retribution, and to his horror Dantes realizes too late that he is as much a victim of his own vengeance as he was a victim of the men who wronged him. He makes peace with his former lover and her son, and sails into the sunset with his devoted servant and a beautiful former slave at his side.

Did You Know?

For his plots Dumas preferred to begin with an idea (in this case, revenge) and find a historical incident that illustrated his theme. He read an account in a police record of a remarkable conspiracy between three friends to frame a fourth man, named Picaud, so that one of the three could marry his fiancé. The innocent Picaud spent seven years in prison, and there grew close to a cleric who left him a vast fortune of three million francs. After his release Picaud staged an elaborate revenge on those who had betrayed him that stretched over a period of twenty years. He was eventually kidnapped and murdered by one of the group, who recounted the whole story on his deathbed. Dumas took this true account as the storyline of *The Count of Monte Cristo*, preserving many of the main elements but reshaping the protagonist, Edmund Dantes, into a kind of superhero.

What Makes it Great?

A great book takes a great idea and gives us an opportunity to examine it in the lives of people like ourselves. Along with the excitement and adventure, we find ourselves wondering what we would do in a similar situation. It is in its tracing of the spiritual struggle of Dantes that the novel rises beyond a simple romantic adventure, and as he is faced at every turn with the impossibility of true revenge, we too are forced to question our own sense of justice. For example, Edmond's rival has married the woman he loved, and they have a son. Should this son of his enemy be destroyed, breaking the heart of his beloved Mercedes? Dantes finds that he cannot exact vengeance on the guilty without harming the innocent. Revenge is never simple.

In the climactic scene where Dantes finally confronts Mercedes, she challenges his notion of justice by reminding him of the collateral damage attendant to revenge, and begs for the life of her son. He comes to the realization that his intricate plans may not have been inspired by God, as he had assumed. On the contrary, he admits, "Providence is now opposed to them when I most thought it would be propitious." (889) As Dantes brings his plan to a close he attempts to mitigate the damage he has set in motion, and finds a place for mercy and forgiveness in his heart.

Another great facet of this novel is its pacing. The action moves so quickly that the book feels like a screenplay—it was cinematic long before there was any such thing as a cinema—and the action is visually exciting. The scenery changes; we move from great houses to deserted islands to terrifying prisons. There are sea voyages, duels, and even an encounter with the great Napoleon himself. It is no wonder that so many adaptations for film and television have been made of this work; it's sheer physicality is irresistible.

In the figure of Edmund Dantes, Dumas created a folk hero whose popularity has never waned. As David Coward says, "Heroes do not come any taller. He is the stuff of adolescent dreams, and will retain his fascination while the boy's heart beats in man." Numerous film versions have been created, and *The Count of Monte Cristo* has been continuously in print and beloved in countless languages since its debut. Of Dumas' unique ability to create characters that crossed national boundaries Victor Hugo said, "The name of Alexandre Dumas is more than French, it is European; and it is more than European, it is Universal." William Thackeray wrote to a friend that he "began to read Monte Cristo at six one morning and never stopped until eleven at night." George Bernard Shaw placed him in the same class with Dickens.

Though I love this book, I have a complaint to register about it. It really bugs me that, after all the high-sounding rhetoric about his undying devotion, Dantes manages to end up abandoning the "love of his life" for a younger woman! Mercedes, (now worn tired and gray with the cares of life) heads off to a convent to pray, and Dantes sails off into the sunset with his gorgeous young slave Haydee. I have never seen this rather disappointing ending used in any of the television or movie versions of the novel, so I was fairly shocked when I finally read the original. Dumas himself had a series of mistresses and one brief, unsuccessful marriage, and he seems content to see his hero find comfort with a sweet young thing rather than remain constant to his lifelong love. That said, there aren't many books that will pull me out of bed for a few extra chapters late at night, but this was one that kept me up way past my bedtime. We love to watch Dantes get his revenge, and just when we become uncomfortable with where things are headed, he relents and shows mercy to the innocent. By following the path of revenge as far as it will take him, Monte Cristo shows us what a dangerous path it is for any of us to tread, and the reason why the scripture counsels, "Vengeance is mine, saith the Lord."

Quotations taken from *The Count of Monte Cristo*. Modern Library Edition, New York. 2002.

Talk About It

The Count of Monte Cristo has been adapted for movies and TV mini series several times, but not one adaptation has ever remained completely faithful to the plot. This brings up the interesting topic of adaptation. How closely should an adaptation follow the plot of the novel? What are your favorite adaptations?

About the Author: Alexandre Dumas

Alexandre Dumas was born in 1802, the son of one of Napoleon's most decorated generals. His father, Thomas, was the illegitimate son of a French nobleman and a Negro seamstress. A dissolute man, Thomas died when Alexandre was only four, leaving his wife to struggle through years of financial hardship. Unfortunately, his brilliant son repeated his example of promiscuity and debauchery. Young Dumas did have one great virtue—he was a tireless worker, writing up to fourteen hours a day. Determined to make his fortune as an author, he succeeded early on with several plays and accounts of his travels.

When newspapers began to serialize novels in the late 1830s, Dumas saw an opportunity and began to write his most famous works, *The Three Musketeers* and *The Count of Monte Cristo*. Though France has produced many great writers, none has been as widely read as Alexandre Dumas. Known for his historical novels of high adventure, Dumas often chose unusual, real characters for historical detail and changed their lives into exciting tales. He wrote over 300 plays, novels, travel books, and memoirs, and he was the most renowned author of his day (more familiar even than Victor Hugo).

In 1870, Dumas died a poor man, having squandered millions of francs on women and high living. He was cheerful to the end, however, and said of Death, "I shall tell her a story, and she will be kind to me." Dumas was buried where he was born, in Villers-Cotterêts. In 2002, French President Chirac led the ceremony to move his remains to the Panthéon of Paris, acknowledging that racism had existed then, and saying that a wrong had now been righted. Dumas was interred alongside such luminaries as Victor Hugo and Emile Zola.

Sources: Gorman, Herbert. *The Incredible Marquis, Alexandre Dumas*. New York: Farrar & Rinehart, 1929.
Hemmings, F.W.J. *Alexandre Dumas, the King of Romance*. New York: Charles Scribner's Sons, 1979.

Anchors Aweigh:
Master and Commander, by Patrick O'Brian

There is no reason why I should love Patrick O'Brian's Aubrey-Maturin series, twenty novels that follow the adventures of a sea captain and ship's surgeon in Nelson's navy in the beginning of the 1800's. To begin with, I don't sail. (My husband sails, and when he persuades me to spend an afternoon on his boat I gasp in horror every time it tips to one side or the other.) Before discovering O'Brian's books, I couldn't tell you the difference between a topsail and a tarpaulin. I have very little interest in ornithology, and even less interest in naval history. No, there is no reason why I should love them, except one. O'Brian writes a ripping good yarn. I have read every one of these twenty novels with the greatest delight, and I predict that you will too.

Synopsis

The Aubrey/Maturin series follows the exploits of Captain Jack Aubrey of the Royal Navy and his ship's surgeon, Steven Maturin. Together they sail the world in the attempt to defeat Napoleon's navy, capture various enemy ships, carry out secret missions for the government (Steven is also a spy) and get themselves into all sorts of trouble with the women in their lives.

In this first novel the two meet at a concert, and Steven eventually signs on as the ship's surgeon to Jack's first assignment as a Post Captain. They are embroiled in war with Napoleon and we are introduced to life at sea, with its terrors and tedium equally portrayed through spare, beautiful prose. We learn more about Steven, who has a secret identity as a spy, and meet the women whose attractions draw them home, occasionally.

What Makes it Great?

These novels are great because of O'Brian's infectious love of the sea and everything to do with ships and sailors, and his ability to bring us into that world. But above all these novels are great because of their endlessly interesting protagonists. If you have not yet made their acquaintance, it is my pleasure to introduce you to two of the most delightful characters in literature: Captain Jack Aubrey and Dr. Stephen Maturin. As our story opens Aubrey, a beefy, florid, friendly sea captain, sits down next to Stephen Maturin, a wiry, eccentric, brilliant physician and ornithologist, at a concert. They immediately begin to annoy one another, and a relationship begins (over their one shared passion, music) that is always electric and engaging. In just a few spare, brilliant lines O'Brian brings these two unique individuals to life:

" . . . They happened to be sitting next to one another. The listener farther to the left was a man of between twenty and thirty whose big form overflowed his seat . . . He was wearing his best uniform . . . and the deep white cuff of his gold-buttoned sleeve beat the time, while his bright blue eyes . . . gazed fixedly at the bow of the first violin.

"If you really must beat the measure sir, let me entreat you to do so in time and not a half beat ahead."

" . . . Only part of Jack's mind paid attention, for the rest of it was anchored to the man at his side. A covert glance showed that he was a small, dark, white-faced creature in a rusty black coat—a civilian. It was difficult to tell his age, for not only had he that kind of face that does not give anything away, but he was wearing a wig, a grizzled wig, apparently made of wire, and quite devoid of powder. Ill-looking . . . to give himself such airs." (13-14)

In Peril on the Sea

After their rather rocky start, these two become fast friends, and Jack persuades Stephen (an abysmal sailor) to go to sea as his ship's surgeon. We'll drop right into the middle of the action, in the teeth of a terrible storm, to get a taste of O'Brian's descriptive powers, his humor, and sense of pacing:

Did You Know?

Two fans of the Aubrey/Maturin series created a cookbook with recipes for the dishes cooked on board the various vessels. The book is titled *Lobscouse and Spotted Dog*, and it offers recipes for such intriguing dishes as Skillygalee, Drowned Baby, Soused Hog's Face, and Jam Roly-Poly. We are obviously on some new culinary ground here, and I haven't had the courage yet to try any of the recipes!

"The seas mounted higher and higher: they were not the height of the great Atlantic rollers, but they were steeper, and in a way more wicked; their heads tore off streaming in front of them so as to race through the *Sophie's* tops, and they were tall enough to becalm her as she lay there a-try, riding it out under a storm staysail. This was something she could do superbly well . . . She was a remarkably dry vessel too, observed Jack, as she climbed the creaming slope of a wave, slipped its roaring top neatly under her bows and traveled smoothly down into the hollow. He stood with an arm round a backstay, wearing a tarpaulin jacket and a pair of calico drawers: his streaming yellow hair, which he wore loose and long as a tribute to Lord Nelson, stood straight out behind him at the top of each wave and sank in the troughs between—a natural anemometer—and he watched the regular, dreamlike procession in the diffused light of the racing moon . . . 'She is remarkably dry,' he said to Stephen who, preferring to die in the open, had crept up on deck, had been made fast to a stanchion and who now stood, mute, sodden and appalled, behind him." (164)

Though the technical terms can be very confusing, O'Brian refuses to talk down to us. He expects us to know our sailing and scientific jargon, and to be able to discern subtle emotional shifts in the characters with little more than a hint here and there. Reading him requires a bit of mental labor for the average landlubber, and perhaps even the use of a dictionary. (Be honest now, when is the last time you used the word anemometer in a sentence?) But he's worth the effort. This is a fascinating period of history, when nations battled for the last open pieces of the planet in wooden ships laden with firepower. O'Brian captures the close, difficult life aboard ship while making us feel the pure excitement of it as well. Here, as the sailors lay siege to a fort using hand-held rockets, O'Brian combines technical detail with such stirring prose that we can literally feel their hearts pounding as the men wait for the order to attack:

"The bosun fixed the three-pronged grapnels to the to the ropes; the coxswain planted the rockets, struck a spark on the tinder and stood by cherishing it; against the tremendous din of the battery there was a little metallic clicking and the easing of belts; the strong panting lessened.

"Ready?" whispered Jack.

"Ready, sir," whispered the officers.

He bent. The fuse hissed, and the rocket went away, and red trail and a high blue burst. "Come on," he shouted, and his voice was drowned in a great roaring cheer." Ooay, Ooay!"

Runnng, running. Dump down into the dry ditch, pistols snapping through the embrasures, men swarming up the ropes onto the parapet, shouting, shouting; a bubbling scream." (249)

I love a book that takes me somewhere I will never be able to go myself, and O'Brian's novels transport me into a world as different from my own as I could imagine. The picture of naval history we see here is, according to his many fans among historians, as close to what the seafaring life was really like as it is possible to achieve in fiction. When I put down one of these books I feel as if I have been on a voyage myself, and returned rich with treasure. Though I'll never be much of a sailor, I love to go to sea with Patrick O'Brian.

Quotations taken from *Master and Commander*. Norton, London. 1999.

Talk About It

Patrick O'Brian's double life raises the topic of the private lives of public men. How much does the private life of the author matter when it comes to his or her work? Do you like to know more, or less, about an author's life and motivations?

About the Author: Patrick O'Brien

Considering the breadth of nautical detail that illustrates these books, it is hard to believe O'Brien himself was not a sailor. He was not. Neither was he a physician, an ornithologist, nor (as he sometimes hinted to friends) a spy for the British. In reality, the author's life was as interesting and mysterious as any of his characters.

Patrick O'Brien was born in England, and his name was Patrick Russ. He grew up a neglected child in a large family, spending hours alone with his books. During World War II, Russ left his wife and two children and disappeared entirely, only to emerge later in a new country under a new name, Patrick O'Brien. He remarried and lived quietly in the south of France, writing novels about the sea battles in the Napoleonic wars. Eventually, his growing fame caused some family members to reveal the truth about his origins, yet even then his concealment of his former life largely succeeded until after his death. O'Brien's portrait of Steven Maturin is often considered to be based upon himself.

Patrick O'Brien died in 2000, just after completing the twentieth novel in his wildly popular Aubrey-Maturin series. Though it took time for the books to gain renown, at his death three million copies had sold worldwide, and O'Brien had been lionized as heir to Melville's genius. Today, newsletters and chat rooms devoted to his books abound, and there are volumes printed to explain his difficult terminology.

Source:
Dean H. King. *Patrick O'Brien—A Life Revealed*. Hodder & Stoughton Ltd., 2001.

Shadows of War:
All Quiet on the Western Front,
by Erich Marie Remarque

We live in the shadow of war. From Iraq to Afghanistan to Africa, hatred seeps across borders of nations, and the nightly newscast is never without a report of battles and bloodshed. Though we advance in every way as a civilization, mankind cannot seem to progress past war. National interests, greed, religious fanaticism, and ethnic hatred are some causes of war, but its effect is always personal: the devastation of the individual, the breaking up of the family, and the loss of that most precious gift, life. One young man who weathered some of the worst fighting of the First World War attempted to recreate his experience through fiction. *All Quiet on the Western Front* deals specifically with the first World War, but because of its unique perspective one feels that it could be about any war at any time in history.

Synopsis

Remarque opens his novel with a simple, two sentence declaration that sets the quiet tone of the narrative and alerts us that we are in for a different kind of war novel: "This book is to be neither an accusation nor a confession, and least of all an adventure, for death is not an adventure to those who stand face to face with it. It will try simply to tell of a generation of men who, even though they may have escaped shells, were destroyed by the war." (1)

All Quiet on the Western Front is the story of a young man, Paul Baumer, full of ideals and enthusiasm, who is inspired by his professor to enlist in the German army, along with his seven classmates. Told in the first person, the novel draws us gradually through Paul's eyes into the horrendous world of the front, where with him we experience every form of death, disease and despair. This is no heroic saga (John Wayne will not be appearing) but only the tragedy of young men forced into a nightmare they did not create and cannot comprehend. The novel ends with the end of the war, and closes Paul's story in a tragic, and curiously ironic manner.

Did You Know?

In 1933, the Nazis banned and burned Remarque's works, and issued propaganda stating that he was a descendant of French Jews. Ten years later, the Nazis arrested his sister, Elfriede Scholz, who had remained in Germany with her husband and two children. Though Remarque had escaped, the Nazis executed his sister in retribution for Remarque's outspoken criticism of Hitler's regime.

What Makes it Great?

It is difficult to absorb the statistics of the First World War. More than sixty-four million men fought, representing nations from northern Europe to northern Africa, western Asia and the United States. Over twenty-one million were wounded, and eight million soldiers died, along with over six million non-combatants. It was the first modern war, meaning that soldiers faced, for the first time, such threats as tanks, U-boats, poison gas, and attacks from the air. Yet it was ultimately a war fought in the trenches, hand-to-hand, by young men hardly out of their teens. An entire generation was drawn into a conflict that left its survivors traumatized and alienated. The greatness of this novel lies in its ability to bring us into a reality that we could otherwise never even imagine. Here we descend into the muddy trenches with these boys, as they await a bombardment.

"We wake up in the middle of the night. The earth booms. Heavy fire is falling on us. We crouch into corners. We distinguish shells of every calibre.

"Each man lays hold of his things and looks again every minute to reassure himself that they are still there. The dug-out heaves, the night roars and flashes. We look at each other in the momentary flashes of light, and with pale faces and pressed lips shake our heads . . . When a shell lands in the trench we note the hollow, furious blast is like a blow from the paw of a raging beast of prey. Already by morning a few of the recruits are green and vomiting. They are too inexperienced." (105-6)

A Lost Generation Finds a Voice

This is a gritty, unsettling, and beautiful book. The horrifying details of death are interspersed with passages of pure poetry. Take for example, a typical moment where Paul lies, face down in the mud, in the middle of an attack, and offers this beautiful description of the earth:

"To no man does the earth mean so much as to the soldier. When he presses himself down upon her long and powerfully, when he buries his face and his limbs deep in her from the fear of death by shell-fire, then she is his only friend, his brother, his mother; he stifles his terror and his cries in her silence and her security; she shelters him and releases him for ten seconds to live, to run, ten seconds of life; receives him again and often forever." (280)

These young German soldiers have been taught to hate their Russian enemies, and Paul is surprised when he lives in close proximity to some prisoners of war to find that they are so similar to his own kind. He is, in fact, sorry to see them starving and suffering.

"Only the dregs [of the soup] that the ladle cannot reach are tipped out and thrown into the garbage tins. This thin miserable dirty garbage is the objective of the prisoners. They pick it out of the stinking tins greedily and go off with it under their blouses.

"It is strange to see these enemies of ours so close up. They have faces that make one think—honest peasant faces, broad foreheads, broad noses, broad mouths, broad hands and thick hair. They ought to be put to threshing, reaping and apple picking. They look just as kindly as our own peasants in Friesland." (189-90)

When *All Quiet on the Western Front* debuted as a film, *Variety* magazine commented that the League of Nations should "buy up the master-print, reproduce it in every language to be shown to every nation every year until the word *war* is taken out of the dictionaries." Unfortunately, no voice, no matter how impassioned, seems capable of holding back the tide of war. Less than a decade after the publication of this book, World War II began. Beaten and weary, Paul sums up the experience of a generation that longed to be heroes and learned instead that war is the worst disease of all.

"Our life alternates between billets and the front. We have almost grown accustomed to it; war is the cause of death like cancer and tuberculosis, like influenza and dysentery. The deaths are merely more frequent, more varied and terrible." (271)

The courage and resilience of the soldiers in this and every war is inspiring, and a reminder that one of the only benefits of war is the bravery and brotherhood it inspires. I chose to include this anti-war novel along with the seafaring stories and the adventures of the Count, because something about our love of "action stories," makes me uneasy. Isn't "action" just a nice way of saying that somebody is going to get killed? Researchers tell us that the average American child will witness 8000 murders on television by the time he or she reaches maturity. We love action movies, novels, and thrilling stories in newspapers and magazines, yet most of us have never really been in a war, or even in the presence of death. While it's great to love a good action novel, it's also important to remember that there is a grim reality behind all that action, with consequences that reach through generations.

Quotations taken from *All Quiet on the Western Front*. Ballantine Books, New York. 1996.

Talk About It

Some novels celebrate the glory of war. *All Quiet on the Western Front* is not one of those. The protagonist wishes only to be relieved of the incessant suffering and meaningless banality of the soldier's life. Is it ever right to go to war? Would you send a child into battle and, if so, for what cause?

About the Author: Erich Maria Remarque

Erich Maria Remarque was born on June 22, 1898, into a German working-class family. At age eighteen, Remarque was conscripted into the army, and in June of 1917 he transferred to the Western Front—the "contested armed frontier" between lands controlled by Germany to the East and the Allies to the West. Six weeks later, after being wounded with shrapnel in his left leg, right arm, and neck, Remarque was repatriated to an army hospital in Germany, where he spent the rest of the war.

Remarque wrote *All Quiet on the Western Front* in a few months in 1927, but he was not immediately able to find a publisher. When the anti-war novel was at last published in 1929, it touched a public nerve and created a storm of political controversy. It sold 1.2 million copies in its first year. H.L. Mencken called it "unquestionably the best story of the World War."

Remarque left Germany in 1931. He bought a villa in Porto Ronco, Switzerland, and lived both there and in France until 1939, when he left Europe for the United States with his first wife.

Over subsequent decades Remarque wrote books, plays, screenplays, and essays, many of which were very successful. One Austrian screenplay told of Hitler's final days in the bunker of the Reich Chancellery. He married the Hollywood actress Paulette Goddard in 1958 and they remained married until his death in Switzerland on September 25, 1970 at the age of 72.

Source: *Dictionary of Literary Biography*, Volume 56: German Fiction Writers, 1914-1945. A Bruccoli Clark Layman Book. Edited by James Hardin, University of South Carolina. The Gale Group, 1987. pp. 222-241.

Action Figures: Take it Personally

Who was the first action hero? Well (even though he was a little slow to get going) when it comes to action, nobody has more to say than Hamlet, that moody fellow with whose words this chapter began. In fact, in order to understand any great novel it helps to understand how the creation of fictional characters was revolutionized by the creation of Hamlet.

Before Shakespeare's time there were stories and plays, but it was Shakespeare who created the first really round, complex, confusing characters that continue to intrigue us after hundreds of years. Scholar Harold Bloom summarizes Shakespeare's contribution to all the literature that follows in terms of character development:

"Literary character before Shakespeare is relatively unchanging; women and men are represented as aging and dying, but not as changing because their relationship to themselves, rather than to the gods or God, has changed. In Shakespeare, characters develop rather than unfold, and they develop because they reconceive themselves." (Harold Bloom, Shakespeare and the Invention of the Human, p. xvii)

The way we experience Hamlet's character development is through his soliloquies. Everybody can quote at least the first two lines of "To be or not to be," but perhaps you haven't thought about how revolutionary that particular moment in drama was. We don't just watch Hamlet, we hear his thoughts and share his inner as well as his outer life. We agonize with him over every choice and challenge. This remarkable idea of entering into the inner life of a character laid the foundation for the fiction we read today. As Hamlet agonizes over whether or not to act we can see the structure of the modern novel being built. Experiencing the inner lives of characters helps to raise the level of these action stories to great literature.

Chapter Seven
Through the Eyes of a Child

The serpent, the king, the tiger, the stinging wasp, the small child, the dog owned by other people, and the fool. These seven ought not to be awakened from sleep.

Chanakya

The question for the child is not, "do I want to be good?" but "whom do I want to be like?"

Bruno Bettleheim

A child is a curly, dimpled lunatic.

Ralph Waldo Emerson

So many books have been written for children, but few have been written about them that stand the test of time. Charles Dickens was a pioneer in this area, and two of his novels represent the first attempts to look at life through the eyes of a hungry, homeless child. The counterpoint to these is the sweet fairy tale of Silas Marner, which shows us what the transformational effect of a child can be on an empty, self-centered soul.

Wanting More: *Oliver Twist,*
by Charles Dickens

In 1837 two figures rose to power in England whose influence would change the world. The diminutive Queen Victoria was crowned, and Charles Dickens published *Oliver Twist,* his second novel and the first to be serialized in his own publication. Its immediate popularity catapulted Dickens to fame. Along with *The Christmas Carol* it is still the most familiar of his novels; its charming, melodramatic plot has been adapted into numerous plays and musicals. The story of the little orphan who is reunited, then separated from, then reunited with with a kind grandfather after countless perils, caught the imagination of Victorian society and has remained a favorite ever since.

Oliver Twist was the first English novel to take a child as its protagonist. Up until Dickens's day, novels were written about people with money, education, and usually good breeding. Dickens chose to view the world through a lens that was unfamiliar to those who bought books; he looked through the eyes of a bright, though helpless child, trapped in a terrible situation. It was a viewpoint he remembered well. Dickens himself was sent by his parents at the age of twelve to work in a blacking factory in the middle of London, when his father became so mired in debt he was forced to take the child out of school. Charles lived alone in a rented room and nearly starved on the meager wages he earned for standing in the window of a blacking factory, pasting labels on bottles of shoe polish. Though within a year his father was able to bring him home again, the terror and humiliation of that experience was so great that Dickens kept it a secret from everyone (even his wife and children) all of his life. He dealt with it instead through his fictional children, particularly Oliver Twist and David Copperfield, and used them to awaken a generation to the plight of the dispossessed.

Synopsis

Oliver Twist, born in a London workhouse in the 1830's, is an unfortunate child. He spends the first nine years of his life miserable and hungry, and when he finally summons the courage to ask for more gruel during a meal, he is farmed out as an apprentice to an undertaker, where he suffers further abuse. Oliver is small but gutsy, and runs away to London. There he is taken up by the Artful Dodger, budding thief and protégée of Fagin, who runs a criminal gang made up of homeless boys like Oliver. Drawn unwillingly into a life of crime, Oliver develops a deep affection for the prostitute Nancy, mistress to Bill Sykes, local psychopath and much-feared associate of Fagin and his gang.

Oliver's mother had been a gentlewoman who got into trouble and died on the streets, and by a Dickensian coincidence Oliver ends up being taken in by her father's best friend. His happiness with them is shortlived; Sykes and Fagin steal him back, and after all the usual plot machinations the action culminates in the death of Nancy, the capture and defeat of Fagan, and the death of Bill Sykes. Oliver eventually ends up in the bosom of his mother's family, safely home at last.

What Makes it Great?

After Shakespeare, Dickens may be the greatest writer in the English language. For sheer mastery of description, characterization and ingenious plot development, he simply cannot be surpassed. Each novel shows us facets of his greatness, but the most impressive quality to me in this work is the tone. Still in his twenties and largely self-educated, we can see Dickens teaching himself to write in this second novel, finding his voice and unique style. In contrast to the light comic subject matter of *The Pickwick Papers, Oliver Twist* deals with the most disturbing, heart wrenching topics imaginable: homeless, defenseless children abused and exploited by criminals, unwanted pregnancies, prostitution, crime and the disease-ridden slums that abounded in London. Dickens was actually writing the end of one novel as he began the other, and would follow a similar pattern for decades, overlapping and interweaving the comic and the serious, the sardonic and the sentimental. So, rather than taking a heavy, serious approach to a weighty subject, Dickens keeps the lighthearted tone of Pickwick—the opening scene is so lighthearted in tone that it could be describing a day on the skating pond rather than the tragic birth of an unwanted child and the death of his mother—and somehow this prevents the narrative from descending into pathos. It is a stroke of genius that draws us in and keeps us engaged. Here is the description of Oliver's birth:

"Although I am not disposed to maintain that being born in a workhouse, is in itself the most fortunate and enviable circumstance that can possibly befall a human being, I do mean to say that in this particular instance, it was the best thing for Oliver Twist that could by possibility have occurred. The fact is, that there was considerable difficulty in inducing Oliver to take upon himself the office of respiration,—a troublesome practice, but one which custom has rendered necessary to our easy existence; and for some time he lay gasping on a little flock mattress, rather unequally poised between this world and the next: the balance being decidedly in favour of the latter. Now, if, during this brief period, Oliver had been surrounded by careful grandmothers, anxious aunts, experienced nurses, and doctors of profound wisdom, he would most inevitably and indubitably have been killed in no time. There being nobody by, however, but a pauper old woman, who was rendered rather misty by an unwonted allowance of beer; and a parish surgeon who did such matters by contract; Oliver and Nature fought out the point between them. The result was, that, after a few struggles, Oliver breathed, sneezed, and proceeded to advertise to the inmates of the workhouse the fact of a new burden having been imposed upon the parish, by setting up as loud a cry as could reasonably have been expected from a male infant who had not been possessed of that very useful appendage, a voice, for a much longer space of time than three minutes and a quarter." (1)

Without an advocate in a hostile world, Oliver survives his first few years out of sheer determination, and Dickens keeps this light tone even as he describes the most horrendous treatment at the hands of the wicked Mr. Bumble and Mrs. Mann. (Nobody names characters more perfectly than Dickens.) Dickens's greatness lies in the way he can turn the mundane into the memorable, and the most famous scene in this book illustrates the way in which a Dickens character can become an emblem for an entire class. Oliver, new to the workhouse, is nudged and encouraged by his fellow boys to do the unthinkable: he asks for more food. (The Poor Law of 1834 actually mandated the pitiful amounts of food allowed to indigent children.) As Oliver struggles to his feet and holds out his empty bowl, Dickens puts a nation on alert that society has gone awry:

"Child as he was, he was desperate with hunger, and reckless with misery. He rose from the table; and advancing to the master, basin and spoon in hand, said: somewhat alarmed at his own temerity: 'Please, Sir, I want some more.'" (12)

Of course, Oliver's simple plea is treated as a criminal act, and he is branded as a troublemaker. His ejection from lawful society, where he has been neglected and abused, is followed by his introduction to the underworld of London, where he is fed, welcomed and even loved. Dickens's point is clear: if society does not care for its own, it will pay the price in increased crime and social unrest. We can be assured that Fagin and his boys have relevance to our day when we view the proliferation of the gang culture in our inner cities, where fatherless children find a family of sorts in criminal groups. Terrorist organizations like Hamas are modern-day Fagins: they feed and care for the widows and fatherless among them, and receive loyal support in return, underscoring again that this is a fairy tale with a message for any age. Rose makes an impassioned plea to save Oliver from going to prison, one that should resonate in any social setting:

"But even if he has been wicked,' pursued Rose, 'think how young he is, think that he may never have known a mother's love, or the comfort of a home; and that ill-usage and blows, or the want of bread, may have driven him to herd with men who have forced him to guilt. Aunt, dear aunt, for mercy's sake, think of this, before you let them drag this sick child to a prison, which in any case must be the grave of all his chances of amendment." (231)

Racial Stereotypes

Fagin, one of the most memorable characters in Dickens, was a repository for all of the fears and prejudices of Victorian society. Dickens plays on racist stereotypes with this Jewish abuser of children who sees in poor defenseless Oliver only a chance for gain. He is described as something reptilian, less than human:

"As he glided stealthily along, creeping beneath the shelter of the walls and doorways, the hideous old man seemed like some loathsome reptile, engendered in the slime and darkness through which he moved: crawling forth, by night, in search of some rich offal for a meal." (345)

Yet, with all his disgusting qualities, there is something strangely likeable about Fagin. Indeed, Dickens lavishes so much creative effort on his villains that they often spring to life with greater believability than his heroes. Norrie Epstein explains:

"Fagin is diseased, satanic, effeminate, greedy, and has a lust for boys. Yet, dare we confess how much we enjoy him? Ironically, it's Fagin, rather than the blandly virtuous characters, who has all the fun in the novel. He's the enticing stranger who hangs around the playground, promising candy and rides in fast cars." (*The Friendly Dickens*, 83.)

A Social Conscience

Like the Artful Dodger himself, Dickens lures us into this nether world in a friendly, offhand fashion, but he has a very serious purpose. Throughout the narrative, Dickens is trying to wake us up to the plight of the poor. First he draws us into the orphanage, and we begin to see the young Oliver as an individual whose life is important, even though he is weak and small. As he begs for "more" we begin to feel his hunger and pain. Next, he bids us follow Oliver into the seamy underbelly of London. We smell the stink of gin on Bill Sykes' breath, and know that Nancy will pay dearly tonight when he stumbles home. We fear for Oliver and even begin to bond with Fagin, who at least offers him some kind of home and protection. This was all new for Victorian readers, and they embraced the orphan boy even as they recoiled at the worldview Dickens presented. But Dickens had an unshakeable faith in human nature, and in his stories there is always hope on the horizon:

"Men who look on nature, and their fellow-men, and cry that all is dark and gloomy, are in the right; but the sombre colours are reflections from their own jaundiced eyes and hearts. The real hues are delicate, and need a clearer vision." (324)

There is a kind of deux ex machina at work in all of Dickens's novels, a heavenly interference (what Wordsworth referred to as a "visionary gleam,") that alters the course of events. At crucial moments in the narrative, such as times of birth, death, or great danger, divine influences are felt that guide the characters and give meaning to their sufferings. Dickens explains it in this way:

"The memories which peaceful country scenes call up, are not of this world, nor of its thoughts and hopes. Their gentle influence may teach us how to weave fresh garlands for the graves of those we loved: may purify our thoughts, and bear down before it old enmity and hatred; but beneath all this, there lingers, in the least reflective mind, a vague and half-formed consciousness of having held such feelings long before, in some remote and distant time, which calls up solemn thoughts of distant times to come, and bends down pride and worldliness beneath it." (409)

Oliver Twist is a good introduction to the hilarious, sentimental, dramatic, ironic, brilliant world of Charles Dickens. You might want to follow it with *David Copperfield*, to see how his genius reaches its height, then *Great Expectations*, to feel how the wisdom and disappointments of age affect his writing. All three are stories of boys who are cast upon a difficult social sea and somehow make their way, illustrating above all Dickens's faith in the resilience and tenacity of the human spirit.

Quotations taken from *Oliver Twist, Penguin Classics Edition*, New York. 1984.

Talk About It

Books reflect the prejudices and racial stereotypes of their times. Fagin, the villain in *Oliver Twist*, resembles Shylock in Shakespeare's *Merchant of Venice*. Each is a bundle of racial stereotypes rolled into one, evil character. Can books be great that perpetuate such stereotypes? If so, how and why?

About the Author: Charles Dickens

Charles Dickens was as interesting as any of the more than two thousand characters he created. Born in 1812 to middle class parents who loved to socialize and tended to live beyond their means, Charles was a deeply imaginative child, weak and somewhat sickly, who enjoyed observing others and exhibited an early gift for theatrics.

When Charles was eleven, his father was sent to debtor's prison, and Charles was forced to work in a dark, miserable blacking warehouse for a year until his father could bring him home. This terrible season of his life had such an impact on Dickens that he never spoke of it, even to his wife. At age fifteen, he had to leave school for good and start out on his own as a journalist. His childhood experiences combined to form a man of great ambition and energy coupled with a deep appreciation for the poor and downtrodden of the world.

Dickens fell in love as a young man but was rejected in favor of a more successful man. He married the next available young lady he met, Catherine Hogarth, the daughter of a well-known man of letters whom Dickens admired. Their courtship, from the first, was rather more practical than romantic, and grew more strained as their family grew to include ten children. After twenty-two years of marriage he separated from his wife, though he remained close to his children, who were fiercely protective of his fame and reputation.

Charles Dickens died at the relatively young age of 58, exhausted by a life of extreme exertion; having written novels, papers and articles at a feverish pace for nearly forty years.

Source: *Dickens*, by Peter Ackroyd. Harper Perennial, 1992.

Innocents Abroad:
The Old Curiosity Shop, by Charles Dickens

Dickens continued his use of the child as protagonist in *The Old Curiosity Shop*. Published in serial form in 1840-1841, the book enthralled readers with its combination of the grotesque and the awe-inspiring. Little Nell Trent is the typical Dickens heroine, "sensitive, frightened, and prematurely responsible," in Paul Schlicke's summation. Adrift in a sea of evil, Nell navigates with a purity of spirit that touches everyone she meets, and foreshadows her doom as a creature too noble for this world.

Synopsis

Conceived as a kind of allegory, the story follows Little Nell as she travels through a sinister world, pursued by the evil dwarf Quilp, whose personality, by turns hilarious and sadistic, colors the landscape she is forced to inhabit. Nell's only protector, her ill-fated grandfather, is ironically also the source of her troubles, since his terrible addiction to gambling places her in constant jeopardy. Like many children of addictive parents, Nell is forced prematurely into adulthood. Together they flee from her Grandfather's shop full of strange "curiosities," where Nell has been raised, and embark on a journey where she encounters their living counterparts. It's a road trip like nothing you've ever imagined.

Like Alice in Wonderland, Nell dwells in a dream world (she is constantly wondering if she is awake or asleep) that really is a nightmare. Besides the maniacal dwarf who pursues her, Nell meets puppeteers, clowns, magicians, and even works for a time as the assistant in a waxwork exhibition. Each of these grotesque characters is drawn in intricate and often hilarious detail. True to style, Dickens gives us plenty of subplots, with Nell's safety threatened as Quilp weaves a scheme to defraud her of a fortune she does not actually possess.

In the process we have the pleasure of meeting another great Dickens creation, Dick Swiveller, the delightfully reckless drunkard who emerges as the unlikely hero of the tale. Besides having one of the best names in fiction, Dick Swiveller is a wonderful bundle of contradictions. He's

Did You Know?

When Dickens passed away suddenly at the age of 58, the nation was devastated. His grave was left open for two days and thousands passed by to look at his simple oak coffin. Later his son said that among the many bouquets of flowers that were tossed into the grave, "were afterwards found several small rough bouquets of flowers tied up with pieces of rag." (*Dickens*, Peter Ackroyd, p. xiv.) The common people loved Dickens; they felt he represented them and felt his loss as a loss of something in them.

lazy and shiftless, but is so likeable that when he is finally forced to go to work we're sorry for him! Mrs. Jarley, the entrepreneur extraordinaire who employs Nell at the waxworks, is another delightful creation. Even Quilp, when he is not terrifying, is very funny. The loose narrative structure allows Dickens to introduce an absolute menagerie of wild characters in startling contrast to the steady, beautiful child. We see, through Nell's eyes, the very human nature of a carnival world. In the end, Nell succumbs to the strain of her journey and dies in one of the most famous, or infamous (depending on your point of view) scenes in literature.

What Makes it Great

The Old Curiosity Shop became a cultural phenomenon comparable to the miniseries *Roots* or to the musical *Les Miserables*. At its height 100,000 copies sold of each number in the series, and for fifty weeks readers on both sides of the Atlantic worried over the fate of Little Nell. In December of 1841 readers began to sense a melancholy turn in the tone of the novel, and Dickens reported to his publishers that they "inundated him with imploring letters recommending poor little Nell to mercy." Dickens was resolute, however, that Nell, as a symbol of purity in an evil world, must be released from her earthly suffering. Summoning up the grief he had suffered three years earlier when his beloved sister-in-law Mary

Hogarth died in his arms, Dickens composed the famous scene. This was a terrible experience for a man who called his characters his "children," and who suffered more over their fates than those of real people in his life. "I am," he wrote to a friend, "for the time, nearly dead with work and grief for the loss of my child . . . I went to bed last night utterly dispirited and done up. All night I have been pursued by the child; and this morning I am unrefreshed and miserable. I do not know what to do with myself." When he finally finished the novel he mourned in a letter, "Nobody shall miss her like I shall." American legend tells of thousands lining the New York docks awaiting the ship transporting the next issue of Nell's saga, crying to those on board, "Is Little Nell dead?" Unfortunately, she was.

Little Nell's legendary demise brings us to the sharpest criticism leveled against this novel, and against Dickens in general, namely, his sentimentality. G.K. Chesterton said of Dickens, "His humor was inspiration, but his pathos was ambition." In other words, Dickens could not help creating wonderful, comic characters, but he created sentimental ones in order to sell books. His long, maudlin death scenes can leave one squirming, and critics, even in his own day, accused him of emotional manipulation. (Oscar Wilde famously quipped that "one must have a heart of stone to read the death of Little Nell without laughing.") Aldous Huxley wrote: "One of Dickens's most striking peculiarities is that, whenever in his writing he becomes emotional, he ceases instantly to use his intelligence. The overflowing of his heart drowns his head and even dims his eyes; for whenever he is in the melting mood, Dickens ceases to be able and probably ceases even to wish to see reality. His one and only desire on these occasions is just to overflow, nothing else." (*Vulgarity in Literature*, 1930)

Is Dickens too sentimental? My own opinion is a firm yes . . . and no. Certainly Dickens has moments of pure sentimentality. Yet remember that Dickens was writing to people who faced death often. One third of the children born in Victorian society died before they were grown. That meant that nearly every family reading the latest installment of his novels had buried, or would bury, at least one child. Dickens, himself no stranger to death, wanted to do something through his writing to help people deal with the loss of loved ones. He wrote, "I resolved to try and do something which might be read by people about whom Death had been,—with a softened feeling, and with consolation." Scholar Arthur Henry King (who as a young boy lost both his father and younger brother) movingly described Dickens's importance in his emotional life:

"I met death in Dickens. It made more of an impression on me than anything else in Dickens. There was the death of Little Nell, the death of Paul Dombey, the death of Barkis in David Copperfield, the death (above all) of Dora. I remember reading about that in the autumn of 1918. It was October; it was a rainy day; and it was late afternoon when I read that chapter. I read it by the light of the fire. I can still remember all that. I can still remember my grief, and I can still remember that it took me several months to overcome that grief about a fictive character in a book—not that I have ever really recovered. That experience at the age of eight prepared me to find value in the passing of loved ones. It helped me to endure and properly experience the real deaths that followed it . . . We need to prepare our children for death. It is one of the things that they need and have a right to learn, and it is from literature that they can best learn it." (*Arm the Children*, 108-9)

The world changes very little, really. People are born, they live, they love, and they die. Through great novels we have an opportunity both to rehearse and to relive some of life's most difficult and tremendous moments. Literature can help us come to terms with life and death, lay down our burden of bitterness and receive wisdom in its stead. *The Old Curiosity Shop* will make you laugh and cry, and both will be, to use my father's expression, "good for what ails you."

Quotations taken from *The Old Curiosity Shop*. Penguin Classic Edition, New York. 1984.

Talk About It

Little Nell is almost too good to be true! Pure, sweet and gullible, she seems doomed to destruction by her very innocence. What do you think of her? Do you like Nell, or like Oscar Wilde, do you find her cloying, or even laughable?

About the Author:
Charles Dickens's London

Filled with restless energy, Dickens walked the streets of London by night, sometimes covering fifteen to twenty miles at a time. He attended executions and visited the prisons. He peered into the back streets and became intimately familiar with the primitive living conditions of the poor. What he saw was heartbreaking. The London that Dickens perambulated had no social services, no public sanitation, and was rife with crime and social unrest. It is estimated that over 40,000 prostitutes walked the streets. Graveyards, unregulated and overfilled by their greedy proprietors, literally overflowed, causing a noxious stench to fill the surrounding streets.

Perhaps the greatest sufferers in Victorian society were the youngsters. Children, unprotected by law, were forced to work long hours in factories, clamber up blackened chimneys as sweeps, or risk their lives in the mines. Unwanted and illegitimate children were sent north to schools where they were abused and underfed. Though his remarkable talent brought Dickens early and lasting success, his humble beginnings caused him to relate with these, the lowest classes of society.

A man whose life was a microcosm of the Victorian ideal, Dickens rose from obscurity to greatness on his own merits, yet never ceased to champion the forgotten masses of poor and suffering people left in the wake of the industrial revolution. When Dickens was born, very few middle class homes had more than a few books; they were too expensive for average families. At the turn of the next century, very few middle class homes were without a complete set of Dickens's novels, since they were considered the foundation of every good education.

Source: *Dickens*, by Peter Ackroyd. Harper Perennial, 1992.

A Little Child Shall Lead Them:
Silas Marner, by George Eliot

"In old days there were angels who came and took men by the hand and led them away from the city of destruction. We see no white-winged angels now. But yet men are led away from threatening destruction: a hand is put in theirs, which leads them forth gently towards a calm and bright land, so that they look no more backward; and the hand may be a little child's." (p?)

The man taken by the hand is Silas Marner, a miserable miser saved by the love of an abandoned child, and the fictional creation of a remarkable woman named George Eliot. Actually, her name was Mary Anne Evans; the *nom de plume* she adopted for her writing allowed her to be taken seriously in a time when women, if they wrote at all, wrote only what she derisively termed "silly novels." Born in 1819 in Warwickshire, England, Mary Anne's philosophical quest mirrored that of her society, which was undergoing a crisis of faith in the wake of the scientific discoveries that seemed to undermine traditional Christian dogma.

From the start Mary Anne was a brilliant and emotional idealist, and she eagerly embraced the Evangelical Christianity of one of her favorite teachers at school, only to make a complete turnaround when she read the highly influential *"The Origins of Christianity,"* which claimed that Christianity was not a revealed religion. At twenty-two years of age she dismayed her family by refusing to accompany them to church, and from then on developed her own philosophy of secular humanism, based on a belief in the natural goodness of the individual. This little novel, *Silas Marner*, is an examination of a similar crisis of faith in the life of a simple weaver.

Synopsis

Silas Marner, raised in one of the dissenting religious sects prevalent in the England of the early 19th century, loses his faith when he is betrayed by his dearest friend and misjudged by his brethren. An outcast from his tribe, Silas wanders alone until he finds a home in Raveloe, a little village where he plies his trade as a weaver. The townspeople are suspicious of this newcomer, since his trade is associated with the devil, and in addition because he suffers from epilepsy, a malady that causes him to freeze in a trance-like state now and then. Again the subject of social ostracism, Silas gradually forms an attachment to the money generated by his craft. His gold becomes his god and his only friend, and he hoards it carefully in his tiny shack on the edge of the Raveloe stone pits.

The life of this unhappy weaver becomes intertwined with the lives of his wealthy landlords, Squire Cass and his sons. One night Silas is robbed of his hoard of gold. At the same time, a woman who has been abandoned by one of the Squire's sons stumbles toward the cabin and dies in the snow. Her little daughter wanders into the cabin, drawn by the firelight, and attaches herself to Marner. He takes the child and raises her as his own, and his life is changed by this loving relationship. The lives of Marner and his neighbors are touched and transformed by their shared part in the raising of this little girl.

What Makes it Great?

George Eliot was a thoughtful, compassionate observer of human nature, and her portrayal of this lonely outcast is a masterpiece of character creation. We see it all come together when the lonely miser returns to his shack one day to find that his precious gold has been stolen from under the hearth of his home, and his world is shattered. Eliot understands that a loss of faith in God is often precipitated by a loss of faith in those whom we have trusted on earth. Since the betrayal of his friends and the decline of his faith, the hoarding of gold has become Silas's reason for being, and the loss of his treasure literally paralyzes him. Standing at the door of his cabin pondering the theft, he is seized with a fit of epilepsy and for a crucial moment remains frozen in the "chasm of his consciousness; holding open his door, powerless to resist either the good or evil that might enter there." (110) In the moment that the door of his home, and his soul, stand wide open, the miracle enters that changes his life forever.

A miracle is defined as "a wonder, or a supernatural event." George Eliot strove to redefine traditional Christianity for herself, and she examined the concept of miracles through the story of Silas and his treasure. Great pains are taken to build a scenario that illustrates the "natural" quality of miracles. Silas is nearsighted and cannot see the woman struggling toward his door with a child. He has epilepsy, which causes a lapse of

Did You Know?

In the romantic novels of the Eliot's time (mostly written by women) the poor were treated as a species apart from "real people." Eliot wrote, "They (the poor) are so many subjects for experimenting on, for reclaiming, improving, being anxious about, and relieving. They have no existence apart from the presence of a curate; they live in order to take tracts and broth." Eliot greatly admired Wordsworth and attempted, like him, to look closely at the lives of people who lacked all of the advantages she enjoyed, sympathetically recording their forms of speech, their customs, superstitions and struggles.

consciousness at a moment when his fire beckons the cold child, stranded in the snow as her mother sinks equally unconscious to the ground. It is only natural that a cold, hungry child should be drawn to the little cabin's bright warmth, and the child toddles to the hearth and falls asleep in front of the fire. As Silas regains his sensibility he sees something glowing on his hearth, and thinks for a moment it is his precious gold:

"Gold!—his own gold—brought back to him as mysteriously as it had been taken away! He felt his heart begin to beat violently; he leaned forward at last, and stretched forth his hand; but instead of the hard coin with the familiar resisting outline, his fingers encountered soft warm curls. In utter amazement, Silas fell on his knees and bent his head low to examine the marvel: it was a sleeping child—a round, fair thing with soft yellow rings all over its head." (110)

Years later, as Silas tries to understand the marvelous gift that was left on his hearth that night, he refers to the fifteen dark years between the loss of his religious faith and the birth of his love for the child: "Since the time the child was sent to me and I've come to love her as myself, I've had light enough to trusten by; and now she says she'll never leave me, I think I shall trusten till I die." (180)

The shabby little cabin where Silas dwells symbolizes the man himself. As the gold is taken from the hearth (or heart) and replaced by a child, Silas turns from miser to a father. The home itself undergoes changes that reflect the changes in the inner man. Eliot was disgusted by the unrealistic portrayal of children in novels, and gives us here a very practical picture of life with a toddler. From our unique vantage point we can see how the daily routine of service to a little child, so familiar to most of us, gradually works its magic on Silas's soul. It is no surprise that over time the shabby cottage transforms itself into a neat, happy home.

The fifteen dark years of spiritual famine are followed by fifteen years of spiritual feasting, and Silas and Eppie form a happy circle of love that draws the other members of the community to them in fellowship. Later, Eppie's future hangs in the balance as two men step forward to claim her—her natural father and her future husband—and Silas realizes he must be willing to share his treasure with another.

An Outsider Looking Inward

Eliot understood a life as a social outcast. As editor of the controversial *Westminster Review*, she enjoyed a rare place for a woman, at the center of intellectual life in society, accepted in many circles. All that changed when she met and fell in love with George Henry Lewes, a prominent literary figure of the time. Lewes was married (though estranged from his wife) and after two years of close companionship they decided to share a life together. This move caused a scandal that turned even the more radical members of society against them. She and Lewes were referred to publicly as "the stinkpots of humanity." Of this ostracism Eliot wrote, "I have counted the cost of the step I have taken and am prepared to bear, without irritation or bitterness, renunciation by all my friends." Her beloved brother Isaac never spoke to her again and Eliot was excluded, for the rest of her life, from "respectable" homes.

It was Lewes who first persuaded Mary Anne to write fiction, and who provided the encouragement and emotional support she desperately craved. (He even hid unfavorable reviews of her novels from her, so she wouldn't become discouraged.) Eliot referred to herself as "Mrs. Henry Lewes" throughout her life, and they remained faithful companions for twenty-five years until his death in 1878.

Like the artisan in her tale, Eliot takes the strands of religious faith, peasant life, aristocratic pride and family love and weaves them into a perfect tapestry. We are drawn into the dilemmas that Silas faces and see them through his myopic vision (symbolically, he can only see up close). Eliot's moments of crisis are often so subtle they slip by us. Consider, for example, the turning point of the novel, when Godfrey Cass confronts his illegitimate daughter, who has wandered onto Silas's hearth. The child simply looks into his face, then, when Cass says nothing, turns her blue eyes to the weaver and clings to him.

The moment passes quickly, and Cass has the illusion of having escaped the consequences of his actions, since his child cannot condemn him for his sins. It appears as if nothing has happened, yet it is this moment that will haunt Godfrey Cass ever after. Eliot believes in the law of the harvest. Each of her novels feature protagonists who cannot escape the consequences of their actions. There are no great villains, no spotless heroes; only, as she called them, "mixed people."

The imagery of weaving and spinning give this tale the dreamy quality of a fairy tale, and the connection to such stories as Sleeping Beauty and Rumplestilskin is deliberate. Eliot is attempting a new kind of fairy tale here, complete with such stock elements as the weaver, the woods, the rich landowner, the poor girl who is really an heiress, and the strange turns of fate that signal an order in the universe unknown to man. She combines these elements with a realistic portrayal of English village life unparalleled in fiction. This unlikely combination of the real with the mythical caused the book to be less popular than some of her other works, yet it has endured as a unique creation by a great and virtuous mind, who believed in the goodness of the human soul even as she searched in vain for a resolution to her own crisis of faith.

Quotations taken from *Silas Marner.* Modern Library Classics, New York. 2001.

Talk About It

Silas Marner's life turns on one remarkable experience. Do you believe in that kind of miraculous "change of heart?" Do people ever really change?

About the Author: George Eliot

Mary Anne Evans was born in Warwickshire, England in 1819. Her father managed the Arbury Hall Estate where his gifted daughter had access to the library and received a classical education. Visiting the estate allowed her to compare the wealth of the local landowner with the impoverished living of those who lived and worked on the estate. She boarded at schools until her mother died in 1836; Evans returned home to keep house for her father until he died in 1849. She immediately moved to Geneva, and then to London to write. Here, she became assistant editor of the left-wing journal, *The Westminster Review,* which profession some considered scandalous for an unmarried young woman, as her colleagues were predominantly male.

In 1954, she and the philosopher and critic George Henry Lewes moved in together, creating quite a scandal, as Lewes was married. To avoid prying eyes, the couple distanced themselves from the London literary society. At this point, Evans vowed to write novels that were realistic, unlike most of the ladies of her era. She hoped her pen name, George Eliot, would ensure her works were taken seriously. Her first complete novel, *Adam Bede* (1859), was an instant success. She continued to write popular novels for the next fifteen years, including *The Mill on the Floss* (1860), *Silas Marner* (1861), and *Middlemarch* (1871). After Lewes died in 1878, Eliot met and married a man twenty years her junior in 1880, and died the same year.

Sources: victorianweb.org, Wikipedia

Through the Eyes of a Child: Take it Personally

For many readers a book becomes a touchstone; an event that marks a change in perspective or even direction. One reader describes how rereading Silas Marner gave her a new perspective on her own life:

"When I read Silas Marner the first time I must not have been able to appreciate what he went through because I had not yet experienced anything that he went through. I had never experienced a trial of faith or the loss of something treasured; my world at that time was very small and untainted. My world and life did not remain innocent. Like Silas I have now experienced periods of times when I questioned my belief in teachings that I had just accepted all my life. I have experienced loss and heartache, but like Silas through that loss I grew and changed, and found peace and love through small miracles in my life. Reading the book again gave me the opportunity remember that sometimes the greatest trials bring the greatest blessings."

Certain experiences in my life are inextricably linked to the book I was reading at the time. I read *The Old Curiosity Shop* when I was bedridden before the birth of our last child. One morning I received word that a dear friend had died, leaving several children motherless. That was a difficult morning, with grief for my friend compounded by my fears for our unborn child. I was comforted by this passage, regarding the sudden death of a little boy:

"There is nothing,' cried her friend, 'no, nothing innocent or good, that dies, and is forgotten. Let us hold to that faith, or none. An infant, a prattling child, dying in its cradle, will live again in the better thoughts of those who loved it; and play its part, through them, in the redeeming actions of the world, though its body be burnt to ashes or drowned in the deepest sea. There is not an angel added to the Host of heaven but does its blessed work on earth in those that loved it here. Forgotten! Oh, if the good deeds of human creatures could be traced to their source, how beautifully would even death appear; for how much charity, mercy, and purified affection, would be seen to have their growth in dusty graves!" (503)

Chapter Eight
Nobody's Perfect

What is wonderful about great literature is that it transforms the man who reads it towards the condition of the man who wrote.

~E.M. Forster

We are all full of weakness and errors; let us mutually pardon each other our follies—it is the first law of nature.

-Voltaire

Heroes are easy to love, but most of us aren't heroes; we're just people. Reading about flawed, failing characters can be strangely uplifting. Yes, maybe we feel better because we are not as deceptive as Becky Sharp, as terrified as Jeremy Pauling or as bitter as Heathcliff, but perhaps it's more than that. It is in the generous acceptance of the frailties and weaknesses of others that we become truly human, and worthy of similar grace at the hands of others.

Each of these novels brings us a soul in shambles. Yet each steadfastly continues to strive, keeps trying to make sense of things, and attempts to reach out to others. In the end this may be the definition of the hero that is most meaningful; one who keeps trying in the face of overwhelming odds. This is what millions of "ordinary" people do every day, and these authors celebrate their tiny, yet significant victories.

Hewn in a Wild Workshop:
Wuthering Heights, by Emily Bronte

Where would English literature be without the Yorkshire moors? These wild, mostly uninhabited lands that stretch across the north of England have provided the setting for some of the greatest stories ever told. They formed the backdrop for Jane Eyre's wanderings and Heathcliff's ravings. It was there that poor intrepid Dr. Herriott made his veterinary rounds, the hound of the Baskervilles howled, and little Mary found her secret garden. Several years ago, while in York on business, we had occasion to drive up to Edinburgh, Scotland for some meetings. On the way up we enjoyed a breathtaking view of the moors, with beautiful patches of heather dotting the craggy hills. That night, as we returned, the same scenery looked entirely different: eerie, forbidding and enshrouded in thick fog.

Clutching our new baby in my arms I peered through the window into the dark night and tried to imagine what it would be like to be raised in that wild, cold country. I thought of the four Bronte children, growing up in virtual isolation on those very moors, creating imaginary characters to fill their lonely existence, and it made sense that the characters they created would be as stormy and forbidding as the moors themselves. It was in this setting that quiet, serious Emily Bronte crafted the remarkable *Wuthering Heights*. Her sister Charlotte said of the book:

"It is rustic all the way through. It is moorish, and wild, and knotty as a root of heath. Nor was it natural that it should be otherwise; the author being herself a native and nursling of the moors."

Synopsis

The title of Emily Bronte's classic comes from a Yorkshire word, "withering," which refers to stormy and changeable weather. There is indeed a great deal of "wither" in this book, most of it bad. The novel's curious structure is laid out in the first three chapters, where a Mr. Lockwood comes as a tenant in a cottage attendant to Wuthering Heights, a great house on the Yorkshire moors. When he hikes up to the main house to meet his new landlord, Heathcliff, he is trapped there by a snowstorm and ends up spending the night in the haunted room of the doomed Catherine, Heathcliff's great love. He meets and is both confused and rather frightened by the strange inhabitants of the house.

By the time he escapes from the various ghosts, dogs, and grumpy old men that inhabit Wuthering Heights, poor Mr. Lockwood is very ill. Safe in his little cottage, he turns to his housekeeper, Mrs. Dean, for entertainment. He persuades her to tell him the story of the weird inhabitants of the infamous hall, and as a result we receive the tale "twice-removed," from Mrs. Dean through Lockwood to us.

The tale is a complicated tangle involving Catherine, her brother Hindley and the orphan Heathcliff, who is being raised in their home. Heathcliff and Catherine love each other, but when Catherine grows up she marries a neighboring gentleman, Edgar Linton. Heathcliff is consumed with bitterness; he has been tortured by Hindley, rejected by Catherine, and in despair goes away to seek his fortune. When he returns he gets his revenge by hounding Hindley to death, inheriting the mansion and tormenting the next generation. Catherine's daughter, also named Catherine, is held prisoner in his home until she marries his invalid son, giving him title to both estates. Heathcliff has gone mad, however, and eventually dies, leaving Catherine (now also widowed) to learn to love and eventually marry Hindley's son, Hareton.

Bronte's convoluted narrative style has been much commented upon, along with the very complex plot line and a challenging time line. Bronte handles the intertwining narrative strains with alacrity to bring us a fascinating story of a strange group of people who are hopelessly intertwined in love, envy and malice.

What's in a Name?

It is surely no coincidence that so many people in this novel share the same names. There are two incarnations of nearly every name, and Catherine herself possesses, at one time or another, the surnames of all three families that form the center of the action. As Mr. Lockwood finds himself imprisoned in the oaken closet that was Catherine's bed, he finds her various names scratched over and over on the wood and in the margins of her books:

Did You Know?

During the first few years after the publication of *Wuthering Heights*, critics did not believe that Emily Bronte was its author. Instead, they chose to think that both *Wuthering Heights* and *The Tenant of Wildfell Hall* (by youngest sister Anne) were earlier, less polished works by the creator of *Jane Eyre*, older sister Charlotte. Since the women lived in almost total seclusion and Emily and Anne died within a few months of each other, it was difficult to persuade the public that there were, in fact, three authors instead of one. Their creative lives were intertwined in a remarkable way, however, as Charlotte described:

"We were wholly dependent on ourselves and each other, on books and study, for the enjoyments and occupations of life. The highest stimulus, as well as the liveliest pleasure we had known from childhood upwards, lay in attempts at literary composition." (*Wuthering Heights*, Penguin Classics Edition, Introduction.)

Catherine Earnshaw, Catherine Heathcliff, and Catherine Linton. There seems to be a deliberate intent to confuse us with the names of the characters, as if their setting, both emotional and physical, causes them to melt into one great bundle of painful emotion. We don't know who they really are.

One of the first reviewers of the novel, Sidney Dobell, saw this repetition of names and histories as a kind of philosophical statement about human nature. He remarks, "There are minds whose crimes and sorrows are not so much the result of intrinsic evil as of a false position in the scheme of things, which clashes their energies with the arrangements of surrounding life. It is difficult to cure such a soul from within. The point of view . . . is in fault." I think this is an important insight about the troubled characters of *Wuthering Heights*. Like many people we know, they are not evil, just out of step somehow with the proper rhythm of happy existence. Their abnormal surroundings make it impossible for them to function in a normal manner.

Again, the moors themselves seem to exert an influence on the personalities of the inhabitants; they are more intense in their passions, more concentrated and fixed in their obsessions. Mr. Lockwood comments:

"I perceive that people in these regions acquire over people in towns the value that a spider in a dungeon does over a spider in a cottage, to their various occupants; and yet the deepened attraction is not entirely owing to the situation of the looker-on. They do live more in earnest, more in themselves, and less in surface, change, and frivolous external things. I could fancy a love for life here almost possible; and I was a fixed unbeliever in any love of a year's standing. One state resembles setting a hungry man down to a single dish, on which he may concentrate his entire appetite and do it justice; the other, introducing him to a table laid out by French cooks: he can perhaps extract as much enjoyment from the whole; but each part is a mere atom in his regard and remembrance." (209)

Love Story, or Horror Story?

When Emily Bronte read the (often harsh) criticism of her wild, violent characters, she was amazed, and could not see why the novel was considered so frightening. She never encountered any of her critics directly, however, since she lived in complete seclusion with her sisters, and died before most people even realized that her novel was not, as many believed, penned by her more famous sister. Later editions of the novel contained a defense of its origin by Charlotte herself, and eventually Emily's genius was duly recognized. Its style is definitely unique to its author. The following passage is just one example of the way Emily gathers in the natural surroundings, the gate, the road, the stones and the "withered turf," to portray the emotional lives of her characters:

"One time I passed the old gate, going out of my way, on a journey to Gimmerton. It was about the period that my narrative has reached: a bright frosty afternoon; the ground bare, and the road hard and dry. I came to a stone where the highway branches off on to the moor at your left hand; a rough sand-pillar, with the letters W. H. cut on its north side, on the east, G., and on the south-west, T. G. It serves as a guidepost to the

Grange, the Heights, and village. The sun shone yellow on its grey head, reminding me of summer; and I cannot say why, but all at once a gush of child's sensations flowed into my heart. Hindley and I held it a favourite spot twenty years before. I gazed long at the weather-worn block; and, stooping down, perceived a hole near the bottom still full of snail-shells and pebbles, which we were fond of storing there with more perishable things; and, as fresh as reality, it appeared that I beheld my early playmate seated on the withered turf: his dark, square head bent forward, and his little hand scooping out the earth with a piece of slate. 'Poor Hindley!' I exclaimed, involuntarily. I started: my bodily eye was cheated into a momentary belief that the child lifted its face and stared straight into mine! It vanished in a twinkling; but immediately I felt an irresistible yearning to be at the Heights." (310)

In response to Emily's critics, Charlotte acknowledged the faults of the work while staunchly defending its honesty and courage. Though she affirmed that over much of the story "there broods a horror of great darkness," Charlotte believed that this was a result of Emily's lonely, melancholy existence, and that "had she lived, her mind would of itself have grown like a strong tree, loftier, straighter, wider-spreading, and its matured fruits would have attained a mellower ripeness and sunnier bloom . . ."

Emily Bronte was a poet as well as a novelist and many of her poems attempt to describe the love she has for her native countryside, and its impact on her psyche. Consider these lines:

> Few hearts to mortals given
> On Earth so wildly pine;
> Yet few would ask a Heaven
> More like this Earth than thine.
> Then let my winds caress thee;
> Thy comrade let me be—
> Since nought beside can bless thee,
> Return and dwell with me.

Wuthering Heights, Charlotte Bronte concluded, "was hewn in a wild workshop, with simple tools, out of homely materials . . . with a rude chisel, and from no model but the vision of his meditations." It is a compelling tale of love gone wrong, and a faithful representation of a wild land, beautiful and dangerous, that shapes the lives and souls of its inhabitants.

Quotations taken from *Wuthering Heights*. Penguin Classics Edition, London. 1995.

Talk About It

Wuthering Heights brings up the discussion of nature versus nurture. Is Heathcliff bad by nature, or was his upbringing as an orphan, tormented by his peers, responsible for the way he behaves as an adult? To what extent are we truly responsible for our own actions?

About the Author: Emily Brontë

Born in 1818, Emily was the middle girl of the three famous Brontë sisters, all novelists. She had four older siblings (Maria, Elizabeth, Charlotte, and Patrick) and one younger sister (Anne). Emily wrote only one novel, *Wuthering Heights*. The family lived in the small, isolated town of Haworth, Yorkshire. A poor Irishman, their father was somewhat eccentric and strict; he became a parish clergyman. Their mother died in 1821 and an aunt brought up the sisters conscientiously but with little understanding and affection.

First published under Emily's pseudonym Ellis Bell and set in eighteenth-century England, her novel is a portrait of the moors. It creates a world of patriarchal values juxtaposed with the natural elements. Brontë explores themes of revenge, religion, class, and prejudice while plumbing the depths of the metaphysical and human psyche.

Both *Jane Eyre* and *Wuthering Heights* were published in 1847. Emily died in 1848 at the age of 30. In the 1850 edition of *Wuthering Heights*, Charlotte wrote an editor's preface and paid tribute to the unique gifts of its creator. "Stronger than a man, simpler than a child, her nature stood alone," she said of Emily.

Source: Glen, Heather, ed. *The Cambridge Companion to the Brontës*. Cambridge, 2002.

A Beautiful Vein of Genius:
Vanity Fair, by
William Makepeace Thackeray

Vanity Fair, by William Makepeace Thackeray, was published in installments in 1847-48: the same year that saw the publication of *Jane Eyre*, by Charlotte Bronte, and the year before *David Copperfield*, by Charles Dickens. All three authors were keenly aware of each other. Dickens was the undisputed master of English novelists; for a decade his novels had appeared in quick succession and had been wildly popular. Bronte idolized Thackeray, to whom she dedicated the second edition of *Jane Eyre*. Thackeray, trained as a critic and essayist, wrote in the serial form popularized by Dickens but in a very different style. Where Dickens was sentimental and even pedantic, Thackeray maintained a cool, ironic stance that both infuriated and delighted readers.

Vanity Fair represented a new kind of novel in English. It was a book that portrayed human nature with all its weaknesses, yet did so against the backdrop of a high moral idealism. Subtitled, "A Novel Without a Hero," the book's title comes from John Bunyan's allegorical story *The Pilgrim's Progress*, first published in 1678 and still widely read at the time of Thackeray's novel. Vanity fair refers to a stop along the pilgrim's progress: a never-ending fair held in a town called Vanity, which is meant to represent man's sinful attachment to worldly things. From the moment that Becky Sharp flings Johnson's dictionary out the window as she leaves boarding school, we know we are in for a wild ride, as she rejects "civilized" society and its restrictions while at the same time longing for its status and advantages.

Synopsis

Becky Sharp, the aptly named "anti-heroine" of *Vanity Fair*, is a surprising, entertaining, and rather unsettling character. Of lowly birth, she is brought up at Miss Pinkerton's fashionable boarding school where her father was once the drawing master. She hates the place, and particularly the snobbish Miss Pinkerton, and the narrative opens with her gleeful, bitter escape.

Becky Sharp has only one friend at Pinkerton's, Amelia Sedley, a sweet, timid, and demure girl that Becky both loves and envies. Amelia falls in love with George Osbourne, a self-centered young soldier, and marries him against his father's wishes. George dies in the Battle of Waterloo and Amelia returns home to her parents to raise their son, George Jr. Meanwhile Betsy marries Rawdon Crawley, a soldier and heir to a fortune, until his aunt disowns him after his marriage to Becky. Rawdon's only talent is cheating at cards, and Becky charms various society figures in order to advance his interests. Osbourne's friend Dobbin adores Amelia, and does everything in his power to help her while she treats him badly and idolizes her late husband. By the end of the novel Becky is impoverished and disgraced. Amelia finally realizes Dobbin's true worth and they marry. Eventually Becky's son by Rawdon inherits the family title and fortune and supports her, though she was an indifferent mother to him.

What Makes it Great?

Thackeray is a master at capturing the subtle gradations in moral character that make life so confusing. There are paradoxes everywhere we look. Sweet, gentle Amelia is Becky's polar opposite, and should, by rights, be the true heroine of the novel, but it doesn't exactly work that way. It is the genius of Thackeray to bring these two girls into all sorts of trying situations where the reader may see their true characters revealed, without ever taking the side of either. Becky is nearly always bad, though she has many endearing qualities. Amelia is nearly always perfect, and rather irritating! Rather than offering us the standard fare of good souls in conflict with evil ones, Thackeray offers us a cast of complex, realistic characters that struggle to make right choices in a confusing world.

To further anchor his characters in the real world, Thackeray places them against the backdrop of the Napoleonic Wars. However, his version of the historical novel is different from Tolstoy's *War and Peace*, or Hugo's *Les Misérables*. In those books the battles are gritty and realistically drawn, and the people are idealized as either good or evil. In Thackeray, the battles are largely ignored, history is merely touched upon, but the everyday struggles in the drawing room, the nursery, the schoolroom, or at the dinner table are shown to be where the real victories and defeats of life take place. Thus, though his story is placed in a historical setting, it would perhaps be more accurate to call Thackeray a moral realist, since ethical behavior is his chief concern.

One quickly gets the impression that it matters very little to Thackeray who wins the battle of Waterloo: what is important is whether George, the young soldier destined to fight and die there, will be faithful to his young wife on the eve of that battle. And the disastrous losses suffered by businessmen who speculated on that war are less important than whether George's father, who profited thereby, will be merciful to those less fortunate than himself. Sometimes his characters succeed, and sometimes they fail, but Thackeray never blinks; we see the whole heart revealed in his masterful prose.

A fine example of this moral realism is the character of George Osbourne, the dashing soldier beloved by Amelia since girlhood. George is handsome but weak, charming but spoiled, and nearly abandons Amelia when her family's financial ruin causes George's father to turn against the match. The one, great, honorable character in the novel, George's friend Dobbin, persuades him that he must go ahead with the marriage. George is constantly disappointing us, yet by viewing him through the adoring Amelia's eyes and the worshipful eyes of the other soldiers, we come to love George in spite of his weakness and mourn his loss. Only Becky sees him without sentimentality, as she sees everyone; just as they are and in terms of how they might benefit her schemes.

We all know a George Osbourne. We know an Amelia, a Becky, and if we are lucky, we may meet one or two people of Dobbin's caliber in the course of our lives. Each character represents a type of person, and yet each character has an endearing individuality that renders them unforgettable. Thackeray has the knack of identifying his characters by certain material objects that surround them, such as Dobbin's cloak, Amelia's miniatures, and Becky's special little box that hides her treasures and will contain the resolution of the novel's plot. These physical clues to inner character abound in Thackeray and are part of the pleasure of his style. For Thackeray, actions often speak louder than words: in a moment of crisis he may say little about how a character feels and instead shows what they do.

Did You Know?

Like many novels of the time, *Vanity Fair* was published as a serial before being sold in book form; it was printed in 20 monthly parts between January 1847 and July 1848. Its canary-yellow cover was Thackeray's signature color (Dickens's was blue-green) and allowed passers-by to notice a new Thackeray number in a bookstall from a distance. It was also the first work that Thackeray published under his own name, and was a bestseller. The original monthly numbers and later bound version featured Thackeray's own illustrations, which at times provided plot hints or symbolically freighted images (a major character shown as a man-eating mermaid, for instance) to which the text does not explicitly refer.

Here, for example, is the scene where George's father reacts to the news of his son's marriage, a union he once promoted but now opposes for purely selfish reasons:

"He opened the book-case, and took down the great red Bible we have spoken of—a pompous book, seldom looked at, and shining all over with gold. There was a frontispiece to the volume, representing Abraham sacrificing Isaac. Here, according to custom, Osborne had recorded on the fly-leaf, and in his large clerk-like hand, the dates of his marriage and his wife's death, and the births and Christian names of his children . . . . Taking a pen, he carefully obliterated George's names from the page; and when the leaf was quite dry, restored the volume to the place from which he had moved it." (p. 272)

Every phrase here is full of emotional information: from the Bible, encrusted in gold but seldom read, to the reference to Abraham and Isaac (George is sacrificed, not on the altar of God through obedience, but on the altar of the world through his father's pride) to his "clerk-like" hand, which reminds us that Osbourne Senior is not a gentleman, but only a small man with a large amount of money. The crowning irony, of course, is that in his most evil moment this father takes his son's name out of the Bible, and by so doing ensures that his own name is struck from the Lamb's Book of Life. Though Thackeray did not espouse religion, he was committed to the idea that the true mark of a "gentleman" was not birth or wealth, but integrity and morality. This notion of the true gentleman looms large in *Vanity Fair*. When young George Junior comes to know his godfather, Major Dobbin, he realizes that Dobbin is in a different class from the fashionable, shallow people that surround him:

"He was a clever lad and afraid of the Major. George could not help admiring his friend's simplicity, his good-humour, his various learning quietly imparted, his general love of truth and justice. He had met no such man as yet in the course of his experience, and he had an instinctive liking for a gentleman." (713)

Becky Sharp, a young person whose moral principles waver when she is thrown on her own resources, is much like the young Thackeray. (Her firm statement that she would have been a moral, upright woman if she had possessed five thousand pounds a year comes right out of a letter Thackeray once wrote to his mother about his own circumstances.) At war with this subtle shrugging off of moral responsibility was a deep idealism about human nature; Thackeray believed that people could be better than they were. William Lilly said that he found irony, but no cynicism in Thackeray: rather an appeal to the higher ideals within us. "To those sympathies, beliefs, instincts, I say, Thackeray ever appealed, to recall us from the worship of Mammon, the worship of rank, the worship of notoriety, to the worship of goodness, and truth and love."(Wm. Samuel Lilly, *Criticism and Interpretations,* Harvard Classics Shelf of Fiction.)

In *Vanity Fair* we have Becky's intelligence and energy juxtaposed upon Amelia's virtue and passivity, yet we are never forced to choose between them. We are allowed to see how each suffers as a result of her failings and enjoys happiness as a result of good choices. These characters feel envy, grief, lust, pride, sorrow and repentance, just as we do. Thackeray brings us along as a part of the crowd, inserting himself jovially into the narrative now and then to comment on their trials and triumphs, and then retreating to allow us to form our own conclusions.

Though he knew he wanted to write a long tale about the world of fashion and society, Thackeray could not think of an appropriate title for his first novel. One night it came to him, and he wrote to a friend that he jumped out of bed in excitement and ran around the room shouting, "Vanity Fair, Vanity Fair, Vanity Fair!" It was a title worth celebrating, for it cleverly refers not only to the vain nature of worldly things, but the entertaining, attractive nature of them. Yes, the world is vain, but it is fair, and it is also a fair, a roiling, exciting, fun place to be. G.K Chesterton said of the book that its principle character was the world. "It produces on the mind," he said, "the same impression of mixed voices and almost maddening competition as a crowded square on market day" (G.K. Chesterton, *Criticism and Interpretations,* Harvard Shelf of Classics.)

This is a wonderful book; funny, enlightening and ultimately uplifting. If you prefer sentimental stories, romance novels, and larger than life heroes, you might not like *Vanity Fair*. But if, like me, you love to experience fully-realized fictional characters that stay with you forever, and prefer to see the human heart mapped honestly and compassionately, you will find a masterpiece in *Vanity Fair*. As Carlyle said of Thackeray, "a beautiful vein of genius lay struggling about in him." That genius is evident here.

Quotations taken from *Vanity Fair.* Penguin Classics Edition, London. 2003.

Talk About It

Vanity Fair gives us a series of flawed characters, none of which really live 'happily ever after.' Did you find the book depressing or uplifting, or both? Did you enjoy spending time with these characters?

About the Author:
William Makepeace Thackeray

William Makepeace Thackeray was born in India in 1811, and after losing his father at an early age, was sent to school in England, where he was miserable and lonely. After his mother remarried and returned to England, mother and son were reunited, though he spent most of his formative years in the often brutal English school system. In 1829, he entered Trinity College at Cambridge University. Not keen on academics, Thackeray left after a year and a half to travel abroad. He had trouble finding a career and dabbled in law and art.

Though possessed of an inheritance at age 21, he squandered his means and was forced to earn a living as a writer. Thus, he was able to observe both sides of the social scene—the privileged life of a gentleman and the scramble for existence faced by an average fellow. Thackeray loved entertainments—gambling, the theater, good food, and drink—and struggled to become a serious, responsible adult. His own life held many sorrows; chief among them the incurable insanity of his wife, Isabella, who grew more unstable with the birth of each of three daughters and was finally placed in a mental institution in 1844.

Thackeray is famous for his satirical works. The author knew that men and women are complex and he avoided oversimplifying them. He also knew "virtuous people can be dull and rascals can be lively." Thackeray believed most people are a mixture of the heroic and the ridiculous. His work skillfully ridicules hypocrites. In fact, his *The Snob Papers*, later collected as *The Book of Snobs*, popularized the modern meaning of the word "snob." A gifted caricaturist, he did his own illustrations for *Vanity Fair*, probably his best novel. He died in London in 1863.

Sources:

Ferris, Ina. *William Makepeace Thackeray*. Boston: Twayne, 1983.

Succoring Us in Our Infirmities:
Celestial Navigation, by Anne Tyler

There is a line in scripture that speaks of the Lord, "succoring his people in their infirmities." What an interesting word; *infirmity*. Webster defines it as "shaky, unstable, or frail," and the Oxford English Dictionary gives it as "weakness, want of strength, or the lack of power to do something." So many of our struggles in life have more to do with weakness than wickedness. Most of us try to do what it right and good, but we fear, we falter, we fail, and we suffer the consequences. It is important, therefore, to understand not only right and wrong, but also something about weakness and infirmity.

It is here that a great novelist like Anne Tyler can help us. She is less interested in the wickedness of the world than in the weaknesses of people like us. Consider, for example, her careful and compassionate description of a man paralyzed by fear. Jeremy, the protagonist of *Celestial Navigation*, is a talented artist and a gentle, kind man, yet his fears completely undermine his ability to live a normal life. Tyler offers a matter-of-fact, almost doctor-like diagnosis of her protagonist:

"These are some of the things that Jeremy Pauling dreaded: using the telephone, answering the doorbell, opening mail, leaving his house, making purchases. Also wearing new clothes, standing in open spaces, meeting the eyes of a stranger, eating in the presence of others, turning on electrical appliances." (*Celestial Navigation*, 86)

There is something incredibly moving about this list for me. Jeremy is a study in fear, and the rippling, damaging effect it can have. In fact, he appears to be the very definition of infirmity. The long paragraph describing his difficulty with nearly every aspect of life concludes with Jeremy's conviction that:

" . . . other people seemed to possess an inner core of hardness that they took for granted. They hardly seemed to notice it was there; they had come by it naturally. Jeremy had been born without it." (87)

Synopsis

Jeremy Pauling, an artist, owns a home and rents out rooms, and in one of them lives Mary, a single mother. She is a study in strength, bearing child after child from various partners and handling everything with aplomb. Jeremy is attracted to her strength, and they eventually marry. Her fatal flaw is a kind of selfish pride that leaves her unwilling to share her parenting relationship with a man, though she relies upon one after another for support. She must own the children; she protects them from their respective fathers and trusts no one—even Jeremy—to enter the circle she creates for herself and her brood.

Jeremy and Mary make a life together, and have children. They interact with the odd collection of people that rent the other rooms in the house. The story is narrated by these characters, and we piece together a picture through their various perspectives. In the end, Jeremy and Mary live separate lives, even in the same house, but Jeremy's art is deeply affected by their relationship.

What Makes it Great?

Ann Tyler has a subtle greatness. Her careful descriptions and insightful snatches of dialogue bring us gradually into the hearts and souls of—in Gail Godwin's words—the "oddballs, visionaries, lonely souls" who invariably populate her fiction. The climactic moment in this novel is the birth of the fourth child (or fifth, we lose count) when Mary goes to the hospital without Jeremy. He has finally been completely excluded from everything but the conception of the child. Every mother understands the sweet circle of two that is formed when a new baby arrives, which then opens to admit the father and complete the family unit. Mary cannot take that step, turning her mothering into a kind of emasculation of the males in her life. Jeremy sees what needs to be done but lacks the power to step up and act. Conversely, Mary sees that she needs help yet lacks the humility to admit her weakness and let her husband be strong. They need each other, yet cannot reach across the divide and create a true married relationship. In the end they

Did You Know?

Agoraphobia (according to Wikipedia) is a term that comes from the Greek word for marketplace. "Sufferers of agoraphobia avoid public and/or unfamiliar places, especially large, open, spaces such as shopping malls or airports where there are few places to hide. In severe cases, the sufferer may become confined to his or her home, experiencing difficulty traveling from this safe place. Approximately 3.2 million adults in the US between the ages of 18 and 54, or about 2.2%, suffer from agoraphobia." This story of an artist with agoraphobia was loosely based on Anne Tyler herself. She suffers from "a touch of agoraphobia" and said in an interview, ""[I am] very, very fond of 'Celestial Navigation,' although it was hardest to write."

are only pretending to be married; they are two separate people in one house.

All of this is brought to life via the interesting narrative structure of this novel: through the voices of the inmates of Jeremy's home, which is let out to renters. The boarding house, with its odd combination of individual lives that bump into each other now and then in communal spaces, feels like one of those dollhouses we played with as children, with the front wall missing from all the rooms. We peer into first one room, then another, observe the inhabitants, and see how they interact. Miss Vinton (who serves a connecting link for the various characters) describes their situation and illuminates Tyler's underlying theme:

"If you want my opinion, our whole society would be better off living in boarding houses. I mean even families, even married couples. Everyone should have his single room with a door that locks, and then a larger room downstairs where people can mingle or not as they please." (141)

By using the boarding house as a metaphor for the larger world, Tyler shows us that we do, in fact, co-exist in much the same way as the inmates of the Pauling home. Our triumphs and failures are more

interconnected than we realize. Jeremy and Mary live out their lives
in a separate spaces, yet many are affected by their actions. Their story
does not end happily, yet somehow there is a hopeful element in their
domestic woes. For though in the long run Jeremy and Mary are unable
to create a stable, happy life together, they do create a family. They have
children, they go forward, and they eventually overcome at least some of
their fears and infirmities.

A World of Their Own

There is a dreamy, contemplative quality about her books that sets
Tyler apart from the plot-driven, sensational literature that crowds the
bestseller lists today. Most of her books center on a woman character, but
that woman is of most interest because of her role in a family unit. Tyler
admitted she is "scared of the very idea of a 'message' in a novel. All I
ever want to do is to tell a story." One rarely has a sense in Tyler's novels
of a particular place and time; in fact, most of her books could take place
anywhere, and they seem suspended in a time zone of their own. Yet in
each of her novels, Tyler has something to teach us about our infirmities,
our weaknesses and our fears.

She also invariably has something hopeful to say about the human
spirit. Though Jeremy fails at relationships, his art expresses something he
is unable to say in language. Though Mary is unable to sustain a marriage,
she is a strong, nurturing mother, and together Jeremy and Mary create
children that may enrich the world through the combination of their
parents' weaknesses and strengths. Even childless spinsters like Miss
Vinton have a vital role to play as they lend support to this struggling
family. The boarding house is a little village, and it takes a village to raise
the children, and support the parents.

In Tyler's world, few people are really evil, and everyone is good for
something. Small victories, like the day when Jeremy walks seven blocks
to see his daughter's play, are celebrated with quiet grace. As Miss
Vinton says, "There are other kinds of heroes than the ones who swim
through burning oil." Her characters may be rife with infirmities, but

Tyler believes in them. As we come to understand their struggles we may take a small step toward conquering our own fears, and receive a kind of succor that lifts us and draws us closer to those we love and seek to understand.

Quotations taken from *Celestial Navigation*. Ballantine Books, New York. 1974.

Talk About It

Everybody seems to have a phobia these days. Conditions that used to just be considered part of life are now treated with medication and therapy. It seems that everything from restless leg syndrome to coulrophobia (fear of clowns) has a name and a pill to cure it. Do you think we actually create infirmities by labeling and paying so much attention to them?

About the Author: Anne Tyler

© Diana Walker

Born in 1941 and raised in a succession of Quaker communes in the mountains of North Carolina, Anne Tyler brings the perspective of an outsider to her observations. Home schooled by brilliant parents, Tyler commented that when she entered public school for the first time at the age of eleven, she had "never used a telephone and could strike a match on the sole of her bare foot." She was also acquainted with home farming, Appalachian crafts, and already deeply immersed in the classics.

Her early years in the commune gave Tyler what she calls "my sense of distance," and one notices in her writing the workings of the inner lives of the contemporary family. This sense of distance, the disciplined quiet of the Quaker upbringing, and the pull of the land are evident in all of her settings, her characters, and her plots. "Daydreaming," she declares, "is the most useful activity I know of, but until now it's been almost universally frowned upon." She graduated at age 19 from Duke University, and completed graduate work at Columbia University in Russian studies.

Tyler's ninth novel, *Dinner at the Homesick Restaurant*, which she considers her best work, was a finalist for both the Pulitzer Prize and the PEN/Faulkner Award in 1983. Her eleventh novel, *Breathing Lessons*, was awarded the Pulitzer Prize in 1988. A mother to two daughters, she lives in Baltimore, Maryland.

Source: *Anne Tyler as Novelist*, Salwak, Dale, ed. University of Iowa Press, 1994.

Nobody's Perfect: Take it Personally

One of the great things a great book can do is cause us to take action in our own lives. Some of the characters in these novels are so dysfunctional that we find ourselves itching to reach into the pages of the novel and fix things for them. After suffering along with Mary and Jeremy in *Celestial Navigation,* one frustrated reader wrote:

"There were times in the book when I wanted to grab Jeremy by the scruff of his neck and kick his rear end from here to eternity. Mary's solution to her problems was to stop the world and get off for awhile, and she managed to do this successfully at least three times, until at last she succeeded in unwittingly destroying those that loved her, Jeremy, Brian and the rest. I am not sure whether I enjoyed the book or not. However, it teaches a powerful lesson; that you cannot quit on yourself, and if you do, you damage many other lives and your own as well."

It is much easier to see what others, especially fictional characters, should do to solve their own problems, than to find solutions for our own. However, a great book can both suggest solutions and enervate us to try again.

Chapter Nine
Chick-Lit for Grown-ups

"When one reads of a witch being ducked, of a woman possessed by devils, of a wise woman selling herbs, or even a very remarkable man who had a mother, then I think we are on the track of a lost novelist, a suppressed poet . . . indeed, I would venture to guess that Anon, who wrote so many poems without signing them, was often a woman."

Virginia Woolf

"I'm not afraid of storms, for I'm learning to sail my ship."

Louisa May Alcott

The term "chick-lit" has come to denote romantic, light books by women, about women; books that men would never find interesting, and so lightweight that they are forgotten almost as soon as we set them down. That's too bad, because there are some great works of literature written by women, about women, that both entertain and enlighten.

Women have so many choices these days that it may be challenging to know just what it is that we really want. Yet it is amazing how many times we, as women, take advice from men on how to be better women! Let's change that right now.

Here are three remarkable women, Jane Austen, Willa Cather and Zora Neale Hurston, writing at the height of their powers about finding mates, making friends, and fashioning independent lives. Their heroines, Fanny, Alexandra and Janie, have something to show us about blooming where you are planted, creating a good life out of less-than-perfect options, and cherishing the people you meet along the way. That's chick-lit for grown-ups.

A Woman of Integrity:
Mansfield Park, by Jane Austen

Jane Austen is a serious reader's writer. By serious reader I don't mean those who pick up a best seller on vacation and breeze through it. I mean the type of reader that lives partly in the real world, and partly in an imaginary world peopled with characters from myriads of books devoured through the years. This kind of reader sometimes has difficulty remembering whether Emma Woodhouse is a fictional character, or a former college roommate. Jane Austen's novels, with their wealth of detail and finely drawn characters, offer a feast of delights for the serious reader; people like you and me. One of the lesser known Austen novels, *Mansfield Park* was published in 1814, just after *Sense and Sensibility* and *Pride and Prejudice*. The least well-known of the novels, it is a study in manners and morals, and how one may, in Hamlet's words, "smile and smile and still be a villain."

Synopsis

Mansfield Park is the Cinderella story of a poor girl who is brought into a great family as an act of charity, and ends by inheriting the central position as mistress of the estate. Fanny Price is an unusual heroine, defined more by her inaction than her actions. She comes to live with her cousins, the cruel shallow sisters Maria and Julia, the drunken wastrel Tom and serious, kind Edmund. Predictably, Fanny worships Edmund and their friendship deepens through the years. Mr. Bertram, the patriarch of the family, leaves for Antigua on business just as some intriguing new neighbors arrive in the area. Henry and Mary Crawford bring a sense of sophistication and a questionable morality to the gathering, and they inspire the group to put on a play in the father's absence. In a confusing triangle, Maria falls for Henry, Henry pursues Fanny (who is in love with Edmund) while Edmund falls in love with Mary.

Fanny resolutely resists participation in the questionable play, and resists Henry's advances as well. Edmund, however, falls more deeply in love with Mary, though she is clearly his moral inferior. When

Mr. Bertram returns suddenly, the play is canceled. Time goes on and Edmund, who wants to enter the clergy, begins to see that Mary's amorality will not change. Maria marries and moves away, and Fanny rejects Henry's proposal, causing her Uncle to send her back to her miserable home. Suddenly, several things happen in quick succession. Henry and Maria run away together briefly, then he abandons her. Julia marries a friend of his, and Tom comes home gravely ill from his life of dissipation. Mary's reaction to these events shows her true lack of character, and Fanny's strength. Edmund ends the relationship, Tom dies, and eventually Edmund and Fanny marry.

What Makes it Great

Austen's novels are mini-masterpieces of construction. Each character is distinct, interesting, and unforgettable, and the plot unfolds with the help of creative staging. Here, in an artistic masterstroke and with an obvious nod to *Hamlet,* Austen borrows Shakespeare's device of the play within a play. Fanny's wealthy cousins and their naughty guests prepare to stage a play, "Lover's Vows," in their father's absence, and through this process truths are revealed about their duplicitous natures that will influence the remainder of the drama. Like young Hamlet, Fanny refuses to act, either in the play or in the backstage dramas that surround it, but keenly observes the actions of those around her, and forms her opinions about whom to trust.

Modern critics have found much to discuss in *Mansfield Park,* from Lord Bertram's involvement in the slave trade to the troubled relationships in Fanny's immediate family. As always Austen touches lightly upon sensitive issues without hammering them. Take, for example, her examination of the effect of Fanny's years at the Bertram estate on her feelings for her family. When, after several years' absence from her humble home, Fanny returns to her parents and siblings in Portsmouth, she expects to find simple happiness in her poor family. Instead, she is appalled by their coarse manners. This is no romanticized English peasant cottage, but a dirty, depressing hovel that literally nauseates its former inhabitant:

Did You Know?

Like many authors, Jane Austen gave her manuscripts to family and friends for review. Here is what her brother and sister-in-law had to say about Mansfield Park:

"We certainly do not think it as a *whole*, equal to P. & P. [Pride and Prejudice]—but it has many & great beauties. Fanny is a delightful Character! and Aunt Norris is a great favourite of mine. The Characters are natural & well supported, & many of the Dialogues excellent.—You need not fear the publication being considered as discreditable to the talents of it's Author."

"She sat in a blaze of oppressive heat, in a cloud of moving dust; and her eyes could only wander from the walls marked by her father's head, to the table cut and knotched by her brothers, where stood the tea-board never thoroughly cleaned, the cups and saucers wiped in streaks, the milk a mixture of motes floating in thin blue, and the bread and butter growing every minute more greasy than even Rebecca's hands had first produced it." (pp. 362-3)

Wealth and education have created a new Fanny Price, who, like Eliza Doolittle, is still poor but is now unfit for a life of poverty. She must determine a new sense of self. For a woman at the turn of the eighteenth century this could only be accomplished through marriage. Like Cinderella, Fanny must be rescued by the handsome prince, and Austen does not disappoint us. *Mansfield Park* is a fascinating study of English life and manners, with wonderful insights into the role of the English clergy in that society. It examines the role of money in our lives, showing how the exposure to wealth and education change our expectations and even our emotional ties. The clever use of playacting in the story reveals the hypocritical character of Henry Crawford (ironically one of the most likeable characters) and illustrates the breadth of Austen's literary powers. Finally, for those of us who are just plain addicted to romance, it's a great story that ends with our heroine living happily ever after. For a serious reader, it doesn't get much better than this.

Late Bloomer

During her lifetime Austen's books were not tremendously popular. Though she is often grouped with Bronte, Dickens and Gaskell, she preceded these great Victorian authors by several decades, and thus her stories reflected a cloistered, ordered world as yet untouched by the industrial revolution. Austen's novels are gentle rambles through great estates where the gentry have dinners, balls, and various family crises. Emma does her match making, Elizabeth Bennett spars with Mr. Darcy, and the Dashwood sisters debate the merits of various poets. In other words, not much happens. (In six novels there is a grand total of two kisses!) It took some time before these subtle stories were taken seriously or became the best sellers that they are today.

Several of Bronte's contemporaries, however, appreciated the genius of the gentle lady's work. Tennyson ranked Austen "next to Shakespeare." Sir Walter Scott read her novels several times each and envied her descriptive powers, and Mrs. Gaskell (eminent Victorian author and Bronte's biographer) was an ardent admirer. Though it is true that Austen's emotions are as tightly circumscribed as her plots (hemmed in by invisible barriers of class, wealth and convention) she reaches the human heart by a route unfamiliar to us today. It is through the very details of mundane existence that Austen leads us to central truths about life and love. Her restraint can be deceiving; it is not Austen's aim to blast convention and custom, but rather to reveal a world of emotion through irony, humor and suggestion. Like many women authors of that century, Austen's novels were published under a *nom de plume*, and it is only in the last one hundred years that she has been recognized as one of the greatest writers in the world.

Of the enduring popularity of Austen, Maureen Corrigan writes:

"These romances continue to captivate readers because they throw together adult men and women with complicated pasts who have to painstakingly work out the terms of their relationships before they achieve wedded harmony. That's the realistic, strikingly contemporary angle to these romances . . ." (*Leave Me Alone, I'm Reading*, p. 96)

When it comes to Chick-Lit on a grown-up level, nobody does it like Jane.

Perhaps her subtlety is the reason Virginia Woolf said of Austen, "Of all great writers, she is the most difficult to catch in the act of greatness."

Jane Austen has been adapted into more TV mini-series and movies than we can count. The latest, and perhaps most creative, iteration of her genius can be found in Seth Grahame-Smith's horrifyingly clever book, "Pride and Prejudice and Zombies." Try this for a great first line: "It is a truth universally acknowledged that a zombie in possession of brains must be in want of more brains."

Talk About It

The heroine of Mansfield Park is a strangely passive figure for an Austen novel. Do you like Fanny? Why or why not?

About the Author: Jane Austen

Biographical information about Jane Austen is "famously scarce." Born in 1775 in England, she grew up in a close family of six brothers and one sister, Cassandra, her lifelong confidant. She was educated primarily by her father and brothers and through her own reading. George Austen apparently gave his daughters access to his large and varied library, was tolerant of Austen's sometimes risqué experiments in writing, and provided both sisters with expensive paper and other tools for writing and drawing. Austen practiced the pianoforte, was an accomplished seamstress, and loved to dance.

From 1811 until 1816, with the release of *Sense and Sensibility* (1811), *Pride and Prejudice* (1813), *Mansfield Park* (1814), and *Emma* (1816), Austen achieved success as a published writer. But because she chose to publish anonymously, her writing brought her little personal fame. She penned two additional novels, *Northanger Abbey* and *Persuasion*, both published posthumously in 1818, and began a third but died before completing it. Her beloved novels feature realism, biting social commentary and use of free indirect speech, burlesque, and irony.

Few authors have sold more books than Jane Austen. Written when still in her early twenties, her most popular novel, *Pride and Prejudice*, has never been out of print, and in 2003 was voted the second favorite novel of all time in England (after Tolkien's *The Lord of the Rings*.) Though occasionally disparaged by critics for her careful, cautious tone, Austen's works speak to women somehow. Her six novels have been repeatedly adapted for television and film, from Bollywood's *Bride and Prejudice* to the campy *Bridget Jones's Diary*, to the latest stormy version with Kiera Knightly as the delightful Elizabeth Bennett. After a slow deterioration in her health, Jane Austen died in 1817 at the age of 41.

Sources: Honan, Park. *Jane Austen: A Life*. New York: St. Martin's Press, 1987.
Le Faye, Deirdre. *Jane Austen: A Family Record*. Second Edition. Cambridge: Cambridge University Press, 2003.

History with Heart:
O, Pioneers! by Willa Cather

"The history of every country begins in the heart of a man or a woman." This famous first line tells us everything we need to know about *O, Pioneers!* In a dramatic departure from the fiction writers of her day, Cather chose the humble, poor settlers of the Nebraska prairie as her subject matter, rather than the more powerful members of urban society. By examining the heart of a pioneer woman and the lives of her family, she sheds a unique light on the history of a nation. Willa Cather's poignant, powerful masterpiece is a perfect example of her subtle artistry.

Synopsis

O, Pioneers! focuses on the lives of four characters in rural Nebraska of the 1890's: the young Emil Bergson; his stalwart older sister, Alexandra; her gloomy friend Carl Linstrum; and a pretty little Bohemian child, Marie Shabata. Alexandra's father, a Swedish immigrant of some stature in the town, leaves his farm and its management to his daughter rather than his two sons, sensing that she alone has the strength to carry on the work that he has begun. Alexandra proves equal to the challenge, and eventually succeeds in growing her farm and securing farms for her two brothers. Carl goes away to live in the city, and Maria, though in love with Emil, marries a sullen drunk and suffers in an abusive relationship.

Sixteen years after the novel opens, Carl returns and rekindles his relationship with Alexandra. Her brothers, jealous of her inheritance, drive him away. Emil and Maria fall more deeply in love and he also flees the town to avoid temptation. A sudden death of a friend causes him to return, however, and Maria's husband, finding them together, shoots and kills them. The novel ends as Alexandra tries to heal the wounds and Carl returns to comfort her. They marry, and life goes on.

What Makes it Great?

Until Willa Cather's day, pioneering had traditionally been viewed as a kind of a battle between the land and its conquerors, who were invariably male. Instead, *O Pioneers!* takes a deeply feminine, almost mythological approach to the subject. Here is no conquering hero, battling savages and subduing nature, but a woman who tames the beast through her love and intelligence. Cather's heroine, Alexandra Bergson, has one great passion, and it is not another human, but the great, unconquered prairie. After her father's death she readily assumes management of the family farm. Though her brothers are ready to give up and return to city life, Alexandra sees that a new world requires a new way of thinking. She knows the land can be made to yield its riches if only she can discern its secrets. Cather's description of Alexandra's feelings toward the land reads like a love poem, with the land personified as the beloved:

"For the first time, perhaps, since that land emerged from the waters of geologic ages, a human face was set toward it with love and yearning. It seemed beautiful to her, rich strong and glorious. Then the Genius of the Divide, the great, free spirit which breathes across it, must have bent lower than it ever bent to a human will before." (44)

As she embraces the land and tries to unravel its secrets, Alexandra prospers. In Cather's beautiful imagery, the land is personified as a creature to be loved, and Alexandra's description of it reveals where her true passion lies:

"We hadn't any of us much to do with it, Carl. The land did it. It had its little joke. It pretended to be poor because nobody knew how to work it right; and then, all at once, it worked itself. It woke up out of its sleep and stretched itself, and it was so big, so rich, that we suddenly found we were rich, just from sitting still." (60)

Alexandra also experiences times of doubt about her chosen path, as when her first love, Carl, returns from the city and causes her to wonder about all she has missed, and she expresses these regrets. In Carl's impassioned response we can feel Cather's love for the land and her deep distrust of urban life. Alexandra says:

"I'd rather have had your freedom than my land."

Did You Know?

The genesis of *O Pioneers!*, can be found in the experiences of the author's youth. In 1881 Willa Cather's family left their home in civilized Virginia and settled in Red Cloud, Nebraska. The great prairie divide, terrifying in its vast spaces, made an indelible impression on nine-year-old Willa, and her keen mind recorded every detail of the lives she saw unfolding around her on the frontier. Hours were spent listening to the older settlers recall their first forays into the wild new land and their attempts to build a world of order in the chaos. Later, after a successful career as a journalist and editor, she mined those memories to create a new kind of fiction.

"Carl shook his head mournfully. "Freedom so often means that one isn't needed anywhere. Here you are an individual, you have a background of your own, you would be missed. But off there in the cities there are thousands of rolling stones like me. We are all alike; we have no ties, we know nobody, we own nothing. When one of us dies, they scarcely know where to bury him. Our landlady and the delicatessen man are our mourners, and we leave nothing behind us but a frock-coat and a fiddle, or an easel, or a typewriter, or whatever tool we got our living by. All we have ever managed to do is pay our rent, the exorbitant rent that one has to pay for a few square feet of space near the heart of things. We have no house, no place, no people of our own. We live in the streets, in the parks, in the theaters. We sit in restaurants and concert halls and look about at the hundreds of our own kind and shudder." (134)

Weary of city life, Carl comes home to the prairie and finds Alexandra stronger but essentially unchanged. Her beauty comes directly from the earth:

"Carl walked rapidly until he came to the crest of the second hill, where the Bergson pasture joined the one that had belonged to his father. There he sat down and waited for the sun to rise. It was just there that he and Alexandra used to do their milking together, he on his side of the fence, she on hers. He could remember exactly how she looked when she came over the close-cropped grass, her skirts pinned up, her head bare, a bright tin pail in either hand, and the milky light of the early morning all about her. Even as a boy he used to feel, when he saw her coming with her free step, her upright head and calm shoulders, that she looked as if she had walked straight out of the morning itself. Since then, when he had happened to see the sun come up in the country or on the water, he had often remembered the young Swedish girl and her milking pails." (66)

As the narrative progresses Alexandra grows in strength until, in Cather's hypnotic prose, she becomes a personification of the land itself:

"Her personal life, her own realization of herself, was almost a subconscious existence; like an underground river that came to the surface only here and there, at intervals months apart, and then sank again to flow on under her own fields." (172)

A Human Tragedy

Another element of greatness in this novel is its elegant treatment of the tragic love story. Juxtaposed on this grand saga of pioneering is the very human tragedy that plays out between Alexandra's brother, Emil, and the Bohemian girl, Marie. Cather's sweet, compassionate portrayal of the lovers and their dilemma refuses to make a villain of any participant. The stumbles and falls of its individual inhabitants balance the great strides taken in colonizing the new land. Yet Cather does not leave us feeling discouraged by human weakness, but rather encouraged by the strength of those who strive to overcome, and the continuity of the new life they build. "We come and go," she reflects, "but the land is always there."

Alexandra Bergson is a woman I am glad to know. Cather closes the novel by saying of her and her beloved land, "fortunate country that is one day to receive hearts like Alexandra's into its bosom, to give them out again in the yellow wheat, in the rustling corn, in the shining eyes of youth!" (210) As the fortunate descendant of courageous pioneers like Alexandra, I marvel at the vision and courage they displayed in a world as different from their own as the moon is from mine. Cather's novels offer an insight into the hearts that first fashioned the life we take for granted. The pioneers of our nation worked a great labor of love, and Willa Cather recaptures their passion in a tribute worthy of their sacrifice.

Quotations taken from *O, Pioneer!* 1st Vintage Classics Edition, New York. 1992.

Talk About It

Alexandra is unusual; a woman and a landowner in the West. In what ways have the contributions of women been ignored by history, and why?

About the Author: Willa Cather

In 1873, Wilella Siebert Cather was born in Back Creek, Virginia, where her family had lived on the land for six generations. Her own repeated "relation with the earth itself," stems from her early experience in rural Virginia. When Cather was nine years old, her family moved northwest of Red Cloud, Nebraska, where her first impressions of the prairie filled her with awe and fear: " . . . I felt a good deal as if we had come to the end of everything—it was a kind of erasure of personality. I would not know how much a child's life is bound up in the woods and hills . . . if I had not been jerked away . . . and thrown out into a country as bare as a piece of sheet iron."

A "genius child," Cather took advantage of frontier life to meet immigrants and other pioneers who spoke different languages. After prairie farming did not take, the family moved into Red Cloud where Cather had access to their neighbor's substantial library. She showed interest in medicine and graduated from high school with two other boys.

At the University of Nebraska in Lincoln she chose to write; after graduation Cather moved to Pittsburgh to work for a magazine and teach English. She came to the attention of the editor S.S. McClure and moved to New York to work at *McClure's Magazine*, finding herself in 1906 at the nexus of professional literary life in the United States. Her "real" first novel, *O Pioneers!,* was published in 1913. The more personal *My Antonía,* followed six years later. She enjoyed an excellent publishing relationship with Alfred Knopf. The watershed novel, *One of Ours*, won Cather the Pulitzer Prize in 1923. She died in 1947 from a cerebral hemorrhage.

Sources:

www.willacather.org

Beauty in a Beastly World:
Their Eyes Were Watching God,
by Zora Neale Hurston

Recently we sold our home and needed to find a place to live for a year. Our agent found a home to rent and sent us to see it, but when we drove by it, I dismissed it right away without bothering to go inside. It was too far away from our business, too small, too this, too that; obviously not the house for us. The next day I got another call from her. "Just come and stand in this home, and tell me you don't want it," she said. So I did. I'm sitting here now, at my desk, in this cozy home that is just perfect for our needs, and I'm so glad she made me step inside the door before I passed it by.

I'm telling you all this because I want you to step inside this little book with me before you pass it by. You might have heard of Zora Neale Hurston's novel, or it might be unfamiliar to you. It might not be a book you would normally select, but then again, it might be one you will never forget. You'll have to step inside to see.

Synopsis

Like most poor blacks in the years following the Civil War, Janie Thompson's life is filled with trial and sorrow. Raised by a grandmother and mother who were both victims of rape, Janie is pushed into marriage with an unfeeling man who works her but does not really care for her. Eventually she leaves him and makes a life with another, more successful, but equally insensitive man. Finally, after his death, she meets Tea Cake, the love of her life. Their story ends tragically as well, as he is bitten rescuing her from a rabid dog, and eventually dies by her hand. She tells her story twenty years later, in the peace and wisdom of older age, and comes to terms with the difficulties and beauties of her life.

What Makes it Great

When I read the first two paragraphs of this book, they startled me with the way they combined homely wisdom with pure poetry, and I read them over and over with delight. If you have some experience with literary devices, notice the use of internal rhyme (ships, distance, wish) and repetition (never, never, remember, remember.) The first line rolls out in perfect iambic pentameter, worthy of a Shakespearean sonnet. Here they are:

"Ships at a distance have every man's wish on board. For some they come in with the tide. For others they sail forever on the horizon, never out of sight, never landing until the Watcher turns his eyes away in resignation, his dreams mocked to death by Time. That is the life of men.

"Now, women forget all those things they don't want to remember, and remember everything they don't want to forget. The dream is the truth. Then they act and do things accordingly." (1)

Hurston writes differently than most authors who are telling a story using occasional images for emphasis. For Hurston, the images *are* the story; the language gives life to the characters in a way I have seldom encountered in literature. There is no distinction in this novel between imagery and reality, between the spiritual and the temporal: it's all one. This woman's writing makes my heart pound. I'll just throw a few more sentences at you:

"Janie saw her life like a great tree in leaf with the things suffered, things enjoyed, things done and undone. Dawn and doom was in the branches." (8)

"There are years that ask questions and years that answer." (20)

"Janie turned from the door without answering, and stood still in the middle of the floor without knowing it. She turned wrongside out just standing there and feeling." (30)

Out of Step

Zora Neale Hurston was out of step with her time. She lived in Harlem in the early 1920's and was educated at a university under the patronage of some sympathetic white women. She worked as an anthropologist and a teacher, and eventually wrote two novels that were harshly criticized because they lacked the angry political stance that both the black and

Did You Know?

In the early 1970s, the great Alice Walker used a secondhand copy of *Their Eyes Were Watching God (1937)* as a text for her literature students. She loved the novel, and was dismayed to learn that Hurston was buried in an unmarked grave, so she traveled to Florida to correct this insult to her memory. Wading through waist-high grass in the segregated cemetery, she found what she thought was Hurston's grave and placed a marker on it which read, "Zora Neale Hurston/A Genius of the South/ Novelist / Folklorist / Anthropologist / 1901-1960." Walker's personal essay about this experience for a national magazine brought the book to the attention of a new generation. The book has been in print continually since then.

white literati felt were essential to a "black novel." Hurston's sweet evocation of the illiterate black working folk seemed to these critics to be a kind of concession to white supremacy in the South. Her quiet, independent heroine, Janie, held no appeal for the angry generation that first read this book. It went quickly out of print, and Zora Hurston ended her life working as a maid, impoverished and defeated by those dreams she so eloquently described. Decades later, when she was "rediscovered" by novelist Alice Walker, critics took a fresh look at Hurston's work, and found a treasure trove of poetic prose, wisdom and insight that, though not politically correct, was spiritually and emotionally full of power.

One of the themes of this beautiful story is the influence of nature. Janie experiences a moment reminiscent of Wordsworth as she watches the union of flower and bee and moves from girlish dreams to womanly understanding. This ecstatic moment (almost graphic in its sexual imagery) creates an ideal of human love for her that she seeks throughout her life:

"[Janie] was stretched on her back beneath the pear tree soaking in the alto chant of the visiting bees, the gold of the sun and the panting breath of the breeze when the inaudible voice of it all came to her. She saw a dust-bearing bee sink into the sanctum of a bloom; the thousand sister-calyxes arch to meet the love embrace and the ecstatic shiver of the tree from root to tiniest branch creaming in every blossom and frothing with delight. So this was a marriage! She had been summoned to behold a revelation. Then Janie felt a pain remorseless sweet that left her limp and languid."

In another take on "nature" Janie and her lover discuss whether it is "natural" for people to be cautious, or whether it is in their nature to move toward danger:

"Listen, Sam, if it was nature, nobody wouldn't have tuh look out for babies touchin' stoves, would they? 'Cause dey just naturally wouldn't touch it. But dey sho will. So it's caution." "Naw it ain't, it's nature, cause nature makes caution. It's de strongest thing dat God ever made, now. Fact is it's de onliest thing God every made. He made nature and nature made everything else."

The title of the novel refers to the helplessness of these post-Civil war black people, caught between slavery and freedom, with few rights and terrible trials to face. Their eyes are watching God, not with simple trust, but with a cautious suspicion. It would be understandable to view a Deity that would allow such suffering as a God to be feared:

"It was inevitable that she should accept any inconsistency and cruelty from her deity as all good worshippers do from theirs. All gods who receive homage are cruel. All gods dispense suffering without reason. Otherwise they would not be worshipped. Through indiscriminate suffering men know fear and fear is the most divine emotion. It is the stones for altars and the beginning of wisdom. Half gods are worshipped in wine and flowers. Real gods require blood . . .

The wind came back with triple fury, and put out the light for the last time. They sat in company with the others in other shanties, their eyes straining against crude walls and their souls asking if He meant to measure their puny might against His. They seemed to be staring at the dark, but their eyes were watching God."(151)

Hurston's characters speak in the dialect of the Deep South, and though the world they inhabit is completely different from our own, she makes us feel that we are part of that world. I love to feel that, through a book, I have entered the essence of another kind of life, and this book offers that experience. Hurston doesn't romanticize these characters; these people are not saints. They are simple folk trying to find the right way. Mistakes are made, but the overwhelming feeling the author invokes is one of faith in the resilience of the human spirit. Here, with timeless wisdom shining through the vernacular, is Janie's philosophy of life:

"Talkin' don't amount tuh uh hill uh beans when yuh can't do nothin' else . . . you got tuh *go* there tuh *know* there. Yo papa and yo moma and nobody else can't tell yuh and show yuh. Two things everybody's got tuh do fuh theyselves. They got tuh go tuh God, and they got tuh find out about livin' fuh theyselves."

Their Eyes Were Watching God chronicles one woman's journey toward a good life, awakening to her own place in the world and learning how to love herself after years of oppression. Having endured abandonment, betrayal, powerlessness, and entrapment, Janie achieves independence and a sense of fulfillment. Even after her one true loving relationship ends with the death of her companion, she finds peace in the memory of their love and in the rightness of her choices. It reminds us that the definition of a good life is not the absence of misery, or even of mistakes, but the journey toward integrity and peace. The novel closes with lines as beautiful as those that opened it:

"Here was peace. She pulled in her horizon like a great fish net. Pulled it from around the waist of the world and draped it over her shoulder. So much of life in its meshes! She called in her soul to come and see." (184)

Quotations taken from *Their Eyes Were Watching God*. Harper Collins, Inc. USA. 1991.

Talk About It

Is Janie an immoral woman? Are the things that happen her fault? Why do you think Hurston's novel was unpopular with black people of her day?

About the Author:
Zora Neale Hurston

Zora Neale Hurston was born in 1891 and lived in Eatonville, Florida, a town founded by African Americans and the nation's first incorporated black township. It was, as Hurston described it, "a city of five lakes, three croquet courts, three hundred brown skins, three hundred good swimmers, plenty guavas, two schools, and no jailhouse." Her idyllic childhood came to an end in 1904 when her mother died. "That hour began my wanderings," she later wrote. "Not so much in geography, but in time. Then not so much in time as in spirit."

In the early 1920s, she lived in Harlem's Renaissance. She studied anthropology at Howard University, Barnard College, and Columbia University. Hurston recognized the significance of the folklore of the southern United States and the Caribbean countries. She worked as an anthropologist, a librarian, a teacher, and a maid.

Hurston also wrote three other novels and an autobiography, *Dust Tracks on a Road*. Each work of fiction shows her interest in Southern black folk customs, her metaphorical language, and her sense of humor.

Sources:

www.zoranealehurston.com

Hemenway, Robert E. *Zora Neale Hurston: A Literary Biography*. Urbana, Ill: University of Illinois Press, 1977.

Chick-lit for Grown-ups:
Take it Personally

Perhaps the problem with our love lives is not in ourselves, but in the men we are choosing as partners, and then what we are expecting from those partners after we are together. On this issue, novels have a great deal to say. In fact, just about every novel ever written contains one or more love stories: boy meets girl, gets girl, loses girl, etc. Over the course of your life you have probably read scores, maybe hundreds of novels, and each of these has affected the way you look at your own life story. Could it be that the stories you read gradually shape the story you live? If you are what you eat, can it be true that you are also what you read?

We call certain books "classics" because they are popular, well written, stand the test of time and offer us wisdom about the human condition. Yet, because these books are also more difficult, most of us choose instead to pick up a bestseller and leave the classics on the shelf. In doing so we may be missing an important component of intelligent living. A classic teaches us to expect complexity, embrace diversity, and mistrust the simplistic solutions. And it might even affect our expectations when it comes to the opposite sex.

No one has more to say about how to find the man of your dreams than Jane Austen, and what she has to say is that the man of your dreams will inevitably turn out to be a nightmare! We've seen so much of Austen onscreen that we may feel that we understand her, but in fact the television and movie versions of her works often portray a very different message than the novels themselves.

So take Jane Austen off the shelf, blow the dust off the cover and peer inside. There you will find a complex, fascinating world of brothers, sisters, parents, lovers and, above all, friends. One of the most important themes of Austen's novels, for me, is her emphasis on friendship, and how our friends can support and influence us for good or evil. You will find a world where marriage is only one component in a fulfilling life. You will discover the intricacies of communication where a glance, or the press of a hand, can convey more meaning than hours of screaming on talk shows. And somewhere between the first meeting of Darcy and Elizabeth and their last muted interview on the walk to Merriton, you may find some wisdom that will impact your next relationship.

Chapter Ten
A Good Man is Hard to Find

Great and good are seldom in the same man.

Thomas Fuller, M.D.

Few will have the greatness to bend history itself; but each of us can work to change a small portion of events, and in the total of all those acts will be written the history of this generation.

Robert Kennedy

What is the value of one good man? These works by Victor Hugo, Anthony Trollope and A. J. Cronin, imply that it requires some connection with divine grace to raise a man from his natural self-centeredness to something finer. Each of these men is unique: eccentric, sometimes myopic in his focus on an objective, and not always likeable. None of them achieve the greatness attained by leaders in politics or business. But the simple, shining goodness exemplified in the lives of Jean Val Jean, Septimus Harding and Father Chisolm changes lives, and continues to offer inspiration to generation after generation of readers.

Can a Work of Art Change Your Life?
Les Miserables, by Victor Hugo

Les Miserables, the great national novel of France and Victor Hugo's masterpiece, is a unique work of art that has touched millions of hearts, inspired various theatrical adaptations, and even spawned a religious movement of its own. This saga of one man's journey from sin to sanctification is both unapologetically sentimental and brutally realistic. The grotesque is coupled with the sublime, and spiritual epiphanies are reported with the same journalistic detail as battle scenes. The novel strives to represent the complete life of a spiritual man, with both seen and unseen forces at work.

Victor Hugo was always active politically, and as a result he was often in trouble with the government, and spent nearly twenty years in exile in Brussels. In 1861, while still an expatriate, he resumed work on a novel he had begun two decades before. Working feverishly, standing at a desk with a cup of hot chocolate beside him each day, he completed the 1200-page work in fourteen months. In a remarkable marketing effort, he arranged to have the book translated into English the same year it was published in France. (C.E. Wilbur's translation still stands as the definitive *Les Miserables*) The double release added to the great popularity of the work. Panned by critics for its sentimentality and condemned by government representatives for its harsh criticism of the legal system, the novel found an immediate place in the hearts of people everywhere.

Synopsis

Jean Val Jean (a true "everyman's" name) is a simple laborer who steals a loaf of bread to feed his sister's children. For this he is sent to prison, and his repeated attempts to escape result in nineteen years at grinding labor, only to be released with the dreaded "yellow passport" that ensures his rejection from every inn and workplace. His fate, however, is not unavoidably tragic (as later more realistic novels would have painted this scenario) because in this story there are heavenly forces at work to save Val Jean. God intervenes to save his soul through a humble priest that

Val Jean has robbed, and as a result Val Jean becomes a new man. In his new guise he becomes a successful businessman, a mayor, and then once again a criminal when he steps forward to reveal his past in order to save an innocent man. He adopts the orphan child of a factory worker he had inadvertently harmed, and devotes his life to her care. Throughout the story, Val Jean is pursued by a relentless minister of justice named Javert. Their struggle, played out against the backdrop of the French revolution, forms the action of the novel. The private spiritual journey of one man is placed against the public history of a nation embroiled in a revolution (inspired by our own) that seesawed back and forth between monarchy and republic.

What Makes it Great?

Les Miserables poses two fundamental questions: First, can man really change for the better? Second, will society as it exists aid, abet, or even allow such change? Hugo's answers are respectively yes, and no. His goals for the work were nothing if not ambitious, as expressed in the introduction:

"So long as there shall exist, by reason of law and custom, a social condemnation which, in the midst of civilization, artificially creates a hell on earth, and complicates with human fatality a destiny that is divine; so long as the three problems of the century—the degradation of man by the exploitation of his labor, the ruin of women by starvation, and the atrophy of childhood by physical and spiritual night—are not solved; so long as, in certain regions, social asphyxia shall be possible; in other words, and from a still broader point of view, so long as ignorance and misery remain on earth, there should be a need for books such as this." (Preface)

There are so many layers to this novel that it is challenging to approach it critically. One of its most interesting facets is the use of the physical settings to portray the spiritual struggles of the characters. The physical settings careen up and down, like a roller coaster, in a mirror of his spiritual journey. Val Jean travels from the tops of trees where he works as a pruner to the depths of the streets where he hides in flight, then back up into the welcoming arms of the Bishop who transforms his life. Later he sinks from the height of prosperity into labor on a ship's galley. He then

Did You Know?

Hugo spent nearly twenty years in exile in Brussels, and during this time he searched for a spiritual philosophy that incorporated his firm faith in God and his passion for social justice and reform. He consulted spiritualists and spent many sessions with mediums, attempting to "channel" the spirits of great figures of the past. There is currently a sect of Buddhism, called Cao Dai, which originated in Vietnam and is based on the writings of Hugo during this period. They believe that Hugo and his two sons return to earth as reincarnated beings occasionally. There are over two thousand temples and millions of followers of this strange faith, another illustration of the tremendous impact of Hugo's work.

climbs to the top of the riggings to rescue a sailor, then plunges back into the sea, into a new death, to begin yet another life in exile. Another time, fleeing the relentless Javert (ultimate symbol of blind justice) he climbs straight up a wall, and then drops into the safety of a convent. Later he descends into a coffin to make an escape.

The pattern of rising and falling is repeated over and over throughout the narrative, and with each incarnation Val Jean strips away more of his benighted, bitter, carnal self and takes on the image the of Master he has vowed to serve. The climactic moment in the novel is symbolic of the death and resurrection of Christ, as Val Jean carries his future son-in-law into the depths of the sewers of Paris, then brings him forth, raising him to life. This final, selfless act completes his progression, as he gives all to save one who will take from him his only joy, his daughter Cosette.

The tremendous physicality of Hugo's writing is one of the reasons we respond to it; it reaches us on a visceral level. Hugo, like Dickens and Dumas, was a visual writer, cinematic (long before cinema existed) as well as literary. People don't just *talk* in this novel, there is always something *happening*. It was this combination of inner and outer drama, no doubt, that inspired Alain Boubil and Claude-Michel Schoenberg to create their rock-opera, *Les Miserables*, which has been performed more times than any musical in history. Faithful to the spirit of the work, it strives to portray the inner struggle of the man as well as the action of the novel, and succeeds beautifully.

The Making of a Masterpiece

By showing the redemption of one man Hugo strives to convince us that redemption for the human race is possible, and that social justice is the first essential step toward that possibility. As the novel draws to a close, Hugo makes its central focus crystal clear:

"The book which the reader has now before his eyes is, from one end to the other, in its whole and in its details, whatever may be the intermissions, the exceptions, or the defaults, the march from evil to good, from injustice to justice, from the false to the true, from night to day, from appetite to conscience, from rottenness to life, from brutality to duty, from Hell to Heaven, from nothingness to God. Starting point: matter; goal: the soul. Hydra at the beginning, angel at the end . . ." (1242)

Though its themes are universal, this is definitely a novel in, of and about Paris, and love for the city and its inhabitants is part of its essence. Whenever possible Hugo roots the action in the city he loves, whether he evokes the beauty of a spring day or describes the unique personality traits of its inhabitants:

"That day was sunshine from start to finish. All nature seemed to be on a vacation. The flower beds and lawns of Saint-Cloud were balmy with perfume; the breeze from the Seine vaguely stirred the leaves; the boughs were gesticulating in the wind; the bees were pillaging the jasmine; a whole bohemian crew of butterflies had settled in the yarrow, clover, and wild oats. The stately park of the King of France was invaded by a swarm of vagabonds, the birds." (p. 127)

"The Parisian is to Frenchmen what the Athenian was to Greeks: Nobody sleeps better than he, nobody is more frivolous and idle than he, nobody seems to forget things more easily than he; but best not trust him nonetheless; he has adapted to all sorts of indolence, but when there is glory to be gained, he is wondrous at every kind of fury." (p. 131-132)

War Within and Without

The action of the novel takes place within the context of the revolutions that shook France over several years. Val Jean finds himself embroiled in battle more than once, and the pitched conflicts on the barricades mirror the internal battles that he fights and wins. Hugo explains:

"Life, misfortunes, isolation, abandonment, poverty, are battlefields that have their heroes; obscure heroes, sometimes greater than the illustrious heroes." (p. 679)

The tumultuous times in which the tale is set make the narrative thrilling on its own; we would be entertained merely with the amount of action involved. However, Hugo's ambitious attempt to portray a truly good man holds us spellbound. As he is relentlessly pursued by Javert, we wonder how much Val Jean can suffer before his integrity gives way. His sweet relationship with his adopted daughter Cosette reveals more weaknesses, as he struggles with a jealous desire to keep her for himself and a more generous desire to have her experience a life separate from his. Hugo takes this opportunity to give us a sweet love story with Marius and Cosette, who remind us that love always brings hope in its wake. His descriptions of the gorgeous couple are unabashedly romantic:

"They were living in that ravishing condition that might be called the dazzling of one soul by another." (p. 1004)

"Love almost replaces thought. Love is a burning forgetfulness of everything else." (p. 1009)

"Marius and Cosette did not ask where this would lead them. They looked at themselves as arrived. It is a strange pretension for men to ask that love should lead them somewhere." (p. 1010)

In stark contrast to the self-questioning Val Jean and the star-struck lovers is the orthodox Javert, a man committed to justice above all else. As Val Jean's unselfish goodness impresses itself upon him, he is unable to reconcile it with his life view. He is destroyed, not by evil, nor by good, but by uncertainty about which is which:

"Before him he saw two roads, both equally straight; but he did see two; and that terrified him—he who had never in his life known anything but one straight line. And, bitter anguish, these two roads were contradictory." (p. 1320)

"Javert's ideal was not to be humane, not to be great, not to be sublime; it was to be irreproachable. Now he had just failed." (p. 1324)

Val Jean is foiled at every turn, yet triumphs. Javert continually triumphs over him, yet fails. Cosette and Marius find true love, yet in their selfish preoccupation with each other they neglect the father that brought them together. What is it about this story that so captivates us? I think it is the very size of the thing; the novel is big, the emotion is over the top, the spiritual dimension is deep and the scope of the story encompasses a wide swath of human history. Hugo put it all in here, and we love it. Through the suffering and redemption of one man Hugo reminded a nation, "He who does not weep does not see." (p. 1220)

Quotations taken from *Les Miserables*. Signet Classics Edition, London. 1987.

Talk About It

In what ways does Jean Val Jean teach his newly found values to Cosette, or does he? Does the comfortable, cushioned lifestyle we create for our children keep them from developing character?

About the Author: Victor Hugo

Victor Hugo's life was even more dramatic than his novels. He was born in 1802. His father, a general in Napoleon's army separated from his mother when he was very young, and his mother took her three sons to live in Paris. Victor fell in love with the girl next door, Adele Foucher, and married her after the death of his mother, who opposed the match. His brother Eugene also desperately loved the girl, and flew into a psychotic rage at their wedding. He spent the rest of his life in an institution. After the births of their four children, Adele refused to live with Hugo as man and wife any longer, and began a relationship with his best friend. Hugo took a mistress, Juliette Drouet, who remained his companion for the next fifty years. (The morals of this family were so decidedly "French" that when Hugo fled to Brussels as a political exile, he took the wife, the family, *and* the mistress along with him!)

Hugo was a devoted father, and was devastated by the death of his daughter, pregnant with his grandchild, and her husband in a boating accident soon after their marriage. His other daughter survived the accident but suffered mental damage. He lived to see her committed to an institution and to watch both of his sons die within three years of each other. Hugo was active in the government and served in the legislature, and was most famous for his poetry and plays. His masterwork was not published until he was sixty years old, but it was an instant success.

Hugo finally returned to Paris in 1870 and received a hero's welcome. When he died in 1885 at the age of 83, two million Frenchmen passed by his coffin under the Arch de Triomphe. He was buried in the Pantheon, the first of a series of cultural heroes to be entombed there. June 1 was declared a national day of mourning and in 1902, on the centenary of his birth, the Maison de Victor Hugo museum was opened in the apartment where he had once lived and worked.

Source: Wikipedia

A Man Without Guile:
The Warden, by Anthony Trollope

In the summer of 1851, Anthony Trollope visited the Salisbury Cathedral. Though he was living comfortably in Ireland with a secure job as a mid-level official in the Postal Service, with a wife and two sons, he was not a happy man. For him, his provincial existence was a prison, and he longed to raise his station in life.

But Trollope had a plan for escape. His chaotic upbringing—a series of catastrophes induced by his father's many financial failures—had been devastating, but also suggested a means of advancing his fortunes. When his family was forced to flee to France to escape their debts, his mother had supported the family by her writing, and Trollope decided that if she could do it, so could he. Determined to succeed as a novelist, he set a goal to write a certain amount every day, and adhered to it with remarkable tenacity. (By the end of his life, he completed 47 novels, several plays and an autobiography.) The first three novels were miserable failures. Then, while on a trip to Salisbury, Trollope toured the cathedral and conceived of the idea for a novel about a clergyman, that would explore what happens when a good man becomes mired in a corrupt system (in this case, the Anglican church.) In 1855, Trollope published *The Warden*, his first successful novel and his first attempt to write about a "truly good man." It was the first in a series of novels that made Trollope famous and established him as one of the premier novelists of his time.

Synopsis

The Warden is the first novel in Trollope's series called the **Chronicles of Barsetshire.** The story revolves around the Reverend Septimus Harding, who is the warden of Hiram's Hospital, a charity home for twelve elderly pensioners. For four hundred years the charity hospital has been funded by the estate on which it stands. Over the years the estate has become so profitable that the warden has a generous salary, which allows Reverend Harding to raise his daughters in comfort and ease. Harding's younger daughter is in love with John Bold, a young doctor who begins a campaign

Did You Know?

Though The Warden appears to be a tame tale about a humble cleric, it takes a humorous shot at nearly everyone. Basically, Trollope is satirizing the power of the church, reformers, the tabloid press, and the power of the sensational novelists of the time—especially Charles Dickens (referred to as "Mr. Popular Sentiment"). Throughout his novels, Trollope uses hilarious and thinly veiled pseudonyms. Besides Mr. Popular Sentiment, The Warden includes characters called Rev. Quiverful and Sir Abraham Haphazard.

against the hospital because he thinks it is a part of a corrupt system that enriches church leaders at the expense of the poor.

Harding's other daughter is married to the Archdeacon Grantly, who eagerly wages a battle against the young doctor, which eventually reaches the national press. Reverend Harding's patients begin to distrust him and he, a very sensitive man, begins to feel doubt about his position and then guilt. Eventually he resigns his position, and although his daughter persuades Bold to drop his opposition, the hospital is neglected. Without the care of their warden, the old pensioners seem to be the real losers in the "moral crusade," but Rev. Harding feels peaceful as he leaves his home. He has been true to his conscience.

What Makes it Great?

One of the most prolific writers of his time, Anthony Trollope had his finger on the pulse of Victorian society. His descriptions of everyday life are so detailed and ingenious that through them we have entry into a world now closed to us. Trollope's novels are invariably filled with social settings; parties, balls, and dinners. Yet each seems to have as a contrast a lonely, struggling individual, often ostracized from the very society Trollope describes so well. The juxtaposition of these two realities creates the tension and accounts for much of the genius in Trollope's work. Critic Robyn Gilmour writes: "Just as contemporaries found in Trollope the man a sensitive nature and feeling heart beneath the bluff, gregarious manner, so the reader of his novels soon becomes accustomed to moving from the comic outer action of the densely realized community to the inner action of the solitary individual." (*The Warden*, Penguin Classics Edition, xiii.)

Like Hugo, Trollope has a poetic sense of setting, and reflects the inner struggles of his hero with the outer landscape of his environment. When Dr. Harding imagines leaving his lovely home, his thoughts run in the course of nature:

"It was so hard that the pleasant waters of his little stream should be disturbed and muddied by rough hands; that his quiet paths should be made a battlefield; that the unobtrusive corner of the world which had been allotted to him, as though by Providence, should be invaded and desecrated, and all within it made miserable and unsound." (45)

Dr. Harding's forebodings prove true. When he leaves his lovely home it falls into neglect, and the old men who inhabit the hospital fight among themselves. Again, nature mirrors their inner decline:

"The warden's garden is a wretched wilderness, the drive and paths are covered with weeds, the flowerbeds are bare, and the unshorn lawn is now a mass of long damp grass and unwholesome moss. The beauty of the place is gone; its attractions have withered. Alas! A very few years since it was the prettiest spot in Barchester, and now it is a disgrace to the city." (183)

Great books often present us with a paradox—placing two realities in front of us that contradict each other—and challenge us to choose between two goods. There is no evil villain in *The Warden*. Archdeacon Grantly is annoying and John Bold is misguided in his enthusiasms, but for the most part they are just people with certain predispositions, whose conflicts cause pain and sorrow to others. It is in the attempt to achieve justice that John Bold inadvertently causes the financial ruin of his future father-in-law. It is in the adherence to his strict conscience that Dr. Harding inadvertently causes suffering to come upon his warders at the charity hospital, and it is through their greed that they lose the one person who has given them loving care through many decades. As much damage is caused in the novel by those trying to do good as by those behaving badly. Trollope simply opens this to us and asks us, as thinking people, to consider the consequences of any attempts at social justice. There is nearly always a downside to every act of reform.

One Good Man

Trollope's Dr. Septimus Harding is a curious soul. He loves his family, his faith, and his cello, which he plays for comfort and solace until his troubles cause his music to dry up within him. Though seemingly humble, he has a deeply stubborn side; he simply refuses to "go along" with the crowd, with his children's wishes, even with the directives of his church superiors. At each turn of events, it is easy to see how Dr. Harding could enjoy the benefits of his position without compromising his integrity too much, but he will not compromise at all. Thus, most people who know him deem him a failure.

The Warden is the first of a wonderful series, commonly referred to as the Barchester novels. Dr. Harding appears in several of them, and toward the end of *Barchester Towers*, Trollope (who has a delightful habit of dropping the "fourth wall" and directly addressing his readers) sums up his protagonist in terms as simple as they are eloquent:

"The Author now leaves [Dr. Harding] in the hands of his readers; not as a hero, not as a man to be admired and talked of, not as a man who should be toasted at public dinners and spoken of with conventional absurdity as a perfect divine, but as a good man without guile, believing humbly in the religion which he has striven to teach, and guided by the precepts which he has striven to learn." (271)

Quotations taken from *The Warden*. Penguin Classics Edition, London. 1986.

Talk About It

Septimus Harding refuses to benefit from his position as Warden only after it is publicized in the papers. Do you think his motives are pure?

About the Author: Anthony Trollope

Born in 1815 in London to a genteel family fallen on hard times, Anthony Trollope lived an unhappy childhood in poverty. His upbringing (a series of catastrophes induced by his father's many financial failures) encouraged him to develop a plan to advance his own fortune. When his family fled to Belgium to escape their debts, his mother supported the family by her writing. Her son vowed to do the same. Raised as a gentleman yet mired in poverty, Trollope was bullied at school and always felt like an outsider.

Before becoming a writer, Trollope worked for many years as a postal clerk where he designed the pillar box—red mailboxes that are still in use in England. He also lived for a time in Ireland. Trollope set a goal to write a certain amount every day, and he became one of the most prolific writers of all time. By the end of his life, he wrote forty-seven novels, several plays, and an autobiography, wherein he admitted he wrote mainly for money.

Trollope became one of the most successful and respected English novelists of the Victorian era. Like Dickens, he developed the capacity to see society both from above and below. Critic Terry Eagleton explains: "The novelist who has a populist ear for the voice of the people, yet at the same time commands the resources of high culture, is likely . . . to outflank all competitors." His first major success came with *The Warden* (1855)—the first of six novels set in fictional "Barsetshire." The best known of these is *Barchester Towers* (1857), a comic masterpiece. George Eliot noted that she could not have embarked on so ambitious a project as *Middlemarch* without the precedent set by Trollope in his own novels. In 1882, Trollope died in London.

Sources:

Glendinning, Victoria. *Anthony Trollope*. Knopf, 1993.

Super, R. H. *Trollope in the Post Office*. Ann Arbor: University of Michigan Press, 1981.

The People's Priest:
The Keys of the Kingdom by A.J. Cronin

We can find counterparts to the Protestant Dr. Harding in other faiths and other novels. Rabbi Saunders in Potok's *The Chosen* possesses the same integrity. The Tibetan lama in *Kim* shares his single-minded devotion to truth. His courage in the face of criticism, even from his own church, is exemplified by a Catholic priest in A.J. Cronin's excellent novel, *The Keys of the Kingdom*.

Though he is not well known today, Cronin was a great favorite with my parents' generation, and one of the keys to the popularity of his work was its timing. *The Keys of the Kingdom* was published in 1941, and Cronin's story of a faithful priest who models his life after the Savior reached number one on the bestseller list the week it was published. In a day when the modern novel was full of cynicism and despair, Cronin told old-fashioned stories of love and loss, stories that reaffirmed belief in the triumph of the individual in an evil world. With the world at war and Hitler's atrocities in the daily papers, readers welcomed his reassuring tone and its underlying religious faith, so rare in more "modern" works of fiction.

Synopsis

The boy Francis Chisolm grows up in the midst of Protestant-Catholic hostility in turn-of-the-century Scotland. His parents are killed by an anti-Catholic mob, and the woman he loves commits suicide, yet Francis resists bitterness. He becomes a priest and departs for China, where he becomes an exemplary missionary. Francis's many adventures in China make up the bulk of the novel's plot, but the book's center of gravity is Francis himself. He is a dedicated, creative, unfailingly humble, and self-effacing priest. He often chides himself for his pride and rebelliousness, but the reader feels that even his mistakes are on the side of right. Francis is not loved by his superiors; they are threatened by his humility and lack of ambition. In the end, he finishes his days as a humble missionary, loved by all he serves and unappreciated by those in power.

What Makes it Great?

Cronin, though not on the level of Hugo or Trollope, was an author who understood his audience. The terrible revelations of cruelty in the Nazi regime, the horrors of World War II and the nagging uncertainty about the future weighed on the hearts and minds of that generation. Cronin was able to take his readers to a simpler, gentler reality through the life of his humble priest. In addition, he satisfied their need to believe in a higher purpose for life, in a heavenly plan that superseded the machinations of men. Though novelists often portray a faithless, cynical view of life, most people believe in something higher and better, and Cronin spoke directly to this faith.

With a knack for characterization, Cronin gives us a complete person in Father Chilsholm. This is no saint. His sincerity is balanced by his stubbornness, and his devotion is balanced by his doubt. We can relate to him as well as admire him. By contrast, the other priests in Francis's life are portrayed much as the Pharisees in Jesus' time: rigid, self-centered and concerned with organizational politics rather than the cause of Christ. In fact, Francis's fellow Catholic priests cause him as much trouble in the Chinese missions as hostile pagans and violent warlords do. Here Cronin shows us the aged Chisolm as seen through the eyes of his Monsignor:

"Dear God," thought Sleeth, "What a pitiable presentation of the priesthood—this shabby old man, with the stained soutane, soiled collar and sallow, desiccated skin! On one cheek was an ugly weal, a kind of cicatrix, which averted the lower eyelid, seemed to tug the head down and sideways. The impression was that of a permanent wry neck, counterpoising the lame and shortened leg. His eyes, usually lowered, took thus—on the rare occasions that he raised them—a penetrating obliqueness which was strangely disconcerting." (7)

One is reminded of Isaiah's poetic description of the Messiah: " . . . He hath no form nor comeliness; and when we shall see him, there is no beauty that we should desire him. He is despised and rejected of men; a man of sorrows and acquainted with grief: and we hid as it were our faces from him; he was despised, and we esteemed him not." (Isaiah 53:2-3, *Holy Bible, King James Version*)

Did You Know?

Cronin drifted away from his religious faith during his medical training and career, but reacquainted himself with it in his thirties. At medical school, as he recounts in his essay "Why I Believe in God," he had become an agnostic: "When I thought of God it was with a superior smile, indicative of biological scorn for such an outworn myth." During his practice in Wales, however, the deep religious faith of the people he worked among made him start to wonder whether "the compass of existence held more than my text-books had revealed, more than I had ever dreamed of. In short I lost my superiority, and this, though I was not then aware of it, is the first step towards finding God."

Religion vs. Faith

Father Chisolm's approach to religious behavior is in stark contrast to the tradition-bound clergy. When he happens upon a Chinese village that has been practicing a unique brand of Christianity (based on the journal of a visiting priest decades before) he takes time to listen and try to understand the needs of this unusual flock. Over time belief in the "Three Precious Ones" (the holy trinity) has melded with their Confucius and Buddhist beliefs, and with pride they describe to him a faith unrecognizable as Catholicism, yet simple and profound in its own way. Father Chisolm is deeply moved:

"He remained at the Liu village for a week. Persuasively, in a manner to hurt no one, he suggested a ratification of all baptisms and marriages. He said mass . . . He spoke to them of many things. In the evenings a fire would be lit outside Liu-Chi's house, and when they had all seated themselves about it, he would rest himself on the doorstep and talk to the silent, flame-like circle . . . he drew no captious differences. It enthralled them when he spoke of the churches of Europe, the great cathedrals, the thousands of worshippers . . . all prostrating themselves before that same Lord of Heaven whom they worshipped . . . This sense of unity, hitherto only dimly surmised, gave them a joyful pride." (167)

In many scenes like this one (obviously modeled on the Sermon on the Mount) Cronin draws a parallel between his priest and Jesus, taking to task the stifling orthodoxy that he felt choked the power of faith. Though Cronin lacks the subtle artistry of Forster or the linguistic mastery of Dickens, he has the instinctive ability to tell a good story in a way that pulls the reader along. He's a realist as well, treating with candor such subjects as incest, abuse, and religious bigotry without sacrificing his hopeful tone. His deep ambivalence about organized religion is balanced by his faith in the gospel of Christ and his interest in the individual. Father Chisholm expresses the feelings of his author when he says:

"If we have the fundamentals—love for God and for our neighbor—surely we're all right? And isn't it time for the religions of the world to cease hating one another, and unite? The world is one living, breathing body, dependent for its health on the billions of cells which comprise it . . . and each tiny cell is the heart of a man." (294)

Note: If you love *Keys of the Kingdom* you will also love *Death Comes for the Archbishop*, by Willa Cather. Same dear, saintly Priest. Different country.

Quotations taken from *The Keys of the Kingdom*. Little Brown and Co. New York. 1941.

Talk About It

Father Chisholm, though often at odds with the leaders and even the precepts of his church, is unceasingly loyal to his faith in Catholicism. Every organized religion has its scandals and its problems. How does the individual maintain integrity and yet remain loyal to a group that acts contrary to his or her principles?

About the Author: A.J. Cronin

A.J. Cronin lived a long and interesting life, with two brilliant careers, first as a doctor and then as one of the most successful authors of the twentieth century. Cronin was born in a small town in Scotland in 1896. His father's early death plunged the family into poverty, and the Cronins were forced to rely on the charity of relatives who despised them for their Catholicism. (His Protestant mother had converted against her family's wishes.) It was in this harsh environment that Archibald formed the two priorities that guided his life, a need for independence and a dream of tolerance between all men.

In that day the only choices available to a poor boy that wanted to rise in the world were the clergy or medicine. Choosing what he termed "the lesser of two evils," Cronin worked his way through medical school and began his practice in the mining towns of Northern England. After nine years he had a lucrative practice in the west end of London, a wife and two sons, but he was unhappy with his life.

Cronin had always loved to write and felt that if he only had the time he could write a novel based on his unique experiences. He sold his practice and moved his family into a cottage in Scotland, and in three months had completed a novel, Hatter's Way, which became an immediate best seller. Cronin went on to write more than a dozen novels that sold in the millions of copies. Several of his books were made into films, and he wrote one of the most successful television series ever to air on British television. A.J. Cronin moved to the United States in the 1930s with his wife and three sons. He later settled in Switzerland. He died in Montreux, Switzerland, in 1981.

Source: Wikipedia

A *Good* Man is Hard to Find:
Take it Personally

As Dr. Harding struggles with his moral dilemma he asks himself, "What would Jesus do?" Beyond its power as a pop-culture slogan, the question of what Jesus would do in any given situation challenges our assumptions about what constitutes a "good" woman or man. This novel gives us an opportunity to think about Jesus, the kind of man he was, and the kind of people we might become if we try to act more like he would act in any given moment.

Recently I posed the question to my family: "If we do as Jesus would do, will we be more or less socially acceptable?" To my surprise, a heated debate ensued. Some felt that Christian principles always benefit us—make us more charitable, easier to talk to, more useful to society in general—and thus would increase our social standing. On the other hand, others pointed out that Jesus was usually on the unpopular side of any given social situation, and that He often caused people to feel very uncomfortable, and even offended many. What do you think?

As each of our children has graduated from high school we have shared a trip together, and as a part of that trip I have taken each one to see "Les Miz" in London, where it has been playing for twenty years or more. To watch each of them experience the closing moments of that musical has been one of the cherished experiences of motherhood for me. The emotional intensity of the musical is perfect for teenagers, and the moral lessons are priceless. It takes Jean Val Jean many years and almost complete destruction before he reaches a level of spiritual understanding that will change his life for the better. As each child has prepared to leave home and face the challenges of adulthood, Les Miserables has offered us an opportunity to talk about what values will take top priority in our lives.

Chapter Eleven
Fantasyland

"Imagination is more important than knowledge. For knowledge is limited to all we now know and understand, while imagination embraces the entire world, and all there ever will be to know and understand."

Albert Einstein

"There are some people who live in a dream world, and there are some who face reality; and then there are those who turn one into the other."

Douglas Everett

What are the uses of enchantment, fantasy, and imagination? Most of what we identify as "real" has less of an impact on us than our thoughts, dreams and perceptions. If a belief can be defined as a thought that we have decided to continue to think, the world of fantasy and imagination can greatly influence our beliefs and even set the standard by which we judge real events.

Three masters of fantasy present three complete worlds, peopled with seers, talking animals, wizards and magical creatures. As we allow the child within us to enter these worlds we regain the wonder and gullibility that made us young. And we emerge with a more childlike faith in good and the eventual triumph of right over wrong.

The Uses of Enchantment:
The *Harry Potter* Novels, by J.K. Rowling

In the summer of 1999, on a family vacation, I noticed a small review in the back of *Time Magazine* for a book about a boy named Harry Potter. I was intrigued, both by the description of the book and the author's rags-to-riches story, so I picked up the book to read aloud to our youngest child, then an avid reader of seven. Well, by the time we finished the first chapter Blake and I were hooked. Our standard twenty minutes per night of reading aloud were forgotten, and instead each night we read until my voice gave out. As the book grew more frightening we had to give up reading at night or Blake couldn't sleep, so we read early in the morning until the pressures of the impending day bore down upon us and we were forced to quit. We told everyone about Harry, and soon realized that we were just a tiny part of a huge groundswell that propelled the Harry Potter series into one of the most amazing phenomena in literary history.

In what seemed the blink of an eye, it was the summer of 2007, and one dark night I gave my tall, lanky sixteen-year old Blake a ride over to Barnes and Noble to attend a midnight celebration and buy the seventh and last volume in the Harry Potter series. As a confirmed bibliophile, it made my heart leap with joy to see a couple of hundred kids standing in line in the middle of the night to buy a book! J.K. Rowling has helped bring reading back to the video game generation, and for this mothers and fathers everywhere will be forever grateful. Children, like Blake, whose entire reading lives have been 'bookended' by these novels, felt a great sense of sadness as they reached the last volume. "I can hardly stand to begin," Blake explained when I asked about the first chapter, "because this is the last Potter book I will ever look forward to reading."

Synopsis

The seven novels of the Harry Potter series were conceived as one story, and follow the seven years between Harry's eleventh and eighteenth

birthdays. Harry, the orphaned son of James and Lily Potter, knows he is
not like other children but doesn't know why. The despicable Dursley's,
Harry's only living relatives who are raising him, understand the secret
that makes him unique. As a result, they distrust and dislike him, and
force him to live in a cupboard under the stairs. In a series of remarkable
events Harry learns that he is descended from witches, and has the right
to attend Hogwarts, the legendary boarding school for those with magical
powers. Albus Dumbledore, the headmaster of Hogwarts, becomes mentor
and second father to Harry. On his first day he meets Hermione Granger
and Ron Weasley, and this threesome becomes the center of the narrative,
as they brave one adventure after another. Harry is a boy of promise, the
miraculous survivor of an attack by the evil Voldemort. The seven volumes
follow Harry's development from frightened, bitter child to a hero of
strength and courage. The novels end with the defeat of Voldemort and
the marriage of Ron and Hermione, with Harry finding love and peace at
last with Ginny, Ron's sister.

What Makes it Great?

There are some good reasons why Harry Potter has bewitched a
generation of readers and their parents. First and foremost is the writing,
for J.K. Rowling has a wonderful talent for telling a tale. She is funny
without being silly and never maudlin. Her characters, from the disgusting
Dursleys to the loveable giant Hagrid to the sage Dumbledore, come to
life as distinct individuals. Rowling has the Dickensian knack of marking
characters with identifying patterns of speech and mannerisms that keep
them separate and memorable, even with a long wait between volumes.
Harry Potter himself is as endearing a character as I have ever encountered
in literature, and he has the complexity of personality to carry the series
without exhausting our interest. Like David Copperfield or Huck Finn,
we want to spend time with Harry, to watch him grow and learn, and even
to watch him make mistakes. A creation like that is rare in literature, and
always an event to be celebrated.

Beyond good writing, Rowling has tapped into a powerful medium
in *Harry Potter*, one that was also understood by George Lucas when he
created the *Star Wars* series; the mythological element in the stories has a

magnetic effect on children. The first chapter of the first volume is titled, "The Boy Who Lived." That remarkable title alone illustrates the subtle genius at work in these books. Without reading a word of the chapter we know we will meet a boy of destiny, someone whose life has been threatened and who, for some special reason, has survived. This story of a chosen, orphaned child raised in the home of his comically stupid and stubborn relatives combines humor and pathos in a way that completely engages the emotions of both parents and children right from the start. Then, when Harry goes to Hogwarts' school for wizards, the intellect and the imagination become involved as well, for the place is full of mysteries and riddles, literary allusions and magical illusions. It is no wonder that millions are entranced by Harry's world. It is so much more interesting than our own!

Though every volume of the Potter series cannot qualify as a "great book," the first and last volumes are, in my opinion, two of the greatest examples of children's literature in print. The last volume does a remarkable job of tying up hundreds of loose ends left dangling throughout the series. Rowling has described her saga as one great novel in seven parts, a story that she envisioned as a whole and which has always been moving in a definite direction. This story did not evolve randomly; it is a complete creation of a gifted author, and this is obvious in the final segment. Though she lacks the artistry of a Dickens or the subtlety of Twain, Rowling possesses something special as an author; she instinctively understands the need of a child in this media-saturated age to wonder, to imagine, and to believe in an unseen world. She speaks to that need with compassion and style.

But, though endlessly fascinating, Harry's world is, after all, a world of witchcraft. Many people are understandably wary of the occult, and others are nervous about scaring young children unnecessarily. Should we be reading to our children about werewolves and wizards? Will years of obsession with *Harry Potter* corrupt children in some way, or give them a skewed take on reality? Some thoughts about the function of fairy tales and fantastic fables may be helpful as we reflect on the effect of this series on the lives of our children.

Did you Know?

Several publishers rejected the first Harry Potter manuscript saying it was too long and literary, but Bloomsbury Publisher finally accepted it in 1996. The book's publisher suggested Rowling use the name "J. K." rather than her real name "Joanne Rowling" to appeal to male readers. As of 2008, Harry Potter books have sold over 400 million copies and have been translated into 67 languages. Rowling is the first person to become a billionaire by writing books.

Once Upon a Time

Many years ago, as I was beginning to raise our five children, I began for the first time to pay attention to the rather alarming nature of fairy tales. Like many parents I was concerned about which types of books and programs to share with small children, and, convinced that peace in the world must begin in the home, I vowed that there would be no toy guns in the house and no violent programs on our television. (This was, of course, before I learned that children could make weapons out of anything, from paper clips to celery sticks.) As I began to read stories to my children, the violent content of nearly every traditional fairy tale and legend alarmed me, and I wondered why parents everywhere were telling and reading stories about wicked witches, villainous step-parents, ghouls, goblins, etc. It seemed bizarre!

I found some insight into this question in the landmark work titled *The Uses of Enchantment: The Meaning and Importance of Fairy Tales,* by the child psychologist, Bruno Bettelheim. He asserts that violent, frightening tales that include magic and mystery are not harmful to children, but instead allow them to experience, in a manageable form, the terrors and confusion of real life, while enjoying a triumphant resolution to conflict through the actions of the hero of the tale. Even critics of Rowling's series would admit that her books fit his description of the ideal children's story:

"For a story truly to hold the child's attention, it must entertain him and arouse his curiosity. But to enrich his life, it must stimulate his imagination; help him to develop his intellect and to clarify his emotions; be attuned to his anxieties and aspirations; give full recognition to his difficulties, while at the same time relate to all aspects of his personality—and this without ever belittling but, on the contrary, giving full credence to the seriousness of the child's predicaments, while simultaneously promoting confidence in himself and in his future." (*The Uses of Enchantment*, p. 5)

Harry Potter—weak, orphaned, and rather nerdy—is a hero to whom every child can relate. By placing Harry in a parallel universe with different rules, Rowling is free to explore the challenge of behaving morally in a foreign environment. This is, of course, the challenge faced by every child, since the adult world is a foreign place where the child must learn to survive and hopefully to thrive. Like Travers's Mary Poppins and Dahl's Willy Wonka, the saintly wizard Dumbledore teaches children to behave better than the adults around them through a magical perspective on life. Without the element of magic the fairy tale becomes just another story. It is the magical element that brings the tale into a deeper realm of the imagination. In a magical world there may be evil, but there is also power available to overcome that evil. This is the reason why, though they are frightening, little children beg to hear these stories. It is *because* they are frightening that they are also empowering.

C.S. Lewis understood this principle and used it to create his wonderful series, *The Chronicles of Narnia*. Lewis was writing a Christian allegory for children, and for this reason it would seem that people of faith would approve of the *Chronicles*, but this is not the case. Because the books are full of witches and magical creatures, orthodox Christians who fear any mention of such matters reject them, along with *The Wizard of Oz*, T.H. White's *The Once and Future King* (on which Disney's movie *The Sword in the Stone* is based) and all of Tolkien's *Hobbit* series. I consider this a tragic mistake. Even a cursory perusal of children's classics shows that magic is an important element in children's literature. If we reject literature because it is magical, we may reject that very element within it that engages the whole child. I suspect that the interest all children have in the magical is connected to their spiritual development. Rather than fear and avoid the magical, we can use it to help the child develop a believing heart. Certainly in the minds of young children there is little difference between God, Santa Claus and Merlin the Magician. As adults we can use the mythical to move toward the truly spiritual, helping our children mature spiritually by understanding the qualities in mythical figures that point us toward the source of all good, whatever we perceive that source to be.

The Child as Hero

The most important use of magical stories, in my opinion, is the empowerment of the child. Fables are destructive, not when they portray violence, but when they are used to discredit faith and destroy hope in the future. Tolkien wrote that four elements were necessary in any good tale: fantasy, recovery, escape, and consolation. Without a detailed explanation of these elements it is enough to say that the great tales of fantasy include magical elements, terrifying losses and obstacles, recovery and escapes, and a satisfying resolution through moral action. All of the great fantasy books I have listed include these elements, including *Harry Potter*. Crucial to such tales is the happy ending, what Tolkien called, the "sudden, joyous turn," that leaves the reader hopeful about the world and his or her place in it. In each volume, Harry and his friends face seemingly insurmountable obstacles and emerge victorious. Though Voldemort may rise again, Harry and his friends will be ready for him, and so will we. It is this resolution that justifies the presence of evil elements in the tale. As Blake (after two solid days of reading) reached the end of the seventh volume and handed it to me he said, "Get ready to be happy." I was delighted to know that Rowling was true to the calling of a great children's author. She had brought her heroes, and her readers, safely home.

There are so many good messages in these books. Rowling is no saint, no prophet; she is merely an author of children's books. Like any author, she has a worldview that may not always coincide with our own. Through the years, however, these books have offered a starting point for great conversations, and I recommend that parents use the remarkable interest in these books to their advantage. Talk with your child about the why of the story: Why does Harry need to act in certain ways? What allegiance, if any, does he owe his relatives? Which of the characters we encounter will turn out to be the "bad guy," and what qualities contribute to his or her downfall? As long as we are talking as we go, imparting our worldview and our chosen perspective, a trip to Hogwarts can be a wonderful experience to share with a child.

A Happy Family

The Weasley family is a fine example of a large, happy family with strong moral values, (rare in modern literature) and Rowling's message is clear here: good parents will guide us the right way. Cloaking it in such humorous magical garb makes the message easier to swallow. Certain characters emerge as villains through their pride, vanity or a lust for power. Others emerge as heroes through humility, curiosity, courage and integrity. Rowling's vision is of a world where goodness will triumph and evil will be overcome, often by the weak and simple. That is a hopeful vision in any age.

One of the many insights to be gained from these books is how each of us may, unwittingly, advance the cause of evil through our pride or our ignorance. In the second volume, Ron's innocent little sister is drawn into Voldemort's nefarious scheme to rule the world. Ginny Weasley finds a fascinating diary that writes back to her when she writes in it. The diary serves as a conduit for the evil Lord Voldemort to emerge anew, and Ginny is horrified to learn at last that she has been his agent. As the story reaches its dramatic climax Rowling softens the lesson with her characteristic humor. Ginny confesses that she has been writing in a diary that writes back to her and is reprimanded by her father:

"*Ginny!*" said Mr. Weasley, flabbergasted. "Haven't I taught you *anything*? What have I always told you? Never trust anything that can think for *itself if you can't see where it keeps its brain?*" (*Harry Potter and the Chamber of Secrets*, p. 329)

The *Harry Potter* books started off scary, and got scarier as Harry got older. The same may be said of the world around us. Every parent wishes to shield the child from the terrifying and horrible realities of life, yet children are aware of these realities from an early age. Many things frighten them and nearly everything is confusing. What they need is confidence that their fears can be overcome and adults will help them find the right way. In Bettelheim's words: "fairy tales are loved by the child because—despite all the angry anxious thoughts in his mind to which the fairy tale gives body and specific content—these stories always result in a happy outcome, which the child cannot imagine on his own." (*Enchantment*, p. 123) J.K. Rowling has given us, through the *Harry Potter* series, another vehicle to help children come to grips with a frightening world and to visualize their ability to overcome the evil and embrace the good. For this reason, as well as for hundreds of happy hours shared with my son, I am an enthusiastic fan.

Quotations taken from *Harry Potter and the Chamber of Secrets*. Bloomsbury Press, London. 1998.

Talk About It

Most fantasy novels are concerned with the battle between the forces of good and the forces of evil. Do you believe that "the forces of evil" actually exist, or is life a more random collection of events that spring from the confusion and weaknesses of mortals, neither all good nor all bad?

About the Author: J.K. Rowling

© JP Masclet

Joanne Rowling was born in 1965 in Gloucestershire, England. She grew up with one sister and enjoyed reading her the fantasy stories Rowling wrote. She attended the University of Exeter to earn a degree in French and Classics. She studied a year in Paris and then moved to London to work as a researcher and bilingual secretary for Amnesty International. In 1990, while she was on a four-hour-delayed train trip from Manchester to London, the idea for a story of a young boy attending a school of wizardry "came fully formed" into her mind. "I really don't know where the idea came from," she told *The Boston Globe*. At home, she began to write; for the next five years she outlined all seven books and began *Harry Potter and the Philosopher's Stone*. She moved to Portugal to teach English, and there, met and married a journalist. She gave birth to a girl and soon after, her marriage ended. Moving to Scotland to be near her sister, Rowling continued writing the *Harry Potter* series in cafés while her baby slept. From 1997 to 2007, she published all seven books in the series; the last four books have consecutively set records as the fastest-selling books in history. Rowling progressed from living on welfare to multi-millionaire status within five years.

In 2000, Rowling established the Volant Charitable Trust, which spends its annual budget of £5.1 million to combat poverty and social inequality. The fund also donates to organizations that assist children, one-parent families, and MS research. Married to an anesthesiologist, she is the mother of three children.

Sources:
www.jkrowling.com
Wikipedia

Down the Rabbit Hole:
Watership Down, by Richard Adams

Watership Down was the *Harry Potter* of the seventies, a publishing phenomenon that entranced a generation of readers. It's author, Richard Adams, was an English civil servant who created the tale to entertain his two daughters on a trip to Stratford-upon-Avon one summer. The girls urged him to write it down, and the task took him about two years, working in his spare time. After several rejections it was finally published in 1972, with a run of only 2,500 copies, and was immediately hailed by critics and readers as a children's classic. By 1985 it was second on Penguin's list of all-time bestsellers with over five million copies in print, and continues to be one of the most popular books ever written for children or adults.

Irritated by the sentimental stories published for children and discouraged by the permissive society of the 1960's, Adams set out to create a fictional world that combined everyday reality and mythical ideals. *Watership Down* is more than just the story of a bunch of bunnies that get crowded out of a field by a housing development and have to find a new place to live. It is a story of love and courage and struggle. It is also a classic retelling of the archetypal myth of the hero, and the most realistic depiction of animals in a children's book you will ever find.

Synopsis

The adventure begins when Hazel, a quiet, unassuming fellow (the lapin equivalent to a civil servant, I suppose) wanders out to *silflay* (graze) one evening with his cousin Fiver. Fiver has a gift—he can sense the future at times—and he has a vision of destruction looming over the warren when he sees a notice board go up in the field. Unable to convince the chief rabbit that danger is imminent, Hazel persuades a few rabbits to flee with him and Fiver in search of a new home. The rabbits of *Watership Down* (a field in the English countryside that becomes their eventual home) are not cuddly or cute; they fight, eat, defecate, mate and generally struggle to stay alive. They contend with an evil, fascist group of rabbits that threatens them, as well as humans and natural disasters. Hazel, an unassuming rabbit with no ambition, emerges as their hero and leader, with the assistance of the prophetic Fiver and some other important friends. Together the rabbits overcome their challenges and eventually find peace. Some survive the struggle, and some die, but they succeed in creating a new society where they can continue to thrive.

What Makes it Great?

Adams used technical information about warrens and their ways (mainly from R.M. Lockley's, *The Private Life of Rabbits*) to give the story a realistic feel. Since this is a fantasy, however, these rabbits also speak, in a language called *lapin*. Every language captures the unique cultural characteristics of its speakers, and *lapin* is no exception. We are given new words to describe activities and emotions unique to rabbits. For example, the word *tharn* refers to the stupefied, frozen fear that rabbits experience when faced with sudden danger. *Silflay* means to go above ground to feed. There may be no more than about fifty words of *lapin* in the text, but the exercise of learning these words helps the reader begin to think, well, like a rabbit, and fully participate in the imaginative world of *Watership Down*.

Even with all the interesting facts and cool bunny language, why would a fantasy tale about rabbits be so popular? It is, of course, because this tale of rabbits tells us a great deal about what it means to be human. As the rabbits journey they encounter various predators; men, dogs, trains, and a whole warren of terrifying fascist rabbits threaten them at every turn. Their struggles against these adversaries mirror our own human conflicts. But above all, *Watership Down* has a memorable hero named Hazel who wins not only the love and respect of his followers, but ours as well. Hazel becomes a Moses (with Fiver as his faithful Aaron) and his character development taps into our collective recognition of the mythic journey of the hero, described by Joseph Campbell:

"There is a certain typical hero sequence of actions which can be detected in stories from all over the world and from many periods of history. Essentially, it might even be said there is but one archetypal

Did You Know?

Adams said of his writing style: "I derived early the idea that one must at all costs tell the truth to children, not so much about mere physical pain and fear, but about the really unanswerable things—what [writer] Thomas Hardy called 'the essential grimness of the human situation.'" It is interesting that Adams chose a story about bunnies to present this realistic worldview.

mythic hero whose life has been replicated in many lands by many, many people. A legendary hero is usually the founder of something—the founder of a new age, the founder of a new religion, the founder of a new city, the founder of a new way of life. In order to found something new, one has to leave the old and go in quest of the seed idea, a germinal idea that will have the potentiality of bringing forth that new thing." (*The Power of Myth*, p.136)

This is one of those books that has so many layers and levels of meaning that it creates a cult following. (In my research I found Watership Down websites with painstaking studies of the religion, myths and customs of the warren.) Interwoven between the action scenes are stories from rabbit mythology about the great El-ahrairah, the first rabbit. Through these various "backstories" Adams creates not only a physical, but also a spiritual and emotional world for these rabbits that is truly believable. It is no accident that the story inspires an almost religious devotion in readers. Like Star Wars and, most recently, the Harry Potter series, these tales create an alternative universe that is more manageable than our own, and thus more attractive in many ways. In the rabbit world, problems are difficult but there is a hero to believe in who will lead the people and bring peace and safety at last. Though the real world may defeat us, we want to believe that the meek truly will inherit the earth, that good will overcome evil and that the last will one day be first. Books that strengthen our faith in these ideas are universally beloved; they are morality plays that speak directly to our ideals. We love Hazel for his leadership, Fiver for his spirituality and Bigwig for his courage. These rabbits become real people to us, and their journey enlightens us about our own life paths. After all, rabbits aren't the only creatures that experience *tharn*. Fear is common to all of us, and these tales give us hope.

Here is a sample of Adams's wonderful writing style, which combines realism, fantasy, humor and pathos to a remarkable degree. Each rabbit in the warren contributes something vital to the survival of the group, and some of the most interesting passages are the ones where the rabbits, with their limited intelligence, work together to solve a problem they have never faced. In this case, they are being chased by the fascist General Woundwort and his army, and actually figure out how to float downriver in an abandoned boat. But, eventually, they are forced to swim to shore, something most rabbits would rather avoid. Often when I read I ask myself how I would describe a certain experience to someone completely unfamiliar with it. What does it feel like for a rabbit to swim for the first time, in a fast-moving stream? Notice how Adams gives us this experience through Hazel's limited frame of reference, which includes little more than temperature, movement, and light and dark:

"There was an instant shock of cold. But more than this, and at once, he felt the pull of the current. He was being drawn away by a force like a high wind, yet smooth and silent. He was drifting helplessly down a suffocating, cold run, with no hold for his feet. Full of fear, he paddled and struggled, got his head up and took a breath, scrabbled his claws against rough bricks under water and lost them again as he was dragged on. Then the current slackened, the run vanished, the dark became light and there were leaves and sky above him once more." (145)

If you have a child or grandchild who likes to read, share *Watership Down* together. I was rather reluctant to begin this book, but so many club members recommended it that my son and I took the plunge. It took me about fifty pages to get involved in the narrative, and by then I was hooked, and was as anxious as my son Blake to find out what happened next. The sweet, final moments when, after a long and courageous life, Hazel is called to the next world are truly fine. Even without Fiver's prophetic gift I can predict you will shed tears, and that you will never look at a bunny in quite the same way again. You will understand why in its initial review of the book one publication stated: "If there is no place for *Watership Down* in children's bookshops, then children's literature is dead."

Quotations taken from *Watership Down*. Sribner and Sons, New York. 1972.

Talk About It

Watership Down and *The Once and Future King* are anti-war novels. Do you think it is fair to couch strong political statements in literature meant for children?

About the Author: Richard Adams

Richard George Adams was born in Berkshire, England in 1920. At age 18, he studied modern history at Worchester College, Oxford, and then joined the British Army soon after the United Kingdom and Nazi Germany declared war. At Arnhem in Holland, Adams participated in heavy fighting with the British Airborne Army. After his discharge in 1946, he returned to Worchester to study, earning a Bachelor of Arts and a Master of Arts degree.

Upon graduation, he accepted a position in government and became a civil servant, eventually working as Assistant Secretary for the Ministry of Housing and Local Government, later part of the Department of the Environment. With the publication of his second novel, he retired from government service to write fulltime. In the 1970s, he was writer-in-residence at University of Florida, Gainesville, and at Hollins College, Virginia.

Adams wove the tale, *Watership Down*, to entertain his two daughters, Juliet and Rosamond, on a trip to Stratford-upon-Avon one summer. The girls urged him to write it down, and the task took him two years, working in his spare time. After thirteen rejections it was published in 1972, with a run of only 2,500 copies, and was immediately hailed by critics and readers as a children's classic. His first book, *Watership Down* won both the Carnegie Medal and the Guardian Children's Fiction Prize. By 1985 it was second on Penguin's list of all-time bestsellers with over five million copies in print, and continues to be one of the most popular books written for children or adults. He also writes poetry, non-fiction, and has served as editor of children's books. In 1973 he received the *Guardian* award; he became a Fellow in the Royal Society of Literature in 1975. Adams now lives within 10 miles of his birthplace.

Sources:

Wikipedia

biography.jrank.org

Return to Camelot:
The Once and Future King, by T.H. White

The legends of King Arthur and his Roundtable lie deep in the consciousness of the Western mind. The young boy, pulling the sword Excalibur from the stone and suddenly finding his birthright, the tragic triangle of King, Queen, and the trusted Knight Lancelot, the brooding, compassionate tutor Merlin; all these images contribute to our view of ourselves and the values upon which our society is built. T.H.White's *The Once and Future King* is a fanciful retelling of the Arthurian legends that served as the basis for Disney's *The Sword in the Stone* and the Broadway play *Camelot*, followed by the Hollywood film. Actually a tetralogy, comprising the first four novels in his series, the book has recently regained popularity as a high school text and is well worth a read. The fifth book in the series, *The Book of Merlyn*, was published separately and finishes the story of Arthur's reign in England.

Synopsis

In Book One, Arthur, nicknamed "Wart," is training to be a squire in the house of his uncle. While lost in the forest one day he meets an eccentric old man named Merlin who comes to tutor at his uncle's castle. Though he is only the squire-in-training, Wart becomes Merlin's protégé', and over the next six years is transformed into a series of animals in order to gain wisdom and strength from each. On a visit to London after the death of the king, Wart is sent to retrieve his knight's sword, and impulsively pulls a sword from a stone in the city square. This fulfills the prophecy about the next successor, and Wart is immediately named King of England.

The second book chronicles Arthur's rise as King, his development of a ruling philosophy and his marriage to Guenivere. Her involvement with Lancelot and the eventual downfall of Camelot are chronicled in the third and fourth books. The saga ends immediately before Arthur's final battle against his illegitimate son Mordred. In the final scenes Arthur strives to defend his kingdom and faces his own demise, yet knows that "Camelot" will live on in the hearts of people who love freedom.

What Makes it Great?

The Once and Future King is an artful blend of Malory's *Le Morte d'Arthur* with the legends of Robin Hood and some clever new inventions of White's (such as Merlin's method of education, which is to transform Arthur into a series of animals). The book also reflects its modern setting, as England was sinking into the second of its great world wars. White was deeply pacifist, and uses the education of Arthur as a way to explore the evils of war and the never-ending cycle of violent nationalism that eventually will destroy any civilization if unchecked by higher principle. In his final lesson from Merlin, Arthur (still 'Wart' at this stage) is transformed into a goose. The wild geese in their migration are a thrilling sight, and White brings us into their quiet, dignified world in order to teach us something about ourselves. Arthur asks a female how battles are fought among the geese. At first she does not understand his question, then is shocked at the notion that geese would fight, not their natural enemies, but among themselves. 'What creature,' she asks, 'could be so low as to go about in bands, to murder others of its own blood?' What creature indeed?

The four novels, though grouped as one now, are very different in tone and scope. The first, *The Sword in the Stone*, is a children's classic, and might easily be read to a young child. It is the book upon which the Disney movie is based and offers us the cranky, magical Merlin, who transforms Arthur both figuratively and literally. The remaining books are aimed at older readers, and offer a chilling portrait of the darker side of chivalry, as Arthur struggles to develop a new philosophy that will become the basis of democratic society in the Western world.

The character of Merlin anchors this series, and the key to Merlin's foresight is that he is actually living backwards, so that the past for him is the future for everyone else. This causes him to be quite muddled at times, and is the basis for both comic and tragic moments in the narrative. White uses Merlin's foresight (actually hindsight) to weave elements of modern life into the fabric of legend. Jousters discuss their tournaments in the jargon of cricket matches, and knights discuss the psychological implications of questing after mythical beasts in the forest. It is a delightful blend of wit, arcane information and romantic legend,

Did You Know?

White wrote to a friend that in autumn 1937, "I got desperate among my books and picked [Malory] up in lack of anything else. Then I was thrilled and astonished to find that (a) The thing was a perfect tragedy, with a beginning, a middle and an end implicit in the beginning and (b) the characters were real people with recognisable reactions which could be forecast[. . .] Anyway, I somehow started writing a book." The novel, which White described as "a preface to Malory", was titled *The Sword in the Stone*.

with some moments of pure inspiration. Here Merlin tries to explain the problem of thinking both backward and forward:

"You see, one gets confused with Time, when it is like that. All one's tenses get muddled, for one thing. If you know what is going to happen to people, and not what has happened to them, it makes it difficult to prevent it happening, if you don't want it to have happened, if you see what I mean? Like drawing in a mirror." (257)

Whenever you have a great teacher paired with a willing student, a situation is created where the author may wax free with his or her philosophy. This is certainly the case here, but White (through Merlin) actually has some very wise things to say. At once a fantasy novel, a political treatise, and a psychological exploration of modern man, *The Once and Future King* is a delightful omnibus to board.

I have carried a quote from *The Once and Future King* in my planner for twenty-five years now. When I happened upon it I had one of those rare moments where I knew that a piece of information would matter to me all my life, and it has. In case it might matter to you as well, I'll share it here:

'The best thing for being sad,' replied Merlin, beginning to puff and blow, 'is to learn something. That is the only thing that never fails. You may grow old and trembling in your anatomies, you may lie awake at night listening to the disorder of your veins, you may miss your only love, you may see the world around you devastated by evil lunatics, or know your honour trampled in the sewers of baser minds. There is only one thing for it then—to learn. Learn why the world wags and what wags it. That is the only thing which the mind can never exhaust, never alienate, never be tortured by, never fear or distrust, and never dream of regretting. Learning is the thing for you.' (342)

Quotations taken from *The Once and Future King*. G. Putnam's Sons, New York. 1987.

Talk About It

Why is Arthur's life so tragic? Why shouldn't *The Once and Future King* end happily, with Camelot thriving, Guinevere faithful and Arthur wisely ruling a democratic kingdom? Why is his project doomed to failure, or is it?

About the Author: T.H. White

Terence Hanbury White was born in 1906 in Bombay (now Mumbai), India, and educated at Cambridge. By nature White was reclusive, sometimes isolating himself for long periods from human society; he spent his time hunting, fishing, and looking after his unusual collection of pets. From 1930 to 1936, he taught as an English master at Stowe School and spent a great deal of time studying obscure subjects such as the Arthurian legends.

He was so fascinated by Sir Thomas Malory's fifteenth-century romance, *Morte d'Arthur*, that he decided to write his own interpretation of the legend of King Arthur. Malory's work was built on a Latin text, written in 1136 by Geoffrey of Monmouth, who traced the line of succession in Britain to a descendant of the Roman Aeneus named Brutus, who conquered a race of giants in Britain. His descendant was Arthur, a Welsh king who conquered the Anglo-Saxons but was eventually adopted as their legendary hero. Monmouth's text was probably drawn from Celtic lore, and Malory expanded the legends to include the romantic ideas of chivalry prevalent in his day.

White, impressed with the depth of Malory's characters and the scope of the narrative, found the story relevant to his day as well. He called his five novels a 'footnote to Malory.' The first novel was *The Sword in the Stone*, which became a modern classic and a 1936 Book-of-the-Month Club selection. *The Once and Future King* was the basis of the Lerner and Loewe musical, "Camelot." White enjoyed a large popular audience in addition to a smaller, but intense, group of admirers that he had from the start of his writing career. On returning from his American lecture tour, he died at the age of 57, onboard ship in Athens, Greece.

Sources:

Wikipedia

www2.netdoor.com/~moulder/thwhite

Fantasyland: Take it Personally

One of the keys to any good relationship is having meaningful interests to share. Reading to a child creates an instant bond, not only because of the time shared, but because the things you read about lead to conversations, and hobbies, and projects that last through the years. Again I quote my beloved teacher, Arthur Henry King:

"It is all very well to read silently to yourself, but the right thing to do with anything worthwhile is to read it aloud to yourself or, even better, to others. Parents who are in the habit of reading to one another and to their children will find that their children respect reading and want to read. Children can even learn to read by being in an atmosphere in which there is reading, in which it is done with them there. They gradually come to follow on the page, and before you know it, they are reading." (*The Abundance of the Heart*, 220.)

We've made plenty of mistakes as parents. (When our kids were younger I used to encourage them to keep a list of all the mistakes I was making so that they could share it with a therapist later!) One thing I am happy about in retrospect is the time we spent reading together and, just as importantly, talking about the things we were reading. The old saying goes that small minds talk about people, average minds talk about events, and great minds talk about ideas. Even very young children can talk about abstract concepts. If you get in the habit of discussing books from the start, you will build a relationship that will transcend all of the stages of life. You'll create a lasting friendship with your child, and you'll always have something interesting to talk about!

Chapter Twelve
The Mystery Makers

"Death in particular seems to provide the minds of
the Anglo-Saxon race with a greater fund of innocent
amusement than any other single subject."

Dorothy L. Sayers

"A mystery is a way of examining the dark side of human
nature, a means by which we can explore, vicariously, the
perplexing questions of crime, guilt and innocence, violence
and justice."

Sue Grafton

Murder, the ultimate human crime for which no reparation can be
made, is the greatest taboo, and also, on a purely visceral level, the most
fascinating subject. Stories fashioned around the commission of a murder
and the subsequent path to justice, in other words, the murder mystery,
have fascinated us since the first account of Cain and Able. How a story
involving terror, murder and mayhem can be relaxing and rejuvenating is a
mystery in itself, but the worldwide popularity of the genre proves it is so.
It seems fitting to end a volume on the classics with some classics of pure
entertainment.

P.D. James remarks, "We do not expect popular literature to be great
literature, but fiction which provides excitement, mystery and humour also
ministers to essential human needs."

The Body in the Library: Why We Love Murder Mysteries

For several years I wrote a monthly column on classic literature, and led an online book club to discuss these works. As the leader of this erstwhile group of bibliophiles, I enjoyed scouting out classic books and doing just enough research and commentary to get a good discussion going. After about five years, however, I found that I began to lose my enthusiasm for the weighty tomes that we were discussing, and had a secret longing that I could no longer deny:

I just wanted to read a good mystery.

So I did. And after that, I read another, then another. Over the next two years I read a truckload of mysteries and found some great authors. So let's nudge Tolstoy and Austen aside for a moment and close this volume with that underrated genre that actually accounts for over one-third of all fiction sold in the English-speaking world: the mystery novel.

Mysteries, Myth and Meaning

Why do we like to read mysteries? The obvious answers are these: we read such stories for entertainment, escape, and in order to solve a puzzle. However, these reasons fail to account for the universal appeal of mystery stories, since a good crossword would satisfy all those requirements. The love of a good mystery crosses all lines of class, race, economic status and lifestyle. Everybody likes them and new mysteries constantly appear to great acclaim. Marie Rodell, in her book *Mystery Fiction*, (1943) digs a little deeper into why everybody likes to find a body in the library. People, she said, read mysteries for four basic reasons:

1. The vicarious thrill of the manhunt . . . carried on intellectually in the cleverness of detective and reader.
2. The satisfaction of seeing the transgressor punished.
3. A sense of identification with the people [the hero principally] and events in the story which will make the reader feel more heroic.
4. A sense of conviction about the reality of the story.

I'm not sure if I buy the fourth reason, (there is nothing very believable about Sherlock Holmes, but we love him) but I do think Ms. Rodell is on to something when she talks about identification with the hero. This leads us into a realm far deeper than mere literary device, and suggests that the modern mystery is an outgrowth of the ancient myth.

Mythical themes, or "functions," are as old as the human ability to tell stories, and the mystery novel ties into one of the oldest: the journey of the hero. In every good mystery the mythical elements are in place. Death (the body in the library) comes as a result of evil (the murderer) and is overcome by reason (the clever work of the detective) and bravery (often facing the criminal alone). Our hero ventures into the world of the crime, is challenged and threatened, then overcomes through reason and courage, and the reader is left with an assurance that the unknown dangers that terrify us (the greatest of which is death) may be faced successfully. So the mystery is more than an escape; it is a way of preparing the mind and spirit to face the next real-life challenge by placing ourselves in the archetypical place of the hero. And you thought you were just killing a couple of hours by the pool!

Mysteries come in all shapes and sizes, but my two favorites are the detective and the "cozy" mystery. A cozy mystery is one that takes place in an enclosed or secluded place (a country house, quaint village, or monastery for example) that we would not normally associate with murder and mayhem. The hero that solves the crime is usually an unlikely character such as an old woman (Agatha Christie's Miss Marple), a priest (Ellis Peters' Brother Cadfael) or even an archaeologist (Elizabeth Peters' Amelia Peabody). Detective mysteries, which range from Sherlock Holmes's elegant, urbane sleuthing to the troubled, wounded P.I.'s of Raymond Chandler and Dashiell Hammett, actually began with a Victorian novel titled *The Moonstone*.

A Priceless Gem:
The Moonstone, by Wilkie Collins

Though many novels of the Victorian period had a mystery as a part of the plot, Wilkie Collins was the first to fashion an entire novel around a crime and its eventual solution by a brilliant detective. In addition to the detective as hero, *The Moonstone* also introduced a unique narrative style. While watching and reporting on a court trial, Collins got the idea to present a mystery through a series of narrators, much as the evidence in a trial is established through a series of witnesses. Collins noted that as each witness bore testimony, a picture of the crime was built in the minds of the listeners. He later wrote:

"It came to me then that a series of events in a novel would lend themselves well to an exposition like this. Certainly by the same means employed here, I thought, one could impart to the reader that acceptance, that sense of belief, which I saw produced here by the succession of testimonies so varied in form and nevertheless so strictly unified by their march towards the same goal. The more I thought about it, the more an effort of this kind struck me as bound to succeed. Consequently, when the case was over I went home determined to make the attempt." (*Moonstone*, xxiii)

The result of this experiment was *The Moonstone*. Published in serial form in Dickens's periodical, *All the Year Round, The Moonstone* caused quite a sensation among the public. According to reports at the time, on publishing days large, anxious crowds waited for the latest number, and bets were placed on where the Moonstone might be found at last, and who the culprit would turn out to be.

Synopsis

The story opens with a brief history of the fabulous gem called the Moonstone, stolen from an Indian raj by a soldier named John Herncastle. The gem is sacred to its owners and the three Brahmins who guard it are murdered in the theft. Fast forward to the mid-1800's, and the gem is left to Herncastle's niece, Rachel Verinder, on her eighteenth birthday.

Franklin Blake, a distant cousin and old acquaintance, comes to deliver the gem and renew his friendship with Rachel. However, the gem is stolen that night. Three Indian characters have been seen lurking around the property and are, of course suspected but nothing can be proved. Rachel reacts so strangely to the theft and is suddenly so cold to him that Blake is mystified, and determines to find the thief.

When the investigation falters, Blake seeks out a famed police inspector and brings him to the Verinder estate to pursue the case. Inspector Cuff suspects a serving maid named Rosanna Spearman, who suddenly commits suicide after hiding something in a dangerous area called the Shivering Sands. Another cousin, Godfrey Ablewhite, courts Rachel and, seemingly in despair, she briefly becomes engaged to him. Rachel's mother passes away and the stone is traced to a moneylender in town. Finally a letter is discovered that reveals the identity of the thief, and Blake is shocked and mystified. (Unlike most classics, where the plot is well-known, to reveal the perpetrator of the crime would ruin the reader's fun, so it will not be told here. You'll just have to read the book!) A local doctor helps him solve the mystery, and eventually the two lovers are reconciled, while the jewel makes its way back to India and into the hands of its rightful owners.

The Moonstone features eleven different narrators: an unnamed cousin of John Herncastle; Gabriel Betteredge (steward to Lady Verinder); Miss Clack (Lady Verinder's niece); Mr. Bruff (Lady Verinder's lawyer); Franklin Blake (Lady Verinder's nephew); Ezra Jennings (assistant to Dr. Candy); Sergeant Cuff; Dr. Candy; Sergeant Cuff's investigator; the Captain of the steamboat *Bewley Castle*; Mr. Murthwaite (traveler to India). Gabriel Betteredge and Franklin Blake narrate more than two sections each. Everyone else narrates one section.

What Makes it Great?

The Moonstone combines several elements of interest: a beautiful young girl with a fabulous gem as an inheritance, sinister figures from the East (who actually have more right to the stolen gem than the hapless girl who inherits it), hypocritical religious "do-gooders" whose charitable acts mask secret lives, and of course, the wonderful Inspector Cuff, dragged out of his beloved rose garden to solve a seemingly unsolvable puzzle. In addition, the Yorkshire dales provide a marvelously eerie setting reminiscent of Wuthering Heights. Collins is adept at using the physical landscape to evoke the emotions of the characters. Here, the "Shivering Sands" (an area of quicksand that will play a terrible role in the story) is described by the first narrator to chilling effect:

"The last of the evening light was fading away; and over all the desolate place there hung a still and awful calm. The heave of the main ocean on the great sand-bank out in the bay, was a heave that made no sound . . . It was now the time of the turn of the tide; and even as I stood there waiting, the broad brown face of the quicksand began to dimple and quiver—the only moving thing in all the horrid place." (131)

Collins also displays a wicked sense of humor. Each of his narrators is satirized in some way by what the author has them reveal of themselves. Most delightful is the butler, Gabriel Betteredge, who narrates the beginning and the end of the story. He often speaks directly to us and even warns us to pay attention:

"Here follows the substance of what I said, written out entirely for your benefit. Pay attention to it, or you will be all abroad, when we get deeper into the story. Clear your mind of the children, or the dinner, or the new bonnet, or what not . . . I hope you won't take this freedom on my part amiss; it's only a way I have of appealing to the gentle reader. Lord! haven't I seen you with the greatest authors in your hands, and don't I know how ready your attention is to wander when it's a book that asks for it, instead of a person?" (43)

Betteredge's description of his less-than-happy marriage is priceless:

"We were not a happy couple, and not a miserable couple. We were six of one and half-a-dozen of the other. How it was I don't understand, but we always seemed to be getting, with the best of motives, in one another's way. When I wanted to go upstairs, there was my wife coming down; or when my wife wanted to go down, there was I coming up. That is married life, according to my experience of it." (25)

Betteredge is deeply devoted to "his Lady," and to the family he has served for fifty years. He brags that he never lets the facts come between him and his duty:

"It was downright frightful to hear him piling up proof after proof against Miss Rachel, and to know, while one was longing to defend her, that there was no disputing the truth of what he said. I am (thank God!)

Did You Know?

Wilkie Collins suffered from gout, and was addicted to the laudanum (a derivative of opium) that he took for the pain. His interest in opium addiction and its attendant hallucinations led to the creation of the character Ezra Jennings (also an opium addict and a rather tragic figure) that saves Franklin Blake through his scientific reasoning.

constitutionally superior to reason. This enabled me to hold firm to my lady's view, which was my view also. This roused my spirit, and made me put a bold face on it before Sergeant Cuff. Profit, good friends, I beseech you, by my example. It will save you from many troubles of the vexing sort. Cultivate a superiority to reason, and see how you pare the claws of all the sensible people when they try to scratch you for your own good!" (444)

From these examples it is obvious that we don't have to trade literary quality for the fun of a mystery: this is a classic piece of superb writing. Collins's use of several narrators keeps the story vibrant and interesting, and each is a complex character in his/her own right. The young "victim" of the crime, Rachel Verinder, is far more than a damsel in distress; she is a strong, self-willed woman, very unlike the swooning heroines of that period. (Her virginal strength and beauty is symbolized by the prized Moonstone.) Betteredge describes her thus:

"She was unlike most other girls of her age, in this—that she had ideas of her own . . . She judged for herself, as few women of twice her age judge in general; never asked your advice; never told you beforehand what she was going to do; never came with secrets and confidences to anybody . . . In little things and great . . . Miss Rachel always went on a way of her own, sufficient for herself in the joys and sorrows of her life." (65)

Collins wrote that he attempted to make the action in the story spring from what the characters would actually have done, rather than simply placing figures in various situations. As a result this book, though set in Victorian drawing rooms, has a strangely modern feel to it. It is as much a psychological study of the hidden motivations and inner desires of its characters as it is a thrilling whodunit. The surprising solution to the mystery adds another layer of interest, confirming T.S. Eliot's description of *The Moonstone* as "the first, the longest and the best of the English detective novel."

Quotations taken from *The Moonstone*. Penguin Classics Edition, London. 1998.

Talk About It

Drug addiction plays a major role in this novel, raising the question of accountability. How much is Franklin Blake responsible for his actions?

About the Author: Wilkie Collins

Born in 1824, William Wilkie Collins was the son of famous landscape artist William Collins, and grew up in the heart of the London literary movement of the 1800s. From ages 12 to 15, he lived with his parents in Italy. At age 22, he studied law and was called to the bar in 1851, the same year in which he first met Charles Dickens; excellent friends, the two novelists are closely associated to this day. Choosing to write, Collins never practiced law. But, write he did. Between 1848 and his death in 1889, he penned 25 novels, more than 50 short stories, at least 15 plays, and more than 100 non-fiction pieces. He was first a playwright and wrote the two plays in which Dickens famously performed.

His best-known works are the novels, *The Woman in White* (1860) and *The Moonstone* (1867). Interestingly, the first weekly serial installment of *The Woman in White* appeared in the same edition of *All the Year Round* as the last installment of *A Tale of Two Cities*. Published in volume form, *The Woman in White* broke all sales records for novels. Hugely popular, Collins was extremely well loved and well paid. Afflicted with rheumatoid arthritis and gout, Collins suffered from chronic pain in his back, and became severely addicted to the opiate laudanum, which he took for pain. Opium figures prominently in *The Moonstone*, and one of the characters, Ezra Jennings (writer and opium addict), is modeled after Collins himself.

He is the inventor of the Sensation Novel, a genre that today is considered a precursor to suspense and detective fiction. *The Moonstone* boasts an unusual narrative structure—portions of the book have different and distinct narrators. It is considered the first detective novel in the English language.

Sources:
victorianweb.org
wilkiecollins.com

The Game's Afoot:
The Complete Sherlock Holmes, by A. Conan Doyle

The Moonstone was the first "detective novel," a genre that has by now grown so large and unwieldy that it is difficult to discuss. However, there are a few classic authors that must not be missed. First and foremost among them is the collection of Sherlock Holmes stories, penned by Arthur Conan Doyle between 1887 and 1927. Over fifty short stories and four novels featured the Baker Street sleuth, and they are still delightful to read. Holmes combines a brilliant mind with a flair for showmanship, and in "The Valley of Fear," he admits as much to his friend Watson:

"Surely our profession . . . would be a drab and sordid one if we did not sometimes set the scene so as to glorify our results. The blunt accusation, the brutal tap upon the shoulder—what can one make of such a denouement? But the quick inference, the subtle trap, the clever forecast of coming events, the triumphant vindication of bold theories—are these not the pride and the justification of our life's work?" (*Valley of Fear*, 67)

Much of the charm of these novels lies in the chemistry between Holmes and his longtime friend, Dr. John Watson. Watson acts as a foil for Holmes, though never as an equal. He is courageous, loyal and somewhat dim. Since Holmes has little love for women, the closest thing he has to an intimate relationship is his friendship with Watson. He enjoys showing off his superior sleuthing skills for his appreciative friend:

"I'm not going to tell you much more of the case, Doctor. You know a conjuror gets no credit when once he has explained his trick, and if I show you too much of my method of working, you will come to the conclusion that I am a very ordinary individual after all." (*A Study in Scarlet*, p. 43)

When Watson is wounded in an encounter with a criminal however, Holmes's deep affection for his longtime friend and chronicler becomes apparent in his agitation. Watson is touched:

"It was worth a wound; it was worth many wounds; to know the depth of loyalty and love which lay behind that cold mask. The clear, hard eyes were dimmed for a moment, and the firm lips were shaking. For the one and only time I caught a glimpse of a great heart as well as of a great brain.

Did You Know?

Conan Doyle grew tired of Sherlock Holmes and wanted to get on to more serious writing, so he killed off his hero in "The Final Problem," published in 1897. At Reichenbach Falls, Holmes has a final confrontation with Moriarty, his arch nemesis, and they both fall to their deaths into the falls. But, the public (and Doyle's publishers) had not had enough of Sherlock Holmes, so Doyle reluctantly brought him back to life. In 1903 he published "The Adventure of the Empty House," claiming that Holmes had survived the fight and rock-climbed up the falls. Fans were delighted and Holmes was back in business for several more adventures.

All my years of humble but single-minded service culminated in that moment of revelation." (*The Adventure of the Three Garridebs, p. 59*)

There is something unique about Sherlock Holmes that has captured the imagination of the public since the first story was published. Holmes's character was loosely based on a real person, Dr. Joseph Bell, who was Conan Doyle's professor at the Medical School of the University of Edinburgh. Doyle worked for Bell as an assistant during his second year, (rather like Dr. Watson) and was impressed by Dr. Bell's powers of observation:

"Dr. Bell observed the way a person moved. The walk of a sailor varied vastly from that of a solider. If he identified a person as a sailor he would look for any tattoos that might assist him in knowing where their travels had taken them. He trained himself to listen for small differences in his patient's accents to help him identify where they were from. Bell studied the hands of his patients because calluses or other marks could help him determine their occupation.

"In teaching the treatment of disease and accident," Dr. Bell stated, "all careful teachers have first to show the student how to recognize accurately the case. The recognition depends in great measure on the accurate and rapid appreciation of *small* points in which the diseased differs from the healthy state. In fact, the student must be taught to observe. To interest him in this kind of work we teachers find it useful to show the student how much a trained use of the observation can discover in ordinary matters such as the previous history, nationality and occupation of a patient." (*The Chronicles of Sir Arthur Conan Doyle*, Website)

Holmes is famously misogynistic, and, with the exception of the lovely Irene Adler (who also outwitted him) sees women only as a necessary evil. Here he is critical of a wife too quickly swayed by a servant:

"She does not shine as a wife even in her own account of what occurred. I am not a whole-souled admirer of womankind, as you are aware, Watson, but my experience of life has taught me that there are few wives having any regard for their husbands who would let any man's spoken word stand between them and that husband's dead body. Should I ever marry, Watson, I should hope to inspire my wife with some feeling which would prevent her from being walked off by a housekeeper when my corpse was lying within a few yards of her." (*Valley of Fear*, p. 120)

With all his failings, Sherlock Holmes has a timeless quality about him; in any age he would be "hip." Begin with "A Study in Scarlet" and move right through the stories to see a truly great character in the making. By the way, though I almost never like books written about famous fictional characters (like those "Mr. Darcy novels"—they just make you miss Austen!) there is a series based on Holmes that is absolutely marvelous. Laurie R. King's Holmes/Russell series pairs the retired detective with a brilliant fifteen-year old orphan, Mary Russell. King's prose is intelligent and her plots are ingenious. If you love Sherlock Holmes you'll have a great time with these books.

About the Author: A. Conan Doyle

Arthur Ignatius Conan Doyle was born in 1859 in Edinburgh, Scotland. His mother, Mary, had a passion for books and was a master storyteller. His father was a chronic alcoholic. Of his mother's influence, Conan Doyle writes: "In my early childhood, as far as I can remember anything at all, the vivid stories she would tell me stand out so clearly that they obscure the real facts of my life." Well educated, he spent seven grueling years at an English boarding school where he excelled in cricket and rebelled at the brutal corporal punishment. Later, he studied medicine at Edinburgh University where he met his mentor Joseph Bell; here, he also made the acquaintance of James Barrie and Robert Louis Stevenson. Conan Doyle traveled with Dr. Bell to Africa as doctor's assistant and ship's doctor. In Bell, he found a master at observation, logic, deduction, and diagnosis, qualities to be found later in the persona of Sherlock Holmes, the investigating detective.

During his studies and after, he wrote numerous stories and articles. In 1882, he settled in Portsmouth to open his own successful medical practice. He married and fathered two children. During his medical practice, he kept up his impressive output of fiction. The same year that *The Adventures of Sherlock Holmes* (1891) was published, the Conan Doyles moved to London. His wife would soon die of tuberculosis. In 1900, he served as a doctor during the South African War. He remarried in 1907 and fathered three more children.

The Sherlock Holmes writings are considered a major innovation in the field of crime fiction. The author wrote four novels and fifty-six short stories that feature Holmes. Dr. Watson narrates all but four stories, in a frame structure. Conan Doyle died in 1930 in East Sussex.

Sources:

sherlockholmesonline.org

online-literature.com

The Mother of All Mystery Writers:
The Agatha Christie Collection

Everybody knows Agatha Christie. From her first novel *The Mysterious Affair at Styles* (1920) to her last, *Sleeping Murder* (1976), she enjoyed a career that spanned over fifty years, and revenues from her books reach into the billions of dollars. Only the Bible has sold more copies than her collected works. Christie's mysteries have been translated to dozens of languages, inspired numerous other authors' works, and have been adapted to radio, the stage, and film. Her two greatest characters, the fussy, debonair Hercule Poirot and the deceptively frumpy Miss Marple, are beloved by millions of readers.

Agatha Christie almost single-handedly created the genre of the "cozy" mystery, with Miss Jane Marple (whom she modeled after her grandmother) as the perfect sleuth: elderly, unassuming, and devastatingly brilliant. Her wry take on the world around her continually delights us, as she avers, "The young people think the old people are fools, but the old people *know* the young people are fools."

Like Sherlock Holmes, Jane Marple has a certain style that is at once old-fashioned and very modern. She appears to be very conservative but is in fact one step ahead of most of the young people around her. Here is a rave about Miss Marple from an unlikely source: a website called "Feminist Review:"

"I celebrate Miss Marple! All feminists should know this character. Miss Marple's stories constantly stir up the hornet's nest of sexism and ageism; this elderly sleuth is treated as "second class" because she's a woman, she's old, and therefore, is seen as unable to contribute anything of worth. When she solves the case, and she always does, the people around her are in shock. The old woman has brains, how strange!" (*Feminist Review*, website)

Though Christie's other hero, Hercule Poirot, is a detective, his adventures seem to fit more into the "cozy" category of mystery, since he almost never gets his manicured hands dirty, and the resolution generally occurs in a drawing room, with all the suspects obediently present for the grand revelation. Hercule Poirot has so many annoying character traits that even Christie grew weary of him. She complained now and then

Did You Know?

In order to be sure that the ultimate fate of her characters was in her control, Christie wrote a final story for each, titled *Curtain* and *Sleeping Murder* respectively, and put them in a bank vault during the 1930's. During the last two years of her life, as her health failed, she published the stories, ending the life of Poirot, and retiring Miss Marple to her home in St. Mary Meade. Hercule Poirot has the distinction of being the only fictional character ever to receive an obituary in the New York Times.

that the character would not leave her alone! (In her diary she called him "insufferable.") But the public loved him and adaptations of the Poirot stories continue to run on public television. The mysteries involving both Poirot and Miss Marple are more about figuring things out than running down the criminal. (The dirty, grimier aspects of justice are left to lesser, more active creatures.) As Poirot says in the very first book:

"This affair must all be unravelled from within." He tapped his forehead. *"These little grey cells. It is 'up to them'—as you say over here."* (Poirot, ch. 10)

One of the most inspiring aspects of Christie's life is, of course, her longevity. She went on producing excellent mysteries long after most people would have retired, and stayed involved in productions of her work right up until the end of her life. She was married twice and spent many years on archaeological digs with her second husband. She spoke about a time of life that is difficult for many women, but for her was a much-needed "second wind."

"I have enjoyed greatly the second blooming that comes when you finish the life of the emotions and of personal relations; and suddenly you find—at the age of fifty, say—that a whole new life has opened before you, filled with things you can think about, study, or read about . . . . It is as if a fresh sap of ideas and thoughts was rising in you."—*An Autobiography* (1977).

If you haven't read Agatha Christie in awhile, I suggest listening to a few of the stories through Recorded Books on Tape, or Audible. com. Christie's prose is so engaging and her dialogue is so believable that recorded versions are a delight. I recently reread *Murder on the Orient Express* and found (though I remember the ending and there was no surprise in store) that the quick, sure creation of character and the delightful interplay between Poirot and his subordinates is continually fresh. Agatha Christie's genius continues to shine even after many readings, and that is the mark of a classic.

About the Author: Agatha Christie

In 1890, Agatha Mary Clarissa Miller was born in Torquay, England. Her father was an outgoing American; her extremely shy mother resembled Agatha in personality. Her mother decided her daughter would not receive a formal education (like Agatha's older sister) but would be taught to read at age eight. By age five, Agatha had taught herself to read. She subsequently learned from tutors, part-time schooling, and French finishing schools. She also trained as a singer and pianist but she was too nervous to perform. When she was eleven years old, her father died. She and her mother grew increasingly close and began to travel, commencing Agatha's lifelong love of travel.

In 1912, Agatha met Archie Christie, an aviator joining the Royal Flying Corps. After a rocky courtship, they married in 1914 on Christmas Eve. During the war, Christie became a volunteer nurse, completing the examination of the Society of Apothecaries. Her sister, Madge, challenged her to write a novel, and thus began her writing career with *The Mysterious Affair at Styles*. Christie's only daughter was born in 1919. By 1926, her life was turned upside down when her mother died and Archie left her for another woman. Christie remarried in 1930 and accompanied her new husband on archeological trips for the next thirty years; they remained happily married for forty-six years.

Agatha Christie is the best-selling author of all time, with over two billion books worldwide. Over half a century, she wrote eighty novels and short story collections and over a dozen plays, including *The Mousetrap*, the longest running play in theatrical history. Her inspiration came from the world she knew. A grandson described her as "a person who listened more than she talked, who saw more than she was seen." She died peacefully in 1976.

Sources:

www.agathachristie.com

A Whimsical Detective:
The Complete Lord Peter Wimsey Stories
by Dorothy L. Sayers

Though I adore Hercule Poirot, I have another brilliant,
monocle-sporting detective that I like even better, Lord Peter Wimsey.
He first appears in a delightful little novel titled, *Whose Body?* published
in 1923. We are introduced to Lord Peter, book collector, confirmed
bachelor and amateur sleuth, when his mother's neighbor finds a body in
his bathtub, "with nothing on but a pair of pince-nez." Peter's mother asks
him to solve the "problem," and the fun begins.

Over the next several years, Dorothy Sayers, scholar, poet and teacher,
published a series of mysteries featuring Lord Peter, his incomparable
butler Bunter (like Jeeves with detective skills) and the love of his life,
Harriet Vane. Harriet is obviously Sayers's alter ego; a scholar/mystery
novelist with grave misgivings about marrying the "Lord of the Manor."
In *Strong Poison*, she is introduced to us as an accused murderess, on trial
for the poisoning death of her lover. It is years, and a few more novels,
before these two tie the knot, but well worth the journey. Harriet is a very
modern character, torn between her desire for independence and a life of
the mind and her love for her rescuer and most ardent admirer, the dapper
Lord Peter. Because this is a series, we trace her development in a deeper
way. Maureen Corrigan, book reviewer for PBS (and a fellow Sayers fan)
explains:

"One of the great, largely unacknowledged advantages of series fiction is
that a story line can be strung out over several novels, allowing a character
to think, falter and reverse direction, as Harriet does." (*Leave Me Alone, I'm
Reading*, P. 110)

Dorothy Sayers brings a meticulous eye for detail to her plots, and
her dry sense of humor combined with her vast knowledge of English
manners, customs and class distinctions, create a world that is always
a joy to visit. In between "Lord Peter" mysteries, Sayers wrote another
excellent novel titled *Nine Tailors*, (which has nothing to do with sewing)
and introduces us to another part of English life that is strange to us:
the ancient art of "change-ringing," in the old churches with their great
bell-ringing tradition. (The "Nine Tailors" are nine bells.)

Did You Know?

Dorothy Sayers was quite a character in her own right. She worked for several years writing advertising copy, until she was able to support herself by the sale of her books and stories. During these years she joined a motorcycle gang, fell in love with a member, and bore him a son, Anthony. Through her study of medieval literature she became friends with C.S. Lewis and J.R.R. Tolkien, and was eventually converted to Christianity.

Dorothy Sayers's modern counterpart is, in my opinion, P.D. James, another woman writer of detective fiction. Her protagonist, Adam Dalgliesh, is a Scottish poet who doubles as a police commander. All of her novels are literate, thoughtful and beautifully constructed.

About the Author: Dorothy L. Sayers

Dorothy Leigh Sayers was born in Oxford, England on June 13, 1893. She was a popular author, as well as a translator, student of classical and modern languages, and Christian humanist.

She is best known for her Lord Peter Wimsey mysteries. Sayers described him as "a mixture of Fred Astaire and Bertie Wooster." Sayers herself considered her translation of Dante's Divina Commedia to be her best work. She also wrote religious essays and plays, and in1943 the Archbishop of Canterbury offered her an honorary doctorate in divinity, which she declined. In 1950, however, she accepted an honorary doctorate in literature from the University of Durham.

Sayers was born in Oxford, where her father was chaplain (and headmaster of the Choir School) of Christ Church College, Oxford. She was educated at Somerville College, Oxford, where she took first-class honors in modern languages, although women could not be granted degrees at that time; she was among the first women to receive a degree when they were allowed a few years later. She worked as a teacher and later as a copywriter in an advertising agency, Benson's, in London, which she used in one of her mysteries, *Murder Must Advertise*.

She gave birth to a child in 1924 while still unmarried and arranged for it to be raised by a cousin. She later married Oswald Arthur "Mac" Fleming (they later adopted her son; but he never lived with them.) She was acquainted with C. S. Lewis and his circle, including J.R.R. Tolkien, and on some occasions joined Lewis at meetings of the Socratic Club. She died of a stroke in 1957.

Source: Wikipedia
Biographybase.com

Other Great Mystery Reads: The Old Bailey to Zebra Drive

If you like the drama of the detective story but want to skip serial killers and the more shocking brutality common today, try some of the novels from the "golden age" of mysteries, such as Margery Allingham's Robert Campion series. In the "cozy" category you must read G.K. Chesterton's Father Brown series and Ellis Peters' Brother Cadfael stories. And if you haven't yet met Rumpole of the Bailey and his beloved wife Hilda ("she who must be obeyed") you are in for a hilarious treat from John Mortimer. A mystery novel that stands on its own, in the same class as *The Moonstone*, is *The Name of the Rose*, by Umberto Eco. Eco is so brilliant that this is the only novel of his that I understand, and I love it for that reason alone!

The Mystery Writers of America recently compiled a list of the hundred best mystery novels, and out of those I would recommend twenty that I particularly love. Cozy and detective mysteries both figure in this list, and most of these are part of a series by a truly talented author so you have lots of reading in store.

Following the mystery list, I'll include a list of Pulitzer Prize winners for literature over the last fifty years. The Internet now makes it possible to find almost any book, even those that have been long out of print. Instead of browsing the bestseller lists, browse these award winners and find some great new books. Enjoy!

Twenty Great Mystery Novels

(in random order)

The Complete Sherlock Holmes, A. Conan Doyle

The Moonstone, by Wilkie Collins

Death in Holy Orders, P.D. James

Rebecca, Daphne du Maurier

The Complete Father Brown, G.K. Chesterton

Murder on the Orient Express, Agatha Christie

Clouds of Witnesses, Dorothy L. Sayers

One Corpse Too Many, Ellis Peters

The Name of the Rose, Umberto Eco

Rumpole of the Bailey, John Mortimer

The Beekeeper's Apprentice, Laurie R. King

The Third Man, Graham Greene

A Thief of Time, Tony Hillerman

Crocodile on the Sandbank, Elizabeth Peters

Judgment in Stone, Ruth Rendell

Time and Again, Jack Finney

The Maltese Falcon, Dashiell Hammett

The Face of a Stranger, Anne Perry

Dancers in Mourning, Margery Allingham

The No. 1 Ladies Detective Agency, Alexander McCall Smith

Pulitzer Prize Winners

2005   *Gilead: A Novel* by Marilynne Robinson
2004   *The Known World* by Edward P. Jones
2003   *Middlesex* by Jeffrey Eugenides
2002   *Empire Falls* by Richard Russo
2001   *The Amazing Adventures of Kavalier & Clay* by Michael Chabon
2000   *Interpreter of Maladies* by Jhumpa Lahiri
1999   *The Hours* by Michael Cunningham
1998   *American Pastoral* by Philip Roth
1997   *Martin Dressler: The Tale of an American Dreamer* by Steven Millhauser
1996   *Independence Day* by Richard Ford
1995   *The Stone Diaries* by Carol Shields
1994   *The Shipping News* by E. Annie Proulx
1993   *A Good Scent from a Strange Mountain* by Robert Olen Butler
1992   *A Thousand Acres* by Jane Smiley
1991   *Rabbit At Rest* by John Updike
1990   *The Mambo Kings Play Songs of Love* by Oscar Hijuelos
1989   *Breathing Lessons* by Anne Tyler
1988   *Beloved* by Toni Morrison
1987   *A Summons to Memphis* by Peter Taylor
1986   *Lonesome Dove* by Larry McMurtry
1985   *Foreign Affairs* by Alison Lurie
1984   *Ironweed* by William Kennedy
1983   *The Color Purple* by Alice Walker
1982   *Rabbit Is Rich* by John Updike, the latest novel in a memorable sequence
1981   *A Confederacy of Dunces* by the late John Kennedy Toole (a posthumous publication)
1980   *The Executioner's Song* by Norman Mailer
1979   *The Stories of John Cheever* by John Cheever
1978   *Elbow Room* by James Alan McPherson
1977   (No Award)
1976   *Humboldt's Gift* by *Saul Bellow*
1975   *The Killer Angels* by Michael Shaara
1974   (No Award)

1973   *The Optimist's Daughter* by Eudora Welty
1972   *Angle of Repose* by Wallace Stegner
1971   (No Award)
1970   *Collected Stories* by Jean Stafford
1969   *House Made of Dawn* by N. Scott Momaday
1968   *The Confessions of Nat Turner* by William Styron
1967   *The Fixer* by Bernard Malamud
1966   *Collected Stories* by Katherine Anne Porter
1965   *The Keepers Of The House* by Shirley Ann Grau
1964   (No Award)
1963   *The Reivers* by *William Faulkner*
1962   *The Edge of Sadness* by Edwin O'Connor
1961   *To Kill A Mockingbird* by Harper Lee
1960   *Advise and Consent* by Allen Drury
1959   *The Travels of Jaimie McPheeters* by Robert Lewis Taylor
1958   *A Death In The Family* by the late James Agee (a posthumous
        publication)
1957   (No Award)
1956   *Andersonville* by MacKinlay Kantor
1955   *A Fable* by *William Faulkner*
1954   (No Award)
1953   *The Old Man and the Sea* by *Ernest Hemingway*
1952   *The Caine Mutiny* by Herman Wouk
1951   *The Town* by Conrad Richter
1950   *The Way West* by A. B. Guthrie, Jr.
1949   *Guard of Honor* by James Gould Cozzens
1948   *Tales of the South Pacific* by James A. Michener

(From 1917-1948, the award was given as the Pulitzer Prizer for Novel)

1947   *All the King's Men* by Robert Penn Warren
1946   (No Award)
1945   *A Bell for Adano* by John Hersey
1944   *Journey in the Dark* by Martin Flavin
1943   *Dragon's Teeth* by Upton Sinclair
1942   *In This Our Life* by Ellen Glasgow
1941   (No Award)

1940 *The Grapes of Wrath* by *John Steinbeck*
1939 *The Yearling* by Marjorie Kinnan Rawlings
1938 *The Late George Apley* by John Phillips Marquand
1937 *Gone With the Wind* by Margaret Mitchell
1936 *Honey in the Horn* by Harold L. Davis
1935 *Now in November* by Josephine Winslow Johnson
1934 *Lamb in His Bosom* by Caroline Miller
1933 *The Store* by T. S. Stribling
1932 *The Good Earth* by *Pearl S. Buck*
1931 *Years of Grace* by Margaret Ayer Barnes
1930 *Laughing Boy* by Oliver Lafarge
1929 *Scarlet Sister Mary* by Julia Peterkin
1928 *The Bridge of San Luis Rey* by Thornton Wilder
1927 *Early Autumn* by Louis Bromfield
1926 *Arrowsmith* by *Sinclair Lewis*
1925 *So Big* by Edna Ferber
1924 *The Able McLaughlins* by Margaret Wilson
1923 *One of Ours* by Willa Cather
1922 *Alice Adams* by Booth Tarkington
1921 *The Age of Innocence* by Edith Wharton
1920 (No Award)
1919 *The Magnificent Ambersons* by Booth Tarkington
1918 *His Family* by Ernest Poole

Edwards Brothers Malloy
Thorofare, NJ USA
December 2, 2013